Manchester Medieval Sources Series

series advisers Rosemary Horrox and Simon MacLean

This series aims to meet a growing need amongst students and teachers of medieval history for translations of key sources that are directly usable in students' own work. It provides texts central to medieval studies courses and focuses upon the diverse cultural and social as well as political conditions that affected the functioning of all levels of medieval society. The basic premise of the new series is that translations must be accompanied by sufficient introductory and explanatory material and each volume therefore includes a comprehensive guide to the sources' interpretation, including discussion of critical linguistic problems and an assessment of the most recent research on the topics being covered.

THE POLITICAL WRITINGS OF ARCHBISHOP WULFSTAN OF YORK

Manchester University Press

MedievalSources*online*

Complementing the printed editions of the Medieval Sources series, Manchester University Press has developed a web-based learning resource which is now available on a yearly subscription basis.

Medieval Sources*online* brings quality history source material to the desktops of students and teachers and allows them open and unrestricted access throughout the entire college or university campus. Designed to be fully integrated with academic courses, this is a one-stop answer for many medieval history students, academics and researchers keeping thousands of pages of source material 'in print' over the Internet for research and teaching.

titles available now at MedievalSources*online include*

Trevor Dean *The towns of Italy in the later Middle Ages*

John Edwards *The Jews in Western Europe, 1400–1600*

Paul Fouracre and Richard A. Gerberding *Late Merovingian France: History and hagiography 640–720*

Chris Given-Wilson *Chronicles of the Revolution 1397–1400: The reign of Richard II*

P. J. P. Goldberg *Women in England, c. 1275–1525*

Janet Hamilton and Bernard Hamilton *Christian dualist heresies in the Byzantine world, c. 650–c. 1450*

Rosemary Horrox *The Black Death*

David Jones *Friars' Tales: Thirteenth-century exempla from the British Isles*

Graham A. Loud and Thomas Wiedemann *The history of the tyrants of Sicily by 'Hugo Falcandus', 1153–69*

A. K. McHardy *The reign of Richard II: From minority to tyranny 1377–97*

Simon MacLean *History and politics in late Carolingian and Ottonian Europe: The* Chronicle *of Regino of Prüm and Adalbert of Magdeburg*

Anthony Musson with Edward Powell *Crime, law and society in the later Middle Ages*

Janet L. Nelson *The Annals of St-Bertin: Ninth-century histories, volume I*

Timothy Reuter *The Annals of Fulda: Ninth-century histories, volume II*

R. N. Swanson *Catholic England: Faith, religion and observance before the Reformation*

Elisabeth van Houts *The Normans in Europe*

Jennifer Ward *Women of the English nobility and gentry 1066–1500*

Visit the site at *www.medievalsources.co.uk* for further information and subscription prices.

THE POLITICAL WRITINGS OF ARCHBISHOP WULFSTAN OF YORK

selected sources edited and translated

by Andrew Rabin

Manchester University Press

Published by Manchester University Press
Altrincham Street, Manchester M1 7JA, UK
www.manchesteruniversitypress.co.uk

British Library Cataloguing-in-Publication Data
A catalogue record for this book is available from the British Library

Library of Congress Cataloging-in-Publication Data applied for

ISBN   978 0 7190 8974 9 *hardback*
          978 0 7190 8975 6 *paperback*

First published 2015

Typeset in Monotype Bell
by Koinonia, Manchester
Printed in Great Britain
by Bell & Bain Ltd, Glasgow

CONTENTS

PREFACE

Although Archbishop Wulfstan's *Sermo lupi ad Anglos* is familiar to every first-year Old English student, his other works have not garnered the same level of attention, even among Anglo-Saxonists. In compiling an anthology of his political writings, many of which are translated here for the first time, my goal has been to make Wulfstan's works accessible to a wider audience of students and professional scholars, both those specialising in Old English and those engaged in the study of medieval legal and political history more generally. A volume of this sort does not have a 'thesis' *per se*, but I do hope that readers will come away from this collection with a greater appreciation for Wulfstan's significance in the history of medieval political theology and, more broadly, for the theoretical sophistication of early English social thought.

If this volume proves to be a useful contribution to the study of Wulfstan and his times, it will be because of the help and support of a large number of people. I am especially grateful to Lisi Oliver, Stefan Jurasinski, Jay Gates, Stephen Harris, Tom Hall, Nicole Marafioti, Bryan Carella, and Bruce O'Brien for sharing their views on Wulfstan, providing clarification on points of law, and suggesting new or better ways of translating problematic passages. At my home institution, the University of Louisville, special thanks are due to Pamela Beattie, Tom Byers, Susan Griffin, Karen Hadley, Aaron Jaffe, Tom Maloney, Glynis Ridley, and Tatjana Soldat-Jaffe, all of whom served as sounding boards for my frequently off-kilter ideas and offered invaluable advice as the project developed. This book is infinitely better for their help; the errors that remain are, of course, my own.

Finally, thanks are due to my parents, Alan and Ellen Rabin, and most especially to my wife Shira and my sons Ari and Eli for their love and patience as this book was written. They've had to share far too much of their time with an eleventh-century archbishop, but without them, this project would never have come to fruition. It is to them that this book is dedicated.

ABBREVIATIONS

Abt.	The Laws of Æthelberht[1]
Admonition	*The Admonition to Bishops*
Af.	The Laws of Alfred
AGu.	*Treaty of Alfred and Guthrum*
As.	The Laws of Æthelstan
Atr.	The Laws of Æthelred
C.C.C.C.	Cambridge, Corpus Christi College
C.U.L.	Cambridge, University Library
Canons	*The Canons of Edgar*
Clerical Compensation	*On Priests' Oaths and Clerical Compensation* (*Hadbot*)
Cn.	The Laws of Cnut
Cn. 1020	Cnut's Proclamation of 1020
Eg.	The Laws of Edgar
EGu.	*The Laws of Edward and Guthrum*
Em.	The Laws of Edmund
Episc.	*Concerning Episcopal Duties* (*Episcopus*)
Ew.	The Laws of Edward the Elder
God's Threat	*God's Threat to a Sinning Israel* (Bethurum 19)
Mercian Law	*Concerning the Law of the Mercians* (*Mircna laga*)
NPL	*The Northumbrian Priests' Law*
On Baptism	*On Baptism and Confirmation* (Napier 24)
On Justice	*On Justice, Virtue, and the Law* (Napier 50)
On Ranks	*Concerning the Ranks of People and Law* (*Geþyncðu*)
On the Laws of God	*On the Laws of God and the World* (Napier 51)

---

1 The abbreviations used for royal legislation were standardised by Felix Liebermann in the *Gesetze der Angelsachsen* (1903–1916). When multiple pieces of legislation have been issued in a king's name, laws are cited according to legislative number, name, clause number, and if applicable, sub-clause number. Thus 'V Atr. 22.1' refers to the first sub-clause of the twenty-second clause of what has been designated Æthelred's fifth law-code. Although the numbering of law-codes was originally intended to indicate chronology, the order suggested by the numbering has been shown to be inaccurate in so many instances that the numbers are now understood as little more than a scholarly convention.

On the Proper Support	*On the Proper Support of the Church*
On Tithes	*On Tithes and Tithing* (Napier 23)
On Wergild	*Concerning Wergild/ The Northpeople's Law* (*Be wergylde/ Norðleoda laga*)
PL	*Patrologia Latina*, ed. J.P. Migne
Polity	*The Institutes of Polity*
Sanctuary	*Concerning Sanctuary* (*Grið*)
Wi.	The Laws of Wihtred

INTRODUCTION

It is a truth nearly universally acknowledged that the legislators of Anglo-Saxon England lacked a sophisticated, theoretical understanding of both law and politics. In early twentieth-century scholarship, this belief underlay such blunt statements as William Dunning's claim that 'the Middle Age [sic] was unpolitical', and Sir Frederick Pollock's more elaborate, if equally damning, assertion that 'an Anglo-Saxon court, whether of public or private justice, was not surrounded with such visible majesty of the law as in our own time, nor furnished with any obvious means of compelling obedience'.[1] Even the great Ernst Kantorowicz concluded that early English lawmakers were 'probably quite unaware of the highly complicated legal and constitutional premises' behind their actions.[2] More recently, the perception of pre-Conquest jurisprudence as primitive and theoretically impoverished has led legal historians to characterise Anglo-Saxon law as 'desperately weak' and 'calculated to avoid reasoned decision-making'.[3] Similar attitudes prevail among scholars of political theory, who often dismiss the study of Anglo-Saxon governmental practices as 'belong[ing] more to the general historian than to the historian of ideas' because of their presumed origin merely in 'practical demands or responses to them'.[4]

The assumption that pre-Conquest legislators understood their duties in only the most primitive way has caused readers to overlook the influence and complexity of the largest corpus of vernacular legal and political prose to survive from the early Middle Ages.[5] Among the

---

1 Dunning 1930: 131; Pollock 1893: 250. Pollock later repeated his criticism in Pollock and Maitland 1968: 14. For a critique of Pollock and Maitland's conclusions, see Wormald 1996: 1–20, and Wormald 1998: 1–25.

2 Kantorowicz 1957: 343.

3 Baker 1990: 4–5; Whitman 2008: 41, 53. For a more extended discussion of Baker's comments, see Rabin 2007: 225–6.

4 Ryan 2012: 219. Ryan is unusual in even mentioning the Anglo-Saxon period. More common in general histories of political thought is the omission of the Anglo-Saxon period entirely, as is the case, for instance, in McClelland 1996 and Klosko 2011. A notable exception is Burns 1988.

5 All told, the pre-Conquest legal corpus is comprised of roughly seventy legislative texts (most of which are included in Felix Liebermann's three-volume *Gesetze*

most significant texts in this corpus are the laws, homilies, and political tracts produced by the early eleventh-century ecclesiastic Archbishop Wulfstan of York. Wulfstan was the leading English churchman of his day, serving as bishop of London from 996 to 1002, bishop of Worcester and archbishop of York from 1002 to 1016, and archbishop of York alone from 1016 until his death in 1023. More than just an ecclesiastical administrator, Wulfstan used his episcopate to advance his vision of a 'Holy Society', one in which the organisation of a Christian state mirrored both the divinely ordained hierarchy of a Christian cosmos and the moral order of the individual Christian soul.[6] This vision took shape in a series of homilies and political tracts that Wulfstan wrote and repeatedly revised throughout his career, as well as in the legislation he composed on behalf of Kings Æthelred (r. 978–1016) and Cnut (r. 1016–1035). Among Anglo-Saxonists, Wulfstan has come to be recognised as a political theorist 'of prodigious abilities',[7] a 'prose stylist of the first importance',[8] 'one of the half dozen leading influences on the formation of Early English culture',[9] and 'the greatest English ideologue of the age'.[10] Yet, despite Wulfstan's influence, many of his works, especially the legal homilies and shorter political tracts, remain unfamiliar to those interested in the history of early medieval social thought.[11] The majority of his writings were last edited more than a century ago, in many cases prior to their attribution to Wulfstan, and published in volumes which are now out-of-print, unreliable, or difficult to use for those not conversant with late nineteenth-century academic German.[12] Accordingly, in making these texts available in new, more accessible translations, it is hoped that this volume will both introduce readers to the range of Wulfstan's political writings and shed light on the development of English law during the early eleventh century.

---

der Angelsachsen) and approximately 1,500 charters. The foremost histories of pre-Conquest law are Wormald 1999d and Hudson 2012. Overviews of the Old English legal corpus can be found in Hough 2001, Rabin 2012, and Oliver 2013.

6 The first, and still most influential, account of Wulfstan's vision of a Holy Society can be found in Wormald 1999a: 244–6.

7 Keynes 1980: 190.

8 Gatch 1977: 18.

9 Wormald 1999a: 225.

10 Blair 2005: 496.

11 On this point, see Abels 1988b: 294; Powell 1994; Wormald 1999d: 330; Orchard 2002: 311–12.

12 This issue has been discussed by, among others, Dammery 1994: 51–61; Lionarons 2004b: 165–8; Orchard 2004: 63–4; Orchard 2007: 318–19; Lionarons 2010: 2.

Background: politics and society in early medieval England

Understanding the origins of Wulfstan's political thought requires some knowledge of the troubled history of later Anglo-Saxon England. His vision of a holy society cannot be separated from the social and intellectual upheavals that radically reshaped English culture between the eighth and tenth centuries.[13] On one hand, the consolidation of the Anglo-Saxon kingdoms, the centralisation of royal authority, and the growth of a vibrant vernacular textual tradition all fostered a sense of cultural identity more self-consciously 'English' than ever before.[14] At the same time, the on-going Viking invasions and the regional aristocracy's resistance to an increasingly ambitious monarchy contributed to a degree of instability that periodically resulted in the failure of the government or worse, the collapse of the state itself. Wulfstan captured the tension between the emergent kingdom's promise and its unstable reality in his image of a throne perched precariously on the three pillars of clergy, aristocracy, and labour. As long as these estates observed their moral and social duties, the throne would stand securely; however, 'if any of them weaken, immediately the throne will tremble; and if any of them fracture, then the throne will crumble to pieces, and that will bring the people all to ruin'.[15] For Wulfstan and his contemporaries, England's recent history vividly illustrated the need for strong governance as well as the constant potential for catastrophe. It was this history that served as the backdrop for Wulfstan's thought and career.

The origins of the eleventh-century English state lay in the clutch of regional kingdoms founded by migrating Germanic tribes in the fifth and sixth centuries. Following the withdrawal of Roman legions from Britain in *ca.* 409–410, invading Saxon, Jute, and Anglian settlers quickly overthrew the remnants of the Romano-Celtic aristocracy and established a series of local chiefdoms that gradually evolved into the principal early Anglo-Saxon kingdoms of Wessex, Sussex, Essex, Kent, Mercia, East Anglia, and Northumbria. This list of kingdoms, sometimes called the 'Heptarchy', should be seen as something of a historical fiction, however: the social and political volatility of this period meant that communities subdivided and combined with a regularity

---

13 For authoritative histories of the Anglo-Saxon period, see Stenton 1971; Blair 1977; Campbell 1982; Fleming 2011; and Higham and Ryan 2013.

14 On the development of a unified notion of an 'English' cultural identity during this period, see Reynolds 1985 and Foot 1996.

15 *Polity* IV.

that left both boundaries and allegiances in a state of constant flux.[16] In the late sixth century, the arrival of Roman and Irish missionaries began the process of Christianisation that led both to the conversion of the Anglo-Saxons and to the establishment of major ecclesiastical foundations at such sites as Canterbury, Whitby, Lindisfarne, York, and Monkwearmouth-Jarrow.[17] These communities supported a thriving textual culture that produced such major figures of early Anglo-Saxon letters as the venerable Bede and Bishop Aldhelm of Sherborne. An equally important consequence of the conversion was the promulgation by King Æthelberht of Kent (r. *ca.* 590–616) of the earliest vernacular written code of English law – composed, in Bede's words, 'after the example of the Romans' ('iuxta exempla Romanorum').[18] By the end of the eighth century, the conversion had taken hold to such an extent that Anglo-Saxon clerics such as Boniface were despatched to the continent to pursue missionary work in the northern Frankish empire, and scholars such as Alcuin of York were invited to join Charlemagne's court school at Aachen.

The eighth century would come to be remembered by Wulfstan and his contemporaries as a golden age, particularly in light of what followed. The Viking raids that began with the destruction of the great abbey at Lindisfarne on 8 June 793, put an end to the first flowering of Anglo-Saxon Christian culture and struck fear into Britain's inhabitants. The anonymous author of the *Anglo-Saxon Chronicle*'s entry for 793 wrote that the Viking attacks were preceded by 'extreme lightning' ('ormete ligræscas') and visions of 'fiery dragons' ('fyrene dracan'), while Alcuin bemoaned that, 'never before has such terror appeared in Britain as we have now suffered'.[19] Over the course of the ninth century, the raids grew more frequent, eventually becoming a full invasion. By the early 870s, most of the earlier Anglo-Saxon kingdoms had collapsed, the principal ecclesiastical foundations of the previous century lay in ruins,

16 On the Anglo-Saxon settlement of Britain and conversion to Christianity, see Blair 1963; Arnold 1988; Kirby 1991; Higham 1997; and Lambert 2010.

17 Although the conversion of the Anglo-Saxon kingdoms brought enhanced prestige to these sites, it should be noted that in many cases – including Canterbury and York – conversion-era foundations were built on locations that had previously been centres of Christian worship during the Roman period.

18 Bede's *Ecclesiastical History*, Bk. II, ch. 5, ed. Colgrave and Mynors 1991: 150. What Bede actually meant by 'the example of the Romans' has been the subject of considerable debate. On this point, see Wormald 1999b and Oliver 2002: 18–20.

19 The references to lightning and dragons occur in the entry for 793 in the *Anglo-Saxon Chronicle*, ed. Irvine 2004: 42. Alcuin's complaint can be found in his second letter to King Æthelred of Northumbria (r. 774–96), tr. in Whitelock 1979: 842.

and Viking armies occupied the majority of northern, central, and eastern Britain. When a young Alfred assumed the throne of Wessex in 871, he ruled little more than a rump state, which was further reduced by Viking victories over the first seven years of his reign.[20] Despite early setbacks, however, Alfred won significant victories in 878 at Edington and Chippenham which enabled him to negotiate a treaty expelling the Vikings from Wessex and large portions of Essex and Mercia. Alfred consolidated the reconquered territories into a single West Saxon kingdom (sometimes referred to as 'greater Wessex' by modern historians), while the area that remained under Viking rule came to be known as the 'Danelaw', a region that would preserve Scandinavian legal and cultural practices well into Wulfstan's own time.[21] Following the pattern of Charlemagne, Alfred used his military success as a catalyst for cultural revival. Famously observing that 'learning had declined so thoroughly in England that there were very few men on this side of the Humber who could understand their divine services in English', Alfred encouraged vernacular literacy among the aristocracy and oversaw the translation into English of works by such authors as Augustine and Pope Gregory I.[22] As part of his project of cultural renewal, Alfred also compiled an extensive code of laws to which he attached a lengthy prologue situating his legislation within a tradition of lawgiving stretching back to Moses on Mount Sinai.[23] The Alfredian *domboc* provided the model for much of the law promulgated over the next hundred years. It would remain the most comprehensive body of English legislation until supplanted by the laws Wulfstan composed on behalf of the conqueror Cnut in the early eleventh century.[24]

The reconquest continued under Alfred's successors, Edward the Elder (r. 899–924) and Æthelstan (r. 924–939), so that by the latter's death, the rulers of greater Wessex had begun to refer to themselves as kings of a united England. More than just political consolidation, though, their military successes also made possible the revival of English religious

---

20 On Alfred's reign, see Abels 1998 and Pratt 2007.

21 See Hadley 2000 and Hadley 2006.

22 Alfred's observation on the decline in learning occurs in the prose preface to his translation of Pope Gregory's *Pastoral Care*, quoted in Keynes and Lapidge 1983: 125.

23 See Liebermann 1908; Wormald 1999d: 416–29; Carella 2011; Jurasinski 2011; Carella 2012; and Jurasinski 2012.

24 The most complete discussion of Alfred's laws remains Wormald 1999d: 265–85, 416–30.

life that scholars now refer to as the Monastic Reform.[25] Begun under Æthelstan and reaching its peak during the reign of King Edgar 'the Peaceable' (r. 959–975), the Reform looked to both Alfredian and continental precedents in order to restore the English Church and reshape the relationship between royal and ecclesiastical authority. Never a unified movement in the modern sense, reformers allied themselves with competing political factions and drew on different sources, but they nonetheless shared certain priorities: antagonism toward lay monastic leadership; nostalgia for the religious life of Bede's Northumbria; advocacy for the uniform observance of the Benedictine Rule in all English monasteries; a desire to recast the episcopacy as a monastic institution; and a portrayal of the king as special patron and guardian of religious life.[26] In particular, the emphasis on royal patronage points to the productive collaboration that developed between the Reformers and the king. Using their influence at court, the leading proponents of the Reform – Archbishop Dunstan of Canterbury, Archbishop Oswald of York, and Bishop Æthelwold of Winchester – sought royal sanction for the seizure of alienated Church lands and the expulsion of regional aristocrats from monastic property. In exchange, they offered financial and ideological support to Edgar's attempts to further centralise the kingdom's government under the authority of the crown. Æthelwold encapsulated this partnership in an imagined address from God to the king: 'because you zealously protect and advance my name and dominion – that is, my Church which I rightly have in my special dominion – as a recompense to you I will glorify your name and increase and advance in prosperity your kingdom which you hold under my dominion'.[27] For Æthelwold and his fellow reformers, this partnership between *rex* and *ecclesia* provided the foundation for a revitalised English Church; for Wulfstan, writing a generation later, it would serve as one of the principal sources for his vision of a holy society.

The Reform encountered its most significant crisis when King Edgar died unexpectedly on 8 July 975, and the resulting dispute between supporters of Edgar's underage sons Edward and Æthelred brought the kingdom to the brink of civil war. Although the succession was finally

---

25 There are a number of excellent studies of the Monastic Reform. See especially John 1966; Parsons 1975; Stafford 1978a; Stafford 1989; Cubitt 1997; and Gretsch 1999.

26 This list taken from Rabin 2013: 225.

27 This passage occurs in Æthelwold's preface to his Old English translation of the Benedictine Rule, edited as 'King Edgar's Establishment of the Monasteries' in Whitelock 1981: 142–54, at 147.

settled in favour of Edward, the young king lacked the means to protect the Church from those who had opposed the consolidation of royal and ecclesiastical authority under his father. The sudden weakening of royal protection left the Church vulnerable to members of the regional aristocracy who had been dispossessed by the Reform, a situation they were quick to exploit through lawsuits and violent attacks on monastic foundations.[28] The trauma of this period was such that Wulfstan, writing the *Institutes of Polity* nearly fifty years later, would refer to it as the moment when the moral character of English government began to unravel: 'since Edgar died, just as God willed, it has come to pass all too much that there are more thieves than righteous people, and it is a terrible thing that they are thieves who should be the shepherds of the Christian people'.[29] The situation reached its nadir with the assassination of Edward by supporters of his brother Æthelred in 978. Though Æthelred was likely innocent of any collusion in the murder, when he assumed the throne later that year it was under a cloud of suspicion that he lacked the political influence or strength of character to dispel.

The legal and extra-legal attacks on Church property continued through the first decade of Æthelred's reign.[30] Although he eventually atoned for his early acquisitiveness and susceptibility to bad companions, Æthelred never escaped his early reputation for being *unræd* ('of poor counsel'). His reputation suffered further from his inability to counter the escalation in Viking raids in the late 980s which led to England being forced to pay an annual tribute to the Danes beginning in 991. The next twenty years were marked by the periodic resumption of the raids until Æthelred could gather enough money to buy off the invaders with an increased tribute. These years also witnessed a series of increasingly horrific events, including the St. Brice's Day Massacre – the government-sanctioned murder of Danes living in England ordered by Æthelred in 1002 – and the martyrdom of Archbishop Alphege of Canterbury in 1012 by a Viking army under the command of Thurkil the Tall.[31] King Sweyn of Denmark launched a formal invasion of England in 1013 which led to the collapse of Æthelred's government, an event

28 The succession crisis and resulting 'anti-monastic reaction' remains one of the most controversial and least understood periods in later Anglo-Saxon history. See especially Fisher 1952; Jayakumar 2009; and Rabin 2013.

29 *Polity* X.

30 On the reign of Æthelred, see Stafford 1978b; Wormald 1978; Keynes 1980; Stafford 1989; Keynes 1991; Lavelle 2002; Williams 2003a; and Keynes 2007.

31 See n. to the first clause of *Cn. 1020* below.

commemorated by Wulfstan in his most famous homily, the *Sermo Lupi ad Anglos* ('The Sermon of the Wolf to the English'). Æthelred resumed the throne the next year following Sweyn's death; however, the invasion continued under Sweyn's son Cnut, whose conquest of England was nearly complete by the time Æthelred died in early 1016. Æthelred's son, Edmund Ironside, continued to resist the Danish invasion, but his own death a few months later left Cnut wholly in control of the kingdom.

Cnut quickly consolidated his rule by forcing the surviving members of the West Saxon royal family into exile in Normandy and marrying Æthelred's widow, Emma (this despite the fact that he was already married to the Northumbrian noblewoman Ælfgifu).[32] The success of his conquest meant that England now formed the centrepiece of an Anglo-Scandinavian empire encompassing Denmark, Norway, and parts of Sweden, and drawing tribute from portions of modern-day Poland, Ireland, France, Scotland, and Germany. Although Cnut based his throne in England, the military and diplomatic demands of an empire this size obliged him to spend much of his reign travelling. As a result, he relied on a number of English deputies and advisors, among the most important of whom was Wulfstan, a leading figure on the royal council and principal author of the legislation promulgated in Cnut's name.[33] Despite his periods of absenteeism and history of invasion, Cnut appears to have been perceived as a successful ruler: he took considerable interest in the just governance of his English subjects and his patronage of the Church earned him a reputation for generosity far exceeding that of his predecessor. Cnut died in 1035 at a relatively young age – his date of birth is unknown, but he seems to have been around forty – and the failure of his sons to secure the kingdom led to the recall of Edward, heir to the West Saxon throne, thus setting in motion a sequence of events that would ultimately lead to the Norman Conquest of 1066.

---

32 On the reign of Cnut, see Stafford 1971; Lawson 1993; and Bolton 2009.

33 Wulfstan's involvement in Cnut's legislation has been widely discussed. See especially Whitelock 1948; Whitelock 1955; Kennedy 1983; Lawson 1992; and Richards 2010.

Wulfstan's life and career

Despite his contemporary prominence, much about Wulfstan's life remains a mystery. Although the *Anglo-Saxon Chronicle* notes his death in its entry for the year 1023, his age and date of birth are unrecorded.[34] Yet while reliable information is scarce, the few surviving facts do allow for some tentative deductions. If we assume that Wulfstan's elevation to the episcopacy in 996 coincided with canonical practice, his birth can be plausibly dated to sometime between 946 and 966.[35] Wulfstan's decision to be buried at Ely and his patronage of Peterborough have given rise to speculation that his family originated in the south-eastern Danelaw; however, the fact that he and several of his relatives were connected to the foundation at Worcester has led some scholars to propose the west midlands as a potential alternative.[36] What little information there is about Wulfstan's early life comes from the twelfth-century *Liber Eliensis*, which records that he 'did not lack either noble birth or worldly honour', that he was born through caesarean section, and that he was reared on cow's milk 'through the industriousness of his kinsmen'.[37] Claims such as these are not uncommon in hagiography of the period – and the *Liber Eliensis* narrative certainly seems to have been composed with Wulfstan's candidacy for sainthood in mind[38] – yet they are not necessarily inaccurate: it is unlikely that Wulfstan could have ascended to a bishopric without an aristocratic background and his letters to Ælfric do reveal an interest in the legality of caesarean procedures, though this may be nothing more than coincidence.[39] Concerning other members of Wulfstan's family, the *Liber Eliensis* notes that Brihteah, a

---

34 The relevant section of *Chronicle* entry for 1023 reads only, 'Here died Archbishop Wulfstan, and Ælfric succeeded [him]'. See Irvine 2004: 75.

35 Prior to the Council of Trent in 1545, the canonical age for ordination varied between thirty and thirty-five, with the former being more common. Age at appointment to a bishopric could vary widely, though: Dunstan became bishop of Worcester in 957 at the age of 48 and Æthelwold was between 54 and 59 when named bishop of Winchester in 963, but his successor Alphege was only 30 at his election in 984.

36 Bethurum 1957: 55; Whitelock 1966: 7; Cooper 1970: 3; Gatch 1977: 18; Williams 2003a: 85; and Wormald 2004: 13. Whitelock notes that further support for a location in the Fenlands or east midlands may be adduced from the fact that Wulfstan's three predecessors as archbishop of York all originated in the same region. Whitelock 1937–45: 170; and Whitelock 1959: 75–6. On the later history of Wulfstan's family, see Williams 1996: 394–7.

37 Blake 1962: II.87.

38 On this point, see Crook 2004: 524.

39 Bethurum 1957: 55 and Cooper 1970: 3.

later bishop of Worcester, was the son of Wulfstan's sister, while the existence of a second sister is attested by a later charter recording her marriage to one Wulfric. Another charter mentions a brother, Elfwige, to whom Wulfstan leased several estates, and the likelihood of a second brother is indicated by a deed in which a certain Wulfmær is referred to as 'the brother of the bishop', who may be tentatively identified with Wulfstan, then bishop of London.[40] Yet, if records such as these suggest that Wulfstan maintained ties with his relatives throughout his career, the nature of those ties, the depth of his affection, and the influence of family members on his intellectual development remain unknown.

Wulfstan's later identification with the Monastic Reform movement and the similarities between his ideas and those of Bishop Æthelwold have led some modern scholars to suggest that he may have been educated as a Benedictine novice at Winchester, although no hard evidence exists to support this supposition.[41] Frank Barlow raises the further possibility that Wulfstan's later correspondence with Ælfric may even 'be due to a common schooling'.[42] However, tempting as it is to imagine a young 'Wulfie' and 'Ælfie' passing notes under Æthelwold's stern, schoolmarm's gaze, such a vision is, sadly, entirely without warrant.[43] John of Worcester records that prior to becoming bishop of London, Wulfstan had been abbot of the monastery at Worcester, which would suggest that he had previously been a monk of that foundation.[44] John's chronicle is inaccurate concerning other details of Wulfstan's career, though, and in the absence of corroborating evidence, this detail must be viewed with suspicion.[45] Nonetheless, whether he was associated with Winchester, Worcester, both, or neither, it remains most likely that Wulfstan lived and was educated as a monk prior to 996. Not only do his writings indicate an extensive knowledge of monastic texts, including both the Benedictine Rule and the *Regularis Concordia*, but

---

40 Whitelock 1930: 136; Robertson 1956: 388–9; Bethurum 1957: 55–6; and Baxter 2007: 24–5.

41 Knowles 1963: 63; Barlow 1979: 68–9. Disputing this supposition, Patrick Wormald writes, 'there is strikingly little evidence that our Wulfstan was educated in the Æthelwoldian style'. Wormald 2004: 13.

42 Barlow 1979: 68.

43 Malcolm Godden has shown that it is unlikely that Ælfric came into contact with Wulfstan prior to their first exchange of letters in 1002. See Godden 2004: 354, 372.

44 See the annal for 1002 in Darlington, McGurk et al. 1995: 452. It should be noted that John confuses the years of Wulfstan's appointment to the see at London with that of his elevation to the sees of Worcester and York.

45 Whitelock 1937: 464–5.

his affiliation with the Reform movement – among the principal tenets of which was the belief that bishops should be chosen from monasteries – make it unlikely that he would have ascended to the episcopacy from anything other than a monastic setting.[46]

Wulfstan's appointment as bishop of London in 996 marks his entrance into the historical record. It was during this time in London that his earliest extant sermons, the eschatological homilies numbered 1–3 in Bethurum's edition, were probably composed. Dorothy Bethurum and Patrick Wormald also assign homilies 4 and 5 to this period, although Sara Pons-Sanz dates these approximately ten years later. Based on linguistic evidence, Pons-Sanz classifies homilies 14, 15, and 19 (the last of which is translated below, pp. 173–6) among Wulfstan's London compositions, yet here Bethurum and Wormald argue for a later date, locating 14 and 15 between 1002 and 1005 and 19 to the period just before Æthelred's brief deposition in 1014.[47] Whatever the precise dating of these homilies may be – and Wulfstanian chronology is, as Wormald concedes, 'a fraught affair'[48] – it appears that even at this stage in his career Wulfstan had already come to be known as a skilled author and homilist, a reputation attested by a surviving letter to the then-bishop praising him for his eloquence and sagacity.[49] These years also witness Wulfstan beginning to circulate his homilies under the pen-name *Lupus*. His reasons for adopting a pseudonym are unclear: the obviousness of *Lupus* (a translation of his name's first syllable) makes a desire for anonymity unlikely, and the fact that he always appears as 'Wulfstan' or 'Wulfstanus' in official documents indicates that he did not see it merely as a convenient Latinisation. It is possible that he adopted a pseudonym to imitate those used by members of the Carolingian court school that grew up around Alcuin, though Simon Keynes has suggested that the reason may be somewhat simpler:

46 Though not conclusive, it is also worth noting that only fourteen of the 116 bishops appointed between 960 and 1066 were non-monastics, none of whom occupied the see of York. Bethurum 1957: 57 and Hill 2004: 311.

47 Bethurum 1957: 101–2; Wormald 2004: 26; and Pons-Sanz 2007: 25.

48 Wormald 2004: 16.

49 The letter is edited in Bethurum 1957: 376–7. Sara Pons-Sans points out that this praise 'should be taken with a pinch of salt because his correspondent was begging off translating materials which Wulfstan had requested; however, it cannot be completely discarded as evidence that his contemporaries were already aware of his characteristic style'. Pons-Sanz 2004: 281n. 281. Wulfstan's rising reputation is also indicated by contemporary charters, in which he is given precedence over all other ecclesiastics except the archbishops and the bishop of Winchester. Williams 2003a: 36–7.

'perhaps one should sense in Archbishop Wulfstan's use of the Latin *Lupus* ('wolf'), as his pen-name, a warning to his flock that he was out on the prowl'.[50]

In 1002, Wulfstan left London to become bishop of Worcester and archbishop of York. Writing a little over a century later, William of Malmesbury condemned Wulfstan's acceptance of this double appointment, which he described as evidence that the newly named archbishop was less than his predecessors 'in both holiness and custom'.[51] The joint holding seems to have been viewed – retroactively, at least – with some suspicion in Worcester as well: one twelfth-century list of bishops labels Wulfstan 'impious' while a second refers to him as 'the reprobate'.[52] It would be wrong to take such subsequent judgments as indicative of contemporary attitudes, though. Wulfstan's predecessors Eadwulf (archbishop from 995 to 1002) and Oswald (archbishop from 971 to 992) also occupied the York and Worcester sees jointly, while Oscytel (archbishop from 958 to 971) held York in plurality with the see of Dorchester. Although pluralism was frowned upon – it later would serve as the justification for the excommunication of Stigand, simultaneously bishop of Winchester and Archbishop of Canterbury – it nonetheless appears to have provided a useful solution to two related problems. Not only was York among the poorer sees in England, but generations of Danish occupation had left it with a long tradition of disloyalty towards the Wessex-based English monarchy. Pairing an archiepiscopal appointment to York with an episcopal appointment to a diocese such as Worcester or Dorchester gave Wulfstan and his predecessors a much-needed extra source of income while also ensuring that they always retained an interest in the more loyal south.[53]

---

50 Keynes 2005: 22. The suggestion that he may have been imitating Carolingian court scholars occurs in Whitelock 1942: 40.

51 Ch. iii.115.11 in Winterbottom 2007: 380.

52 The first of these occurs on fol. 2 of the Worcester Cartulary. See Darlington 1968: 1. The second is quoted in Whitelock 1966: 8–9. Stephen Baxter has recently found evidence that Wulfstan's accession was viewed much more positively at the time. A short piece of Latin doggerel copied into a Worcester cartulary wishes 'peace, long life, and also salvation for the Wolf'. Baxter 2004: 161. See also Barrow 1992: 53–74.

53 On this point, see Bethurum 1957: 59–60; Whitelock 1959: 72–6; and Whitelock 1966: 10. It is possible that in Wulfstan's case, though, one may see the reverse of this pattern: instead of an effort to ensure that a northern cleric retained a southern interest, Wulfstan's appointment may indicate an attempt to place an ecclesiastic with southern loyalties and affiliations in a position of power over a northern see. For this theory, see Stafford 1978b: 34. The difficulties in governing the north have been usefully illustrated in Fletcher 2003.

Although Worcester was a prosperous diocese with extensive real estate holdings, the scant evidence that survives for York Minster during this period suggests that Wulfstan would have found a relatively impoverished church suffering from a series of recent property losses and a clergy accustomed to more heterodox practices than the new archbishop was prepared to countenance.[54] Wulfstan's actions as a Church administrator and manager of ecclesiastical property remain among the least understood aspects of his career;[55] nonetheless, he appears to have been, in the words of one historian, 'someone who took estate administration seriously' and who engaged in 'extraordinarily well-conceived and innovative' strategies for securing the tenurial rights of the properties he oversaw.[56] At Worcester, Wulfstan almost certainly commissioned the production of the *Liber Wigorniensis*, the oldest surviving Anglo-Saxon cartulary, as a means of ensuring that leased ecclesiastical property would revert to the Church when current tenancy agreements ended.[57] Likewise, at York, he aggressively pursued the recovery of alienated Church property, expanded the foundation's endowment, and consolidated the minster's real estate holdings.[58] It cannot be a coincidence that Wulfstan's early years at York and Worcester also witnessed his first forays into legal composition, including the *Laws of Edward and Guthrum*, *Concerning Episcopal Duties* (*Episcopus*), the 'Compilation on Status', and the initial version of the *Canons of Edgar*.[59] It is likely that the shared focus of these texts on clerical status, the moral obligations of priests, Church property rights, and episcopal duties provided an ideological framework for Wulfstan's approach to ecclesiastical administration.[60] In the demands that these texts place on clergy and communicants, as well as in their nostalgic vision of the early tenth century, the vision of a revived Christian community in the northern diocese becomes a model for the restoration of a holy society in England as a whole.

---

54 Brooke 1977: 12–43; Keynes 1986: 89–90; Baxter 2004: 161–206; Norton 2004: 207–34; and Woodman 2012: 55ff.

55 Those who have addressed this topic include Whitelock 1965: 214–31; Keynes 1986: 81–99; Barrow 2004: 141–60; Baxter 2004: 161–207; and Woodman 2012: 61–4.

56 Baxter 2004: 190.

57 Ker 1948: 49–75; Stafford 1978a: 23; Baxter 2004: 175–6; and Woodman 2012: 62.

58 Keynes 1986: 88–91 and Baxter 2004: 186–7.

59 Whitelock 1941: 1–21 and Bethurum 1950: 449–63.On the dating of these texts, see Wormald 2004: 26 and Pons-Sanz 2007: 25.

60 Cf. Stephen Baxter, who argues that 'Wulfstan regarded the protection of God's property to be an integral element of his wider programme for the regeneration of Christian society'. Baxter 2004: 163.

The years between 1008 and 1016 were a critical period in Wulfstan's development as a lawmaker and political theorist. Although the archbishop had long served as one of Æthelred's advisors – charter witness-lists produced during his London years record his frequent attendance upon the king and participation in the royal council[61] – it is with the Council of Enham in 1008 that he begins to make his mark as a legislator. The laws promulgated after Enham, edited by Felix Lieber-mann as V and VI Æthelred, are the first to be composed in Wulfstan's distinctive homiletic style, indicating his principal role in the texts' composition.[62] The meeting at Enham may also have been the occasion on which Wulfstan preached the earliest of his surviving addresses to the royal council (translated below, pp. 127–30).[63] The Enham texts bear witness to Wulfstan's newfound pre-eminence as a legislator, yet they also mark both a significant evolution in his political thought and the emergence of a new form of Old English legal composition. V and VI Æthelred initiate what Wormald has described as 'the last phase' of Anglo-Saxon legislation, characterised by increasing sophistication in expression and content.[64] More specifically, the laws' fusion of legal and homiletic rhetoric as well as their rigorous emphasis on the practices necessary to lead a Christian life point to Wulfstan's growing recogni-tion of legislation's potential as a vehicle for realising his vision of a holy society.[65]

Over the course of the next eight years, though, the fulfilment of this vision must have seemed increasingly unlikely as Wulfstan found himself confronted with Æthelred's diminishing power and the mounting aggressiveness of the Viking invasions. The impact of these trends on Wulfstan's thought can be seen in the works he produces during this period, including the law-codes VII–X Æthelred, the first version of the *Institutes of Polity*, as well as such homilies as the *Sermo ad Populum* (Bethurum 13) and Wulfstan's most famous work, the *Sermo Lupi ad Anglos* (Bethurum 20). These writings are characterised by a movement away from the general admonitions and eschatological prophesying of

---

61 See, for instance, S 877, 878, 879, 887, 888, 889, 892, 895, 896, 897, 898, and 899. Charters are cited according to the number assigned to them in Sawyer 1968.

62 Wormald 1978: 49–58; Lawson 1992: 573–8; Wormald 1999d: 332–5; Williams 2003a: 92–3; and Keynes 2007: 177–9.

63 On the date of this text, see Jost 1950: 108. Wormald has proposed 1014 as an alter-native, but concedes the possibility of the earlier date. Wormald 1999d: 337n. 344.

64 Wormald 1999d: 330. On this point, see also Schwyter 1998: 221–2.

65 Wormald 1999d: 345 and Wormald 1999a: 244.

his early works and towards more specific calls for moral and polit-ical transformation. As a result, by 1016, Wulfstan had, in Wormald's words, 'moved from herald of Antichrist and the end of all things, through apprentice welder of English canonical tradition, to prophet and engineer of social reconstruction and political transition. It was an astonishing intellectual odyssey with few parallels in the history of the medieval West'.[66] Wulfstan's emergence as a political thinker of the first order would have practical consequences: the collapse of the West Saxon monarchy in 1016 left Wulfstan as the country's foremost legis-lator, and thus in a perfect position to influence the laws of England's new ruler, King Cnut of Denmark.

Among the greatest mysteries of Wulfstan's career is the question of how he negotiated the period of Danish conquest between 1014 and 1016. The uneven documentary record has left it impossible to discern how his loyalties evolved, when he transferred his allegiance, whether he submitted to Cnut's regime willingly or out of political necessity, and if he sought out the new king on his own or if the young conqueror instead approached the more experienced archbishop for counsel and support.[67] What is clear, however, is that Wulfstan weathered these years with his prestige undiminished. Although he retired as Bishop of Worcester in 1016, he retained his influence over the diocese through his replacement Leofsige, who likely acted only as a suffragan.[68] More importantly, not only did he continue to be the principal author of English legislation, but evidence of Wulfstan's revisions to Cnut's proclamation of 1020 (translated below, pp. 192–6) suggests that he served as one of the principal intermediaries between the Anglo-Saxons and their new Danish king.[69] Wulfstan's service to Cnut provides the backdrop for the composition of many of his most important works, including I and II Cnut, the series of homilies preserved in the York Gospels (translated below, pp. 154–64), and the revised versions of the

---

66 Wormald 1999a: 246. On this point, see also Godden 1994: 142–60; Rabin 2006: 388–414; and Keynes 2007: 170–89. Wormald elsewhere notes the effect of this transition on Wulfstan's prose style: 'The contrast between 1008 and 1014 is impor-tant. It is part of the evidence that Wulfstan was moving from a basically homiletic mode to one with a more evenly balanced blend of the conventions of preaching and law-making'. Wormald 1999d: 340–1.

67 These questions have been usefully explored by M.K. Lawson, whose study of Cnut's reign highlights the political interdependence of Crown and Church during the period of conquest. Lawson 1993: 117–60.

68 Whitelock 1966: 9.

69 Bethurum 1957: 63–4; Lawson 1993: 125–9; and Bolton 2009: 83–4.

Canons of Edgar and the *Institutes of Polity* (translated below, pp. 85–100 and 101–24). This last, which sets forth Wulfstan's view of the three orders of society and argues for the central importance of the episcopacy to a Christian polity, provides the most extensive elaboration of his social vision and represents the most sophisticated work of English political theory before John of Salisbury's *Policraticus*.

Wulfstan died at York on 28 May 1023. In accordance with his wishes, his body was transported to Ely, where he was buried in the cathedral. Renovations to the cathedral over the succeeding centuries resulted in his remains being reinterred several times before reaching their current resting place in the chantry chapel of Bishop Nicholas West in 1771.[70]

Style and canon

Unlike his contemporary Ælfric, relatively few of Wulfstan's writings circulated under his own name. Even those attributed to *Lupus* do not link the pseudonymous author with the archbishop of York. As a result, the establishment of Wulfstan's canon is an on-going project, and the past half-century has witnessed a number of scholars arguing for or against particular Wulfstanian attributions.[71] In the absence of historical or contextual evidence, the principal forms of proof brought to bear on such arguments concern Wulfstan's distinctive prose style. Although Wulfstan's writings encompass a range of genres, his rhetorical practices remained largely consistent. Accordingly, even as Wulfstan is rightly praised as one of Anglo-Saxon England's most sophisticated prose stylists, he may also be considered one of its most easily identifiable.[72] Unfortunately, translation into modern English obscures many of the most important features of Wulfstan's prose; nonetheless, the centrality of the archbishop's mode of expression to his meaning makes it useful to enumerate some of those features here.

---

70 Wulfstan shares his tomb with six other prominent figures in Ely's early history, including Byrhtnoth, leader of the Anglo-Saxon forces at the Battle of Maldon in 991. On the history of Wulfstan's remains, see Crook 2004: 501–24.

71 The list of contributions to this discussion is far too lengthy to be recounted here, but some classic examples include Whitelock 1941; Bethurum 1950; and Whitelock 1955. For more recent instances, see Wilcox 1992; Wormald 1999f; Orchard 2002; Hall 2004; Clayton 2008; and Rabin 2010a.

72 For general overviews of Wulfstan's style, see Kinard 1897: 19–31 and McIntosh 1949; Bethurum 1957: 87–98; Bethurum 1966: 229–35; Orchard 1992; Orchard 2002; Dance 2004; Orchard 2004; and Gates 2010: §22–§33.

Perhaps the most striking aspect of Wulfstan's writing – and certainly the one that most reflects his training as a preacher and rhetorician – is his appropriation of the alliterative and rhythmic elements of Old English verse. Like the authors of Anglo-Saxon poetry, Wulfstan composed much of his work in two-stress phrases bound together by alliteration. To cite just one example, Wulfstan begins the dramatic peroration of his homily *Evil Rulers* (Bethurum 21, translated below, pp. 177–9) with a series of two- and three-stress alliterative units (distinguished here by slash marks), each of which ends with a rhyming infinitive verb: 'utan God gladian/ 7 Godes lage healdan/ 7 anræde weorðan/ to gemænelican þearfan' ('let us please God, adhere to God's laws, and grow steadfast for the common benefit').[73] The effect, as Bethurum has noted, is to make the sound of his language as much a part of his meaning as the sense: 'his sentences must be heard to be understood, and perhaps a modern reader whose sense of rhythm has atrophied from reading the printed page can never realise how these sermons sounded in the churches of Worcester and York'.[74] The importance of poetic rhythm to Wulfstan's writing has led some scholars to suggest that his works ought to be edited using a two-column format similar to that found in editions of Old English verse.[75] So, for example, in Karl Jost's edition, the opening sentence of *Polity*, ch. X reads:

| Riht is, ðæt gerefan | geornlice tylian |
| And symle heora hlafordan | strynan mid rihte. |

| [It is right that reeves | toil assiduously |
| and always for their lord | provide properly.][76] |

Those favouring a poetic layout observe that many of the manuscripts associated with Wulfstan feature patterns of scribal punctuation that offer a visual correlative to the aural effects produced by the prose's rhythm.[77] This approach has not been widely accepted, however. As its critics note, Wulfstan's writing, though verse-like, is not verse: he does not employ the conventional vocabulary and verbal formulae of Old English poetry and his use of rhythm and alliteration is neither regular

73 On the rhythmic patterns in this homily, see Orchard 2002: 314–27.

74 Bethurum 1957: 92. On this point, see also Clemoes 1970: 21–4.

75 For arguments in favour of this approach, see Einenkel 1884: 200–3; McIntosh 1949: 114–22; Jost 1959: 34–6; Orchard 2002: 311–40; and Orchard 2004: 63–91.

76 Jost 1959: 81. For the translation, see below, p. 111.

77 Orchard 2004: 65–70.

nor consistent.[78] To adopt the editorial conventions of Old English verse erases the significant distinctions between rhythmic prose and poetry while imposing potentially inappropriate formal and interpretive paradigms.[79] As such, it remains a common, though admittedly problematic, editorial practice to edit Wulfstan's works without any explicit acknowledgment of their sonic elements.

Other distinctive features of Wulfstan's writing include his frequent use of adverbial intensifiers such as *georne* (translated variously as 'urgently', 'eagerly', 'earnestly', 'diligently', 'assiduously', and 'willingly') and *swiðe* ('very', 'exceedingly'), recapitulation (most commonly signalled by clauses beginning with the words, 'that is'), and echoic pairs such as *godcund/ woruldcund* (divine/ secular) and *manswica/ manswora* (traitor/ perjurer).[80] Perhaps as a result of the northern context in which they were written, Wulfstan's political works are also characterised by a high density of Old Norse borrowings, most notably legal terms such as *þræl* (slave), *grið* (peace), and *lagu* (law).[81] Finally, among the most memorable aspects of Wulfstan's style, even to those relying on translation, is his practice of punctuating both his legal and homiletic writings with ominous lists of sins, sinners, or impending disasters.[82] Rhythmic, alliterative, and constructed of rhyming or echoic compounds, such lists often provide the text's dramatic climax, as in the homily *On Heathen Practices* (Napier 60, translated below, pp. 159–61):

> Her syndan on earde godcundnessæ wiðersacan and godes lage oferhogan, manslagan and mægslagan, cychatan and sacerdbana, hadbrecan and æwbrecan, mytestran and bearnmyrðran, þeofas and þeodscaðan, ryperas and reaferas, leogeras and liceteras and leodhatan hetele ealles to manege, þe ðurh mansylene barjað þas þeode, and wedlogan and wærlogan and lytle getrywða to wide mid mannum.

> [Here in this land are enemies of the divine and despisers of God's law, murderers and parricides, church-haters and priest-killers, violators of holy orders and violators of their marriage vows, prostitutes and child-killers, thieves and criminals, robbers and vandals, perjurers and hypocrites and all too many evil tyrants who empty the realm through their butchery,

78 Bethurum 1957: 94; Whitelock 1961; Funke 1962: 317–18; and Orchard 2007: 321. The problems involved in distinguishing Old English verse and rhythmic homiletic prose have been discussed in Stanley 1985: 363–92.

79 Whitelock 1966: 19n. 12.

80 Bethurum 1957: 89–90; Bethurum 1966: 231–2; Whitelock 1966: 18; Hattori 1990: 195–207; Orchard 1992: 247–50; Chapman 2002: 1–18; and Pons-Sanz 2004: 281–96.

81 Whitelock 1965: 226; Whitelock 1966: 44; and Loyn 1994: 79.

82 See especially Meaney 2004: 479–81 and Davis-Secord 2008: 65–96.

breakers of oaths and violators of trusts, and all too widely there has been little faith among men.]

Wulfstan's reliance on lists of this sort is not limited by genre: similar passages appear in both his early and late homilies, in political tracts such as *Polity*, and in his law-codes, most notably II Cnut. Many of the compounds on these lists are unique to Wulfstan's writings, and it is likely that they were coined by the archbishop in the process of composing the list. Although such passages might seem overwrought to the modern reader, they serve a crucial rhetorical purpose. As Jonathan Davis-Secord has pointed out, 'his compound-laden lists and the unique compounds ... stress the point of social stability but through different means. The lists add weight and authority to the general exhortations, and the content of the unique compounds ... bring to the forefront the threats to social stability'.[83] Much of the force of Wulfstan's writing lies in his power to overwhelm his audience with the magnitude and immediacy of the moral peril confronting them; this urgency results as much from the style of his prose as from the substance of his text.

The consistency and distinctiveness of Wulfstan's style has enabled scholars to establish the corpus of his writings with some confidence. It is generally agreed that he wrote the twenty-one Old English homilies (some in multiple versions) edited by Bethurum, the eleven additional Latin homilies identified by Thomas N. Hall and J.E. Cross, and items 1, 23, 24, 25, 27, 35, 50, 51, 52, 53, 59, 60, and 61 in Arthur Napier's 1883 edition. He is also responsible for the series of short fragmentary texts preserved in Copenhagen, Kongelige Bibliotek, Gl. Kgl. S. 1595, fol. 66v and London, British Library, Additional MS. 38651, fols. 57–58.[84] Jonathan Wilcox includes Napier 36 and 38 in the corpus, albeit with question marks; however, these attributions have since been challenged by Joyce Tally Lionarons, who argues that they contain too many features not found elsewhere in the archbishop's work.[85] In addition to his homiletic writings, Wulfstan also served as the principle author of the law-codes V–X Æthelred, I–II Cnut, Cnut's laws of 1018, and portions of Cnut's proclamation of 1020.[86] Wulfstan's political writings consist of the so-called *Laws of Edward and Guthrum*,

---

83 Davis-Secord 2008: 95.

84 Wilcox 1992: 200–1; Hall 2004: 94–8; Pons-Sanz 2007: 8–10; and Lionarons 2010: 27.

85 Lionarons 2010: 31–2.

86 Whitelock 1948: 433–52; Whitelock 1955: 72–85; Kennedy 1983: 57–81; Keynes 1986: 95–6; and Wormald 1999d: 330–65.

Concerning Episcopal Duties (*Episcopus*), the 'Compilation on Status' (*On Ranks, On Clerical Compensation,* and the second half of *On Wergild*[87] are original compositions by Wulfstan which he then combined with the *Laws of the Mercians, The Mercian Oath,* and the first half of *On Wergild*), *On Sanctuary, The Canons of Edgar,* the Old English *Regula Canonicorum,* and *The Institutes of Polity.*[88] The brevity of *Northumbrian Church-Sanctuary* makes a firm attribution more difficult, yet its similarity to VIII Æthelred 5.2 points to Wulfstan as the most likely author.[89] Also attributable to the archbishop are the short tracts edited by Jost as appendices a, b, c, e, f, g, i, and l in his edition of *Polity* (the last of which is translated below as *An Admonition to Bishops*, pp. 180–3), the Latin letters included in Bethurum's edition of the homilies, the Old English Benedictine Office, the entries for 959 and 975 in the *Anglo-Saxon Chronicle,* and portions of the Old English translation of Ælfric's first Old English pastoral letter. Additionally, Wulfstan likely oversaw revisions to the Old English *Handbook for a Confessor* (formerly called the *Penitential of Pseudo-Egbert*), the law-codes I Æthelstan, II Edmund, and II–III Edgar, and the *Promissio Regis.*[90] Finally, he has been shown to be responsible for the compilation previously identified as the *Excerptiones Pseudo-Egberti,* but re-edited by J.E. Cross and Andrew Hamer as *Wulfstan's Canon Law Collection.*[91] Other texts attributed to Wulfstan include several homilies edited by Napier, the tracts *Rectitudines Singularum Personarum* and *Gerefa,* and the *Northumbrian Priests' Law;* however, these attributions have since been shown to be erroneous.[92]

Manuscripts

The texts translated in this volume survive in twelve manuscripts, which can be usefully divided into three categories:[93]

87 Also referred to as the *Law of the North People.* See below, pp. 70–1.

88 Whitelock 1941: 1–21; Bethurum 1950: 449–63; Jost 1959: 23–4; Wormald 1999d: 389–96; and Rabin 2010a: 43–52.

89 Dammery 1994: 257 and Wormald 1999d: 395.

90 Bethurum 1957: 374–7; Ure 1957: 25–46; Jost 1959: 167–268; Wilcox 1992: 201; Pons-Sanz 2007: 10–17; Clayton 2008: 91–150; and Lionarons 2010: 79–80.

91 Cross and Hamer 1999: 3–6.

92 Cf. Scragg 1977: 197–211; Wilcox 1991: 1–19; Harvey 1993: 1–22; Scragg 1998: 8ff; Wormald 1999d: 387–8, 396–8; and Wormald 1999f: 247–51.

93 Contents lists for these manuscripts can be found in the appendix. The brief descrip-

a. Manuscripts used or copied from those used by Wulfstan[94]

i. Cambridge, University Library, Additional 3206

Fragments of two leaves from the second half of the eleventh century. The manuscript from which these came probably originated in southwest England. The fragments contain passages from *The Canons of Edgar* and *The Institutes of Polity*, likely copied from Junius 121 or a related manuscript.

ii. Cambridge, Corpus Christi College 190

Originally two distinct manuscripts bound together before 1327. The older material was probably compiled in the early eleventh century, the newer material perhaps twenty-five years later. The manuscript is most likely of Worcester origin. Contents include *The Mercian Law* (*Mircna Laga*), *On Oaths* (*Að*), and *Concerning Clerical Compensation* (*Hadbot*) of the 'Compilation on Status'.

iii. London, British Library, Cotton Nero A.i

Two volumes, the first dating to the years around 1066 and the second compiled between 1003 and 1023 in either Worcester or York. Contents include *On Sanctuary* (*Grið*), *Northumbrian Church-Sanctuary* (*Norgrið*), *The Institutes of Polity*, *An Admonition to Bishops*, *God's Threat to a Sinning Israel* (Bethurum 19), and *Evil Rulers* (Bethurum 21).

iv. Oxford, Bodleian Library, Junius 121

Compiled sometime during the second half of the eleventh century in Worcester. Contents include *Concerning Episcopal Duties* (*Episcopus*), *The Canons of Edgar*, *The Institutes of Polity*, and *God's Threat to a Sinning Israel* (Bethurum 19).

v. York, Minster Library, Additional 1

A Gospel book compiled between the end of the tenth and the beginning of the eleventh century. Possibly produced at Christ Church, Canterbury, but in the possession of York Minster by 1023. A series of Old English texts, some annotated by Wulfstan, have been added on the last six leaves of the MS. Contents include *On the Duties of the Laity* (Napier 59), *On Heathen Practices* (Napier 60), *On Christian Practices* (Napier 61), and *Cnut 1020*.

tions found here based on those in Ker 1957 and Gneuss 2001.

94 A useful summary of the evidence for Wulfstan's manuscript use can be found in Whitelock 1965: 215–21.

Of the five manuscripts in this category, four – C.U.L. Additional 3206, Cotton Nero A.i, C.C.C.C. 190, and Junius 121 – form part of a family of manuscripts somewhat misleadingly referred to as Wulfstan's 'commonplace books', compilations consisting of Old English legal and homiletic material, extracts from Carolingian canonists, and versions of Wulfstan's own writings. Although the organisation and contents of the manuscripts may be attributed to Wulfstan, in at least two cases – C.U.L Additional 3206 and Junius 121 – the surviving manuscripts are copies made after the archbishop's death. The coherence of the 'commonplace book' family of manuscripts, though not its association with Wulfstan, was first noted in an 1895 article by Mary Bateson, who identified five compilations with similar content seemingly produced as 'a kind of theological commonplace-book specially intended for a bishop's use'.[95] Dorothy Bethurum subsequently demonstrated that the manuscripts had either been compiled by Wulfstan or copied from manuscripts compiled by him, possibly to provide source or reference material during his early tenure as archbishop.[96] More compilations of this type have since been identified, and twelve manuscripts are now recognised as members of the 'commonplace book' family.[97]

Wulfstan's reasons for producing manuscript compilations of this sort remain the subject of some debate. The term 'commonplace book' – connoting an eclectic notebook consisting of random quotations reflecting the idiosyncratic interests of its compiler – fails to capture the particular organisation of these compilations and the care that went into selecting their component texts. Possibly originating as attempts to gather material for what would become the *Canons of Edgar*, the commonplace books grew into a project echoing the great *compilationes* of the Carolingian canonists.[98] As Patrick Wormald has pointed out, 'what was taking shape was something like the canon collections of Regino of Prüm, Abbo of Fleury, and Burchard of Worms: assemblages of ecclesiastical law and custom that exploited patristic as readily as decretal or

95 Bateson 1895: 712.

96 Bethurum 1942.

97 In addition to the four manuscripts noted above, the group includes: C.C.C.C. 265; Copenhagen, Kongelige Bibliotek, G.K.S. 1595; Rouen, Bibliothèque Municipale 1382 (U. 109); Oxford, Bodleian Library, Bodley 718; London, British Library, Cotton Vespasian A.xiv; Paris, Bibliothèque Nationale, lat. 3182; Brussels, Bibliothèque Royale, 8558–63; and Oxford, Bodleian Library, Barlow 37. For a discussion of these manuscripts, see Bethurum 1942: 917–29; Cross 1992: 63–73; Jones 1998a: 77–82; Wormald 1999d: 214–15; Sauer 2000: 340–3; and Hill 2004: 320–2.

98 Fowler 1963: 9–10 and Hill 2004: 322–3.

conciliar prescriptions'.[99] Indeed, it is striking that the manuscripts of the 'commonplace book' family draw no distinction between different genres of text and freely intermingle legal and homiletic material. The blending of genres so characteristic of Wulfstan's writing and so central to his vision of a Holy Society is no less present in the manuscripts he commissioned. In this sense, the 'commonplace books' may be more than merely collections of extracts that caught the archbishop's interest; rather, they may indicate instead a self-conscious attempt to compile and organise the textual materials of Wulfstan's political programme.

b. Posthumous compilations and miscellanies

i. Cambridge, Corpus Christi College 201

A miscellany comprised of three parts compiled over the course of the eleventh century, possibly at New Minster, Winchester though it may have links to Worcester or York. Contents include the 'Compilation on Status', *The Canons of Edgar, The Institutes of Polity, On the Proper Support of the Church* (Napier 22), *On Tithes and Tithing* (Napier 23), *On Baptism and Confirmation* (Napier 24), *On Various Misfortunes* (Napier 35), VIIa Æthelred, *God's Threat to a Sinning Israel* (Bethurum 19), *Evil Rulers* (Bethrurm 21), and the *Northumbrian Priests' Law.*

ii. Cambridge, Corpus Christi College 419

A companion to C.C.C.C. 421. Compiled in the first half of the eleventh century, perhaps at Christ Church, though it entered the library at Exeter Cathedral shortly thereafter. Contents include *On the Proper Support of the Church* (Napier 22), *On Tithes and Tithing* (Napier 23), and *On Baptism and Confirmation* (Napier 24).

iii. Cambridge, Corpus Christi College 421

A companion to C.C.C.C. 419. Compiled in the first half of the eleventh century, perhaps at Christ Church, though it entered the library at Exeter Cathedral shortly thereafter. Contents include *On Justice, Virtue, and the Law* (Napier 50).

iv. London, British Library, Cotton Tiberius A.iii

Compiled in the mid-eleventh century, likely at Christ Church, Canterbury. Contents include *On the Laws of God and the World* (Napier 51), *On the Duties of the Clergy* (Napier 52), *On the Sins of the Clergy* (Napier 53), *On the Proper Support of the Church*

---

99 Wormald 1999a: 239–40.

(Napier 22), *On Tithes and Tithing* (Napier 23), and *On Baptism and Confirmation* (Napier 24).

v. Oxford, Bodleian Library, Hatton 113
Compiled at the end of the eleventh century at Worcester for the use of Bishop (later Saint) Wulfstan, nephew of Archbishop Wulfstan. Contents include *On the Proper Support of the Church* (Napier 22), *On Baptism and Confirmation* (Napier 24), *On Various Misfortunes* (Napier 35), and *Evil Rulers* (Bethurum 21).

The manuscripts in this category attest to the circulation of Wulfstan's writings from the height of his career to the period shortly after his death in 1023.[100] Although the scribes behind these manuscripts may have been familiar with Wulfstan's 'commonplace books', Wulfstan himself knew nothing of these manuscripts nor did he have any direct influence over their contents or organisation. They thus provide useful evidence for the reception of Wulfstan's writings and perception of his career in the mid- to late eleventh century. What this evidence indicates is that Wulfstan's works, particularly his homilies, were seen as valuable source material by subsequent authors. The revising of homilies such as *On Various Misfortunes*, the breaking up and repurposing of textual groups such as the *Sermones ad Populum* (Napier 19–25), and in the most extreme cases, the cobbling together of entirely new homilies out of the spare parts of other texts (as was the case with Napier 30) suggest that later writers not only saw his works as useful but felt little compunction about plundering them for their own needs.[101] Equally important is the fact that the compilers of several of these manuscripts intersperse the homiletic material with extracts from Wulfstan's political writings, including the *Canons of Edgar* and the *Institutes of Polity*. The production of manuscripts of this sort in such foundations as Christ Church, Canterbury or New Minster, Winchester – 'nurseries of monk-bishops', in Wormald's words – points to the extent to which Wulfstan's works were seen as guides for careers that unified ecclesiastic and secular responsibilities.[102]

c. Twelfth-century legal anthologies

i. Cambridge, Corpus Christi College 383

---

100 On the immediate posthumous reception of Wulfstan's writings, see Wilcox 1992: 199–217.

101 Scragg 1977: 197–8; Wilcox 1992: 204; Lionarons 2004b: 159–65; and Lionarons 2010: 30–1.

102 Wormald 1999d: 210. See also Budny 1997: Vol. I, p. 475; Lionarons 2010: 14.

Compiled in the early twelfth century, probably at St. Paul's in London. Contents include *The Laws of Edward and Guthrum.*

ii. Strood, Medway Archive and Local Studies Centre, MS. DRc/R1
(*Textus Roffensis*)
Compiled in either 1123 or 1124 at Rochester at the behest of Bishop Ernulf. A two-part manuscript containing legislation (part I) and the cartulary of Rochester Cathedral (part II), *Textus Roffensis* was probably produced in order to serve as evidence in property litigation. Contents include *The Laws of Edward and Guthrum* and the 'Compilation on Status'.

The manuscripts in this category were produced as what Wormald has labelled 'legal encyclopedias' by Anglo-Norman ecclesiastics in the twelfth century.[103] They are characterised by their contents which, unlike the manuscripts of the previous two categories, consist entirely of legal material selected and organised to demonstrate a continuity of authority between the pre- and post-Conquest periods.[104] The compilers of these manuscripts betray little knowledge of Wulfstan's career or intentions as a writer, and the fact that they freely intermingle historical forgeries such as *Edward-Guthrum* with political tracts and royal legislation suggests that they recognised little distinction between prescriptive law and other forms of legal composition produced under the Anglo-Saxons. These manuscripts are the most comprehensive sources for pre-Conquest legislation, yet the manner in which their compilers reorganised and reworked texts has been the cause of considerable confusion among modern legal historians, not least because their treatment of Wulfstan's writings tended to disguise their original contexts and obscure the archbishop's involvement in their composition.[105]

Sources and influences

Two principal difficulties confront those seeking to identify the sources Wulfstan used in his writings: first, unlike his contemporary Ælfric, the majority of whose career was spent in a single location, Wulfstan

103 Wormald 1999d: 224.

104 Richards 1986: 181–6; Richards 1988: 43–60; Richards 1997: 55–6; O'Brien 1999: 7; Wormald 1999b: 115–39; Wormald 1999d: 224–52; and Hough 2006: 114–31.

105 See below, pp. 45–6.

divided his time between London, the various diocesan properties of York and Worcester, and the itinerant courts of Æthelred and Cnut. Consequently, not only can he not be identified with a single library or manuscript repository, but it is likely that much of his writing took place in the saddle under conditions in which a wide range of texts would not have been readily at hand.[106] Second, again unlike Ælfric, Wulfstan rarely identifies his sources by name – other than Biblical citations, his only explicit mention of a source is a single reference to Pope Gregory I[107] – and, in the process of translating passages into his distinctive rhythmic prose, he often revises his material to such an extent that the original source becomes almost unrecognisable.[108] Indeed, it is telling that Wulfstan is one of the few major authors omitted from Michael Lapidge's otherwise comprehensive study of the contents of pre-Conquest libraries.[109] Yet, if a complete list of the texts known to Wulfstan remains elusive, enough of his sources have been identified to convey some sense of his learning and his habits as a reader.

Among English sources, Wulfstan relies most on texts associated with the Monastic Reform of the tenth and eleventh centuries.[110] Although familiar with earlier materials – his writings reveal knowledge of such texts as Bede's *Ecclesiastical History*, the penitential of Theodore, the works of Aldhelm and Alcuin, the canons of Oda of Canterbury, the decrees of the synods of Hertford (672) and Chelsea (816), and a variety of royal and papal letters[111] – his frame of reference appears to have

---

106 The peripatetic nature of Wulfstan's career led Christopher Hohler to reject many of the attributions then being proposed by Whitelock and Bethurum, as he did not believe that such texts could have been produced under those circumstances. This argument has not found wide acceptance, however. Hohler 1975: 225n. 259.

107 Bethurum 10c, l. 48. See Orchard 1992: 240. It's worth noting that Wulfstan did occasionally note his sources in the margins of manuscript copies of his texts. See Ker 1971: 323.

108 Sauer 1978: 118–19; Orchard 1992: 257; Hill 1993: 20–1; Scragg 1998: 12; and Orchard 2007: 334–5.

109 The authors whose libraries are catalogued in Lapidge's book are Theodore and Hadrian of Canterbury, Aldhelm, Bede, Alcuin, the anonymous author of the *Old English Martyrology*, Asser, Lantfred, Abbo of Fleury, Wulfstan of Winchester, Ælfric, and Byrhtferth. Lapidge 2006: 174–274. The topic of Wulfstan's library has been taken up by Andy Orchard; however, as he concedes, Wulfstan's habit of extensively revising his sources means any speculation on this topic is largely limited to the contents of the 'commonplace book' manuscripts. See Orchard 2012: 694–700.

110 For useful overviews of the Monastic Reform, see Knowles 1963: 31–57; Stenton 1971: 433–67; Cubitt 1997: 77–94; and Gretsch 1999.

111 Whitelock 1966: 32–3.

been shaped by texts produced from the 940s onwards. Reformist texts such as the *Regularis Concordia* influenced his approach to the liturgy and the regulation of monastic life, while his practice of assembling manuscript *compilationes* may have been modelled on pontifical anthologies produced by the Reformist Bishop Oswald, one of his predecessors at Worcester.[112] Of particular importance, however, was the legislation promulgated under the kings most associated with the Reform, Edmund and Edgar. Wulfstan may have drawn on these laws in part because they mark the first attempt to link secular and ecclesiastical authority through a blending of legal and homiletic rhetoric.[113] Equally important, though, is the fact that the relative stability of the reigns of Edmund and Edgar, along with the latter's close ties to such venerated Church figures as Archbishop Dunstan of Canterbury and Bishop Æthelwold of Winchester, led churchmen of Wulfstan's generation to view the years from 940 to 975 as something of a golden age.[114] In *Polity*, Wulfstan writes that the kingdom's decline began with Edgar's death, while elsewhere he admonishes his readers to 'faithfully obey the law of Edgar'.[115] Likewise, the rubric to the earliest version of the *Canons of Edgar* – which may have been conceived initially as a historical forgery similar to the *Laws of Edward and Guthrum* – reads, 'Here now are the practices fitting for those in orders according to the decrees of Edgar'.[116] References such as these indicate the extent to which Wulfstan understood himself as part of a Reformist tradition: in aligning his work with that of the previous generation of ecclesiastical Reformers, Wulfstan grounds his vision in an established precedent. The return to religious orthodoxy, preservation of Church privileges, elevation of episcopal authority, and vision of holy kingship so important to the first generation of English Reformers here serves as the basis for Wulfstan's own social programme. More broadly, in acknowledging his intellectual debt to the legal, political, and religious inheritance of the mid-tenth century so explicitly, Wulfstan signals its importance as both model and inspiration for his attempt to establish a new golden age in eleventh-century England.

112 Dumville 1992: 75–6; Hill 1992: 106; Hill 2004: 315–17, 320–3; and Jones 2004: 328.

113 Wormald 1999d: 308–20.

114 Whitelock 1942: 29; Bethurum Loomis 1971: 129–47; Hill 2004: 313; and Rabin 2013: 230–1.

115 Cf. *Polity* X, *Cn. 1020* 13, *On Justice*, n. 43; and *On Christian Practices*, n. 6. On Wulfstan's references to the 'law of Edgar', see Wormald 1999d: 132.

116 See below, *Canons* n. 2. See also Fowler 1972: xxvi–xxvii.

The most significant Reformist influence on Wulfstan came not from his tenth-century predecessors, however, but from his contemporary, Abbot Ælfric of Eynsham. The only prose writer of the later Anglo-Saxon period to rival Wulfstan in output and accomplishment, Ælfric provided Wulfstan with much of the moral and theological framework around which he constructed his political edifice. Among modern scholars, the two are often taken to represent the twin poles of later Anglo-Saxon intellectual life, 'one as standing for the Law and the other as standing for the Gospel', in the words of Eric Stanley.[117] While Wulfstan's career took place in the world, as an advisor of kings and member of the royal council, Ælfric spent his career in the cloister where he focused his mental energies on problems of theology rather than politics.[118] The extent of Ælfric's influence on Wulfstan's thought is indicated by the fact that he is one of the few people whose opinions the archbishop is known to have solicited directly. Between 1002 and 1006, at Wulfstan's request, Ælfric composed a series of pastoral letters detailing his views on a variety of doctrinal issues ranging from clerical celibacy to the proper length of time between birth and baptism. Five of these letters have survived, three in Latin and two in Old English translations.[119] Beyond the pastoral letters, Wulfstan was also familiar with many of Ælfric's other writings, including a pastoral letter he had composed for Bishop Wulfsige of Sherborne, his Latin commentary on the Decalogue, and twelve of his homilies.[120] Wulfstan mined these texts extensively over the course of his career: nine of the homilies in Bethurum's edition are based on texts by Ælfric, the pastoral letters serve as sources or analogues for thirty-seven of the seventy clauses in the *Canons of Edgar*, and Ælfric's *Book on the Old and New Testament* is most likely the immediate source for the 'Orders of Society' in the

---

117 Stanley 2004: 430.

118 On Ælfric's career and its parallels with that of Wulfstan, see Gatch 1977: 12–17; Stafford 1978a: 11–32; Gneuss 2009: 2–6; and Magennis and Swan 2009.

119 Fehr 1914: 35–227. Four of these letters (two of the Latin and the two Old English adaptations) were written as 'public' letters designed for circulation, while one (Fehr's *Briefe* 2A) was written as a private response to a more specific series of questions. The 'private' designation of this last letter originated with its editor, Bernard Fehr; however, Malcolm Godden has suggested that that this letter was composed for public circulation also. See Godden 2004: 357–8. One of the Old English letters was then further adapted by Wulfstan. See the C.C.C.C. 201 version of Ælfric's first Old English letter to Wulfstan, Fehr 1914: 68–145. The circumstances under which the letters came to be written has been discussed extensively. See Hill 1992: 103–17; Godden 2004: 354–62; Hill 2004: 313–14; and Gneuss 2009: 28–9.

120 Clemoes 1960: 253–83 and Godden 2004: 363–4.

Institutes of Polity, to cite just a few examples.[121] Why Wulfstan relied so heavily on Ælfric's writings remains the subject of some debate. Modern readers have ascribed Wulfstan's use of Ælfric to insecurity, to ignorance, or simply to a desire to confirm and document orthodox practices before implementing his proposed reforms.[122] Any one of these reasons might be correct, yet it is equally likely that Ælfric's writings fulfilled a more practical need. The *imprimatur* of one of the most respected ecclesiastics in England provided a powerful warrant for an archbishop with Reformist tendencies. Moreover, the rigorous orthodoxy of Ælfric's theology may have served as something of an inspiration, even provocation, for Wulfstan's desire to import a similar orthodoxy into English political life. This is not to suggest either that Wulfstan merely ventriloquised Ælfric or that Ælfric was little more than an ideological facilitator for Wulfstan's political agenda. The two often disagreed: Wulfstan differed from Ælfric on many details of Church ritual, while the latter was deeply suspicious of clerical involvement in matters of government, especially criminal prosecution.[123] However, Wulfstan's willingness to repurpose Ælfric's views suggests that such points of disagreement may have been no less useful to his thinking than the confirmation the latter's works offered on the points on which they agreed. In other words, much of the value of Ælfric's writings for Wulfstan may have lain in the way in which they encouraged him to rethink the abbot's monastic theology for use in the secular world. In this way, even as Ælfric served Wulfstan as a resource on Church doctrine, his works also provided the archbishop with an intellectual foil against which to test his own ideas and reforms.

Among non-English sources, Wulfstan relied most on Carolingian works of the ninth and tenth centuries. As was the case with his use of English sources, Wulfstan appears to have preferred more recent writers despite having extensive familiarity with earlier texts, including the decrees of the Church councils, the writings of the Church fathers, and canon law compilations such as the eighth-century *Collectio canonum Hibernensis*.[124] Especially influential on Wulfstan's thought were Alcuin, Hincmar of Reims, Theodulf of Orléans, Atto of Vercelli,

---

121 See Fowler 1972: xxxix–xl and Godden 2004: 364 as well as *Canons* and *Polity* below.

122 Fehr 1914: cix; Godden 2004: 374; and Hill 2004: 314.

123 Godden even goes so far as to suggest that their correspondence may have ended because Ælfric discovered how much Wulfstan had altered his views in the course of repurposing his writings. Godden 2004: 373–4 and Marafioti 2008: 42–50.

124 Bethurum 1957: 61; Whitelock 1966: 31; Gatch 1977: 62; and Hill 1993: 20–1.

Adso of Montier-en-Der, Ghaerbald of Liège, Abbo of Saint-Germain-des-Prés, Sedulius Scottus, Jesse of Amiens, and Amalarius of Metz.[125] Works by these authors were available at Worcester's monastic library, and in several cases, excerpts of their writings occur in one or more of Wulfstan's 'commonplace books'.[126] What Wulfstan took from these writers, in Wormald's words, was a desire 'to bring order to the accumulated law of the Church, and to assert its relevance to a society [he] felt to be threatened'.[127] Canonists such as Theodulf and Amalarius offered Wulfstan a model for organising ecclesiastical authority and situating the law of the Church in relation to that of the crown. Meanwhile, political theorists such as Alcuin, Hincmar, and Sedulius Scottus provided him with the ideal of the 'just king', a divinely appointed ruler bound to safeguard the prerogatives of the Church and preserve peace through the righteous governance of a properly ordered society.[128] In texts such as the *Institutes of Polity*, Wulfstan combined these two trends in Carolingian thought while also introducing his own, Reformist-inspired policies, most notably the elevation of episcopal authority to a higher status than that accorded it by his continental predecessors.[129] In this sense, Wulfstan was, as Wormald called him, '*par excellence* a Carolingian ideologue', yet one who inflected his thought with the theology and priorities of the English Monastic Reform.[130]

The picture of Wulfstan conveyed by his sources and influences is of a learned individual, yet one who viewed his reading principally as a means of engaging with contemporary issues of just governance and the regulation of authority, both Christian and secular. The combined influence of Carolingian political thought and the theology of the Monastic Reform enabled Wulfstan to generate a social vision responsive to what he saw as the particular needs of early eleventh-century England. No less important is what Wulfstan's treatment of his sources reveals about him as a writer: the freedom with which he revised his

---

125 Whitelock 1942: 29–30; Whitelock 1943: 125–6; Bethurum 1957: 61; Whitelock 1966: 31–2; Bethurum Loomis 1971: 130–1; Emmerson 1983: 1–10; Cross and Brown 1989: 270–91; Cross 1993: 237–46; Cross and Brown 1993 for 1989: 71–91; Jones 1998b: 681–3; and Elliott 2010: 161–5.

126 Bethurum 1942: 916–29; Bethurum 1957: 61; Cross and Brown 1989: 271–2; Cross and Brown 1993 for 1989: 238–9; Jones 1998b: 681–3; Wormald 1999d: 198–223; Hill 2004: 320–3; and Mann 2004: 235–78.

127 Wormald 1999d: 457.

128 Bethurum Loomis 1971: 131–2; Stafford 1971: 183–4; and Wormald 1999d: 457–8.

129 Bethurum Loomis 1971: 134 and Wormald 1999d: 457.

130 Wormald 1999d: 464. On this point, see also Hill 2004: 323–4.

material and concealed his debts, all in a unique rhythmic prose strikingly different from that of his contemporaries, points to a deep investment in the creation of his own distinctive authorial voice. As Joyce Hill observes, 'Wulfstan's writings are not in the main presented as texts in dialogue with other texts, whatever may be the reality of their mode of composition behind the scenes. It feels like, and in important ways it is, a textual world and a lived world which is significantly different from those of the figures who provide us with our dominant terms of reference for the Reform in England'.[131] Yet, if Wulfstan wears his learning lightly, it is nonetheless present; and in reworking his material for his own ends he undertakes in miniature the larger project which consumed his career, his remaking of the archbishop's role into an instrument for the reformation of English society as a whole.

Homilist and statesman

Wulfstan occupied a unique position at the juncture of England's ecclesiastical hierarchy and the later Anglo-Saxon state apparatus. More than any other pre-Conquest churchman, he sought to shape both the legal and religious lives of his countrymen. It was the dual nature of this project that gave form to his writings. The importance of this duality in Wulfstan's works was first explored by Dorothy Whitelock in an influential 1942 article that described the archbishop's pursuit of a reformist agenda through his complementary roles as (in the words of her title) 'Homilist and Statesman'. According to Whitelock,

> Enough remains on record of this prelate for us to see him as a man of fiery zeal who, convinced that the misfortunes of his country were a retribution for sin, strove by all means to bring about reform, not confining himself to impassioned denunciation, though of this he was a master. He toiled to improve the standard of learning and morality of the clergy and to bring all classes to an understanding of the Christian faith and a due observance of the laws of the church, and to put an end to the abuses of contemporary life.[132]

As Whitelock perceptively observed, the moral agenda Wulfstan advocated in his sermons cannot be separated from the behavioural prescriptions set forth in his legal writings any more that underlying social vision of his laws can be distinguished from the Christian idealism

131 Hill 2004: 311.
132 Whitelock 1942: 42.

of his homilies. Indeed, the legal and religious strands in Wulfstan's thought are so intertwined that, in Wormald's words, the very duality implied by Whitelock's title, 'tends to bifurcate what was (or became) a unitary enterprise'.[133] This is not to say that Wulfstan recognised no distinction between law and homily as rhetorical genres;[134] rather, it is to suggest that any attempt to understand the development of Wulfstan's ideas and his significance as a political thinker must take into account his works' unique blending of the legal and the homiletic.

In part, Wulfstan's view of his roles as ecclesiastic and statesman can be seen in the way in which he transforms his legal and political writings for homiletic purposes. Much of what occurred prior to the promulgation of a law-code in the early eleventh century remains unclear, yet it seems likely that the process began with the king setting forth a series of specific prescriptions with the advice of his council, of which Wulfstan was a leading member. Wulfstan then redrafted these prescriptions in a quasi-homiletic style that situated the specific royal decrees within a Christian framework. Portions of the resulting legislation then could be incorporated into homilies in which the most important original prescriptions were retained, yet divorced from the specific occasion of law-making and subordinated to the archbishop's larger moral vision.[135] Evidence for this process survives in the form of the three versions of Æthelred's 'penitential edict' of 1009: a Latin text preserved in the twelfth-century compilation *Quadripartitus* (designated VII Æthelred; translated below, pp. 186–8), an Old English 'draft' produced by Wulfstan sometime around the Latin's original date of promulgation (designated VIIa Æthelred; translated below, pp. 189–91), and a subsequent homily of Wulfstan's which draws on the Old English (translated below, pp. 130–2). The Latin version, likely a reasonably accurate translation of an Old English original,[136] opens with a prologue specifying that it was established ('instituerunt') by King Æthelred and his councillors ('Æþelredus rex et sapientes') at a meeting of the royal council at Bath ('apud Badam').[137] The first clause

---

133 Wormald 1999a: 226.

134 On this point, see Wormald 1999d: 339.

135 Cf. Liebermann 1913; Stafford 1978a: 29–30; Lawson 1992: 576–8; Richards 1997: 54; Wormald 1999d: 330–9; and Lionarons 2010: 164.

136 Wormald points out that the prologue retains the introductory formula found in other early Wulfstanian legislation and that the distinctive features of the archbishop's prose are still visible 'shining through the frosted glass of the *Quadripartitus* Latin'. Wormald 1999d: 331.

137 VII Atr. Pr.

enjoins subjects to 'obey their king' ('regi suo pareant') and to 'protect his realm along with him' ('cum eo pariter defendant regnum suum').[138] The remainder of the code then lists a series of communal penitential rituals designed to engage the entire community in the spiritual defence of the kingdom.[139] In contrast, the Old English version omits all reference to the king, his councillors, and the political obligations of subjects to their royal lord; instead, the text begins with a rubric situating it within a moment of national crisis: 'This was decreed when the great army came to this land'. Wulfstan then replaces the loyalty clause with a demand for Christian fidelity: 'We all must strive diligently so that we may receive God's mercy and compassion and, with his help, withstand our enemies'.[140] The subsequent penitential injunctions hereby acquire a new significance. As Wormald points out, the text no longer described 'what a ruler did in a recollected spatial context, and became what was agreed in a predicament that must at all costs not recur'.[141] Its scope becomes even broader in the homiletic version, headed only with the vague phrase *Concerning Various Misfortunes*. The text opens, 'if it comes about that a great misfortune befalls the realm because of the people's deeds – war or hunger, fire or bloodshed, crop failure or bad weather, the death of men or cattle from a sudden plague – then amends always is to be made to God himself'. The specific laws of VII Æthelred thus come to be transformed into a broader account of a people's penitential obligations when faced with a communal threat.[142] The porousness between genres illustrated by these texts indicates the extent to which Wulfstan brought the obligations of his different roles to bear upon one another. For Wulfstan, the political act of law-making could not be distinguished from his larger religious project, the moral regeneration of the kingdom.

This combination of roles emerges, not only in Wulfstan's writings, but also in the manuscripts in which they are preserved. Many of the earliest manuscripts to contain Wulfstan's works, particularly those in the 'commonplace book' tradition discussed above, likely were produced for his own use, and the presence of annotations and corrections in his handwriting reveals how closely he supervised their production.[143] As

138 VII Atr. 1.
139 See Keynes 2007: 187–8.
140 VIIa Atr. Pr.
141 Wormald 1999d: 331–2.
142 Cf. Wormald 1999d: 332; Keynes 2007: 189; and Lionarons 2010: 144–5.
143 Ker 1971: 319.

such, it is striking that these manuscripts draw no visual or organisational distinction between legal, political, and homiletic texts. Not
only are law-codes, sermons, and political tracts intermingled without
reference to genre, but different genres are not distinguished by layout
or scribal practice.[144] For instance, in the York Gospels, ff. 158r–160v,
Napier homilies 59–61 (translated below, pp. 154–64) are presented
in a manner identical to Cnut's proclamation of 1020, such that the
perusing reader is unable to tell that the texts represent different
genres or that one is an official state document while the others are
ecclesiastical pronouncements.[145] Likewise, in British Library, Cotton
Nero A.i, homilies and law-codes are similarly made to resemble one
another in form and presentation: both are presented in identical text
blocks, divided into clauses by means of initials highlighted in red,
and identified by nearly identical rubrics.[146] However, though common
in Wulfstan-associated manuscripts, it must be emphasised that this
sort of blending of genres – not only intermingling texts, but doing
so in a manner that erases the visual cues that might enable the reader
to distinguish between genres – does not occur in other analogous
manuscripts of the period. Moreover, other genres of text found in
these manuscripts, such as lists or historical records, were not treated
in this fashion.[147]

Wulfstan's self-conscious mingling of genres parallels his blending of
the roles of homilist and statesman, yet it also marks one of the crucial
components of his larger vision of a holy society. For Wulfstan, unifying
the legal and the religious makes possible a political model that encom-
passes both the organisation of the community and the orientation of
the individual soul. In doing so, he draws upon developments in legal
composition of the preceding four decades. During the middle years
of the tenth century, the close affiliation between Crown and Church
championed by supporters of the Monastic Reform movement resulted
in legislation increasingly characterised by its ecclesiastical orientation and sermonic language. The laws of Kings Edmund and Edgar
promoted Christian ritual and enjoin proper Christian behaviour to an

144 On this point, see Richards 1986: 176–81 and Wormald 1999a: 240–2.

145 See the facsimile, Barker 1986. See also Keynes 1986: 81–100; Wormald 1999a:
     241–2; and Treharne 2012: 25–6.

146 See the facsimile, Loyn 1971b. See also Richards 1986: 177–8 and Wormald 1999a:
     241.

147 Richards 1986: 176.

extent not seen in the decrees of earlier rulers.[148] Under Æthelred and Cnut, Wulfstan incorporated this Reformist view of law as an instrument of Church policy into a broader vision of a Christian polity. The outline of this vision is illustrated by the injunction with which he concludes the final version of the *Institutes of Polity*: 'let us order our words and deeds rightly, fervently cleanse our inmost thoughts, truly keep our oath and pledge, and frequently reflect on the great judgment to which we all must go'.[149] In this passage, Wulfstan draws together the legal, moral, and political into a single set of social prescriptions. The juridical demand to 'truly keep [one's] oath and pledge', a reference to the subject's oath of loyalty taken from the laws of King Alfred, here comes to be paired with the ethical obligation to 'order ... words and deeds rightly', the moral responsibility to 'cleanse [one's] inmost thoughts', and the Christian duty to meditate on 'the great judgment to which we all must go'.[150] For Wulfstan, the moral regeneration of society relies upon the spiritual condition of the individual as much as it does upon the traditions of the community, the rituals of the Church, and the enactments of the State.[151] In this way, Wulfstan's writings anticipate the emergence in the thirteenth century of what Anthony Musson has called English 'legal consciousness', a new understanding of law as 'an active element shaping people's values, beliefs and aspirations and also as a passive agent providing a reserve of knowledge, memory and reflective thought, influencing not simply the development of the law and legal system, but also political attitudes'.[152] Wulfstan could not have foreseen the changes to English political thought brought about by the Conquest and *Magna Carta*; however, viewed within an eleventh-century context, his melding of the political and homiletic laid the intellectual groundwork for the most sophisticated vision of English society since the reign of Alfred the Great.

148 Richards 1986: 177; Wormald 1999d: 308–29; and Keynes 2008: 10–13.

149 The significance of this formulation in Wulfstan's thought is indicated by it recurrence elsewhere in his work, most notably as part of the conclusion to the *Sermo Lupi ad Anglos*. See below, *Polity* n. 126.

150 On Wulfstan's use of the phrases 'words and deeds' and 'oath and pledge', see Clemoes 1995: 164–5.

151 Cf. Harris 2003: 119.

152 Musson 2001: 1–2.

Major themes

Although Wulfstan expressed his opinions on a wide range of topics over the course of his career, certain themes recur frequently enough in his writings to indicate that he saw them as particularly important.

The rights of the Church

The holy society imagined by Wulfstan depended upon a proper adherence to religious ritual and the due recognition of Church prerogatives. In the archbishop's writings, both of these categories of observance come to be understood as different forms of what he calls *Godes gerihta*. The collocation lacks a precise modern English equivalent, but it can refer to the dues owed to the Church, the respect to which God or the Church is entitled, and the Church's legal privileges or prerogatives (though *geriht* should not be confused with the related word *riht*, 'right' or 'just').[153] In Wulfstan's earlier writings, the phrase *Godes gerihta* serves merely as shorthand for the list of ecclesiastical dues first enumerated in II Edgar 1–4.[154] As Wulfstan elaborates upon Edgar's list in his later works, he incorporates additional obligations, ritual as well as financial, and additional occasions on which these obligations were to be performed.[155] In so doing, he extends the meaning of *Godes gerihta* beyond simply the regular payment of Church dues; instead, it marks the formal acknowledgement of ecclesiastical rights and privileges. Depending on context, *Godes gerihta* encompass the tithes collected on designated saints' days, the inviolability of Church sanctuary, and the precedence owed to the Church in various circumstances.[156] Although some historians have professed themselves 'repelled by those churchmen who seize the occasion for the constant reiteration of the duty of all men to pay their Church dues', to understand *Godes gerihta* merely as a set of financial obligations is to miss the point.[157] That Wulfstan should employ this phrase so capaciously indicates the way in which he

153 The difficulties involved in translating *Godes gerihta* have been discussed in Stanley 2004: 430.

154 See, for instance, *EGu.* 5.1.

155 Detailed accounts of Wulfstan's additions can be found in Bethurum Loomis 1971: 140–1; Blair 2005: 441–4.

156 Cf. in this volume, the homilies *On Justice, On the Duties of the Laity* and *On Christian Practices*, and the law-codes VIIa Atr. 8 and *Cn 1020*, clauses 2 and 8. See also V Atr. 11 and 12.2; VI Atr. 16, 21.1, and 43; VIII Atr. 14; I Cn. 8 and 14; Bethurum 20.1, ll. 22–5 and 33–5; Bethurum 20.2, ll. 26–30 and 39–43; and Bethurum 20.3, ll. 25–9 and 37–45.

157 Richardson and Sayles 1966: 26.

understood the relationship between the Church's worldly institutional status and its place in the spiritual identity of the kingdom. As Eric Stanley has pointed out, *Godes gerihta* are not merely 'divine exactions, in money or goods'; rather, they are 'the rightful service owed to God because of his supreme place in the eternal scheme of justice'.[158] The fulfilment of this rightful service marks the measurement of the ecclesiastical year, the acknowledgement of ecclesiastical privileges, and the differentiation of ecclesiastical from secular land. The rigorous observance of *Godes gerihta* – the timely payment of Church dues, the proper performance of Church rituals, and the scrupulous respect for Church privileges, especially the right of sanctuary – thus serves as a means of organising time and space according to a spiritual order defined by the supreme rule of God.

The obligations of the bishop

For Wulfstan, primary responsibility for safeguarding the Church's rights and overseeing the kingdom's moral regeneration lay with the upper echelons of the Church hierarchy, especially the bishops. Drawing on the work of Carolingian canonists such as Theodulf of Orléans and Amalarius of Metz, Wulfstan characterised the episcopacy as the cornerstone of a holy society.[159] As he writes in *Polity*:

> bishops are the messengers and teachers of God's law, and they must proclaim justice and forbid injustice. He who disdains to listen to them may take issue about that with God himself. If bishops fail, in that they do not curb sin or forbid injustice, and they do not make known God's law, but mumble with their mouths when they should shout, woe to them for that silence![160]

Wulfstan allots to bishops such diverse responsibilities as participating in shire and hundred courts, supervising the standardisation of weights and measures, examining candidates for the priesthood, providing guidance to kings, hearing confession, distributing alms and washing the feet of the needy, preaching Church doctrine, overseeing fasts and holy days, collecting dues and tithes from local parishes, attending Church synods, even mastering a handicraft.[161] This list of obligations

---

158 Stanley 2004: 430.

159 Cf. Bethurum Loomis 1971: 140–1; Loyn 1975: 100–1; and Wormald 1999d: 464–5.

160 *Polity* V.

161 See *Polity* VI, *Episc.* 1–7, *Canons* 5–7, *Admonition*, *EGu.* 4–4.2, 10, and 12, and the homilies *On the Laws of God* and *On Baptism*. See also Bethurum Loomis 1971: 139–45; Loyn 1975: 101–2; Barlow 1979: 270; Wormald 1999d: 454–7; Williams 2003a: 86–7; and Blair 2005: 494–5.

is striking, not only in its range, but in the extent to which it calls
upon bishops to assume responsibility for secular as well as ecclesiastical governance. It is not just that Wulfstan's thought 'reveals no
obvious sign of conflict between Church and State', as Henry Loyn
argued, but that the Church supersedes the secular aristocracy as
the entity principally responsible for the kingdom's wellbeing.[162] As
Wulfstan writes in *Concerning Episcopal Duties*, one of the texts that
circulated with *Polity*, it is proper for a bishop 'to offer guidance in all
things, both in religious and secular matters'.[163] Signs of this implied
precedence permeate Wulfstan writings. In the hierarchically organised *Polity*, for instance, the single chapter dedicated to the nobility
follows three chapters on earthly kingship and four chapters outlining
episcopal duties.[164] Likewise, the political tract *On Sanctuary* assigns
elevenfold compensation for violation of an archbishop's property and
a mere ninefold compensation for damage to the king's.[165] Although it
is possible, as some have argued, that Wulfstan's emphasis on episcopal
power reflects his experience with the inept Æthelred as well as the
broader clerical mistrust of the secular aristocracy following the 'Anti-
Monastic Reaction' of the 970s and 980s, it seems more likely that
this combination of secular and religious authority emerges from his
own experience blending the roles of 'homilist and statesman'.[166] The
inextricable link between moral and secular governance in Wulfstan's
thought leaves the episcopacy as the only institution fully capable of
ensuring that the law of God be upheld with the same vigilance as the
law of the king.

The history of law

Wulfstan grounds his social vision in an idealised account of England's
legal past. The importance of legal history in Wulfstan's writings has not
always been recognised; instead, it has become a critical commonplace

162 Loyn 1975: 100.

163 *Episc.* 1.

164 See *Polity* II–X.

165 *Sanctuary* 7. Bethurum points out that this clause is based on the first clause of
Æthelbert's law-code, but that the earlier text 'says that a *bishop's* property must be
repaid elevenfold and does not mention the king's. Obviously, these codes are aimed
at elevating the status of the upper clergy'. Bethurum Loomis 1971: 140.

166 The influence of Æthelred *Unræd* on Wulfstan's vision for the episcopacy has been
discussed in Bethurum Loomis 1971: 138–9. It should be noted, however, that more
recent scholars have argued that Æthelred's ineptitude may have been overrated.
See Keynes 1991: 67–81.

to allude (often with a note of surprise or dismissal) to the archbishop's nostalgia for the more orthodox religiosity of Bede's Northumbria or the more reliably Christian reigns of Alfred or Edgar. Bethurum, for example, found 'a certain irony' in the fact that the works of a legal innovator like Wulfstan would 'invoke[e] the past with nostalgia' and Wormald viewed the archbishop's outlook as 'decidedly old-fashioned'.[167] Yet to reduce Wulfstan's frequent historical references simply to a form of nostalgia fails to appreciate the past's central role in his political programme. For Wulfstan, the history of English law – a history he romanticised and, often as not, invented – offers a precedent exercising both moral and prescriptive force on contemporary juridical practice.

The extent to which Wulfstan employs fictions of the past to shape his vision of the present and future can be briefly illustrated by one of his most historically-informed projects, the 'Compilation on Status' (translated below, pp. 65–75). The 'Compilation' consists of three ninth-century texts on social status, two from Mercia and one from Northumbria, which have been revised by Wulfstan and bracketed between two texts of his own composition. Yet the 'Compilation' is more than simply a nostalgic collection of defunct regional legislation: as in the case of law-codes such as VII Æthelred, Wulfstan's revisions extract the Status tracts from their original historical and cultural contexts in order to resituate them within a broader Christian framework. In reshaping the texts to fit his 'Compilation', Wulfstan adds clauses, changes rubrics, and incorporates passages of Christian admonishment, all of which result in a picture of early Anglo-Saxon legal culture as more coherent, more unified, and more resolute in its Christianity than ever it was in reality.[168] Wulfstan thus recreates the texts of the 'Compilation' as evidence of a virtuous community that once existed and now needs only to be reclaimed. Accordingly, the 'Compilation's opening and concluding clauses, that 'in the laws of the English, it once was that people and law were ordered by status; and the people's councillors were treated with dignity' and that 'wise were the councillors who added these laws to the ecclesiastical canons for the guidance of the people', reflect neither strict historical fact nor accurate recollections of

167 Bethurum Loomis 1971: 129 and Wormald 1999d: 393. See also p. 131. For similar comments, see Bethurum 1950: 458; Brown 1969: 141; and Faith 1997: 126–7.

168 For a complete account of Wulfstan's revisions, see the notes to the translation below. In this context, it is worth bearing in mind Richards's observation that Wulfstan lends legitimacy to his legal writings by providing 'a sense of continuity with the Anglo-Saxon cultural context defined in the earliest codes'. Richards 1997: 54.

earlier legal practice.[169] Rather, in evoking a vision of the past in which just laws resulted in a properly ordered social hierarchy, they offer a statement of precedent imposing an ethical and juridical demand upon contemporary legislators. The revisions to the Status tracts indicate how English legal history offered Wulfstan, in the words of Nicholas Howe, a 'theory of causation':[170] as he did elsewhere in texts such as the *Laws of Edward and Guthrum, On Sanctuary,* and *The Canons of Edgar,* Wulfstan created a legal exemplar in the past in order to establish both precedent and paradigm for legislating the present.

The imminence of the apocalypse

If appealing to legal history provided Wulfstan's social agenda with a precedent, evoking the coming apocalypse imbued it with urgency. Drawing especially on the *De antichristo* of Abbot Adso of Montier-en-Der, Wulfstan's eschatology emphasised the imminence of divine judgment and the immediacy of the dangers posed by the Antichrist.[171] In so doing, it situated the experience of the English within the broader arc of Christian history and emphasised the pressing need for reform. The evolution of Wulfstan's eschatology is among the aspects of his career most frequently discussed by modern scholars.[172] This interest is hardly surprising, given the extent to which ruminations on the End Times pervade Wulfstan's writings. The apocalypse forms the subject of his earliest surviving homilies, in which he proclaims that 'it appears to us that the time [of the Antichrist] is very near at hand, for from day to day this world grows ever the worse'.[173] Even towards the end of his career, though, he still reminds his audience that 'preachers of God [must] frequently warn God's people against the horror at hand for mankind, namely the archenemy Antichrist'.[174] Wulfstan's persistent emphasis on the imminence of the End Times even after the turn of the

---

169 *On Ranks* 1, *Clerical Compensation* 11. On the historical accuracy of these texts, see Abels 1988a: 108–11; Lawson 1993: 60; Hadley 2000: 104–5; Rabin 2010a: 50–2; and Rabin forthcoming.

170 Howe 2001: 18. Lionarons notes that Wulfstan employs Biblical history in a similar fashion. See Lionarons 2010: 5.

171 On Wulfstan's use of Adso, see Bethurum 1942: 925; Bethurum 1957: 282; Emmerson 1983: 1–10; Wilcox 1991: 12; and Lionarons 2010: 58–62.

172 See, for instance, Gatch 1977: 105–17; Emmerson 1983: 1–10; Godden 1994: 142–62; Lees 1999: 101–4; Atkinson and Burton 2002: 49–62; Richards 2002: 41–8; Prideaux-Collins 2003: 289–310; Lionarons 2004a: 413–28; and Lionarons 2010: 75–107.

173 Bethurum 1b, ll. 22–4.

174 *On Justice,* n. 56.

millennium has led some to question whether he truly thought that a literal apocalypse would occur in the year 1000.[175] Whatever he believed early in his career, however, by the time he preached the sermon *On Justice, Virtue, and the Law* (Napier 50, translated below, pp. 143–53) in 1018 or shortly thereafter, the continued prevalence of eschatological themes in his writings suggests that he had come to see the apocalypse less as an immediate event than as a metaphor for the inevitable downfall of an unregenerate society.[176] The homily consists of excerpts from his laws and *Polity*, yet it ends by reminding his audience of the nearness of the apocalypse, since 'the devil deceives men's thoughts, so that they remember it too rarely'. He then proceeds to admonish them that 'this world is in haste and storm, in disease and bad weather, so that now there cannot be many altogether of whom some are not sick and weak ... [T]his world is not worthy to be loved all too much'. The cause of these misfortunes, he continues, is the absence of those who might 'uplift the people through their teaching so that they all might not perish together'.[177] As the conclusion of a homily on the nature of just governance, this passage links the fate of sinful world with the collapse of a poorly governed kingdom. Implicitly, the end of the world here becomes a vision of England's potential ruin, the destruction of a community that fails as a holy society. As Lionarons writes, 'if the homily contains his hopes for the social reconstruction of England and the creation of a 'holy society' governed by the laws that he had written, it also expresses his unshakeable conviction of that society's end'.[178] Eschatology thus serves as both the catalyst and dominant metaphor of Wulfstan's social vision: it invests his political programme with urgency even as it provides the moral context within which that programme transpires.

The necessity of penance

Underlying Wulfstan's vision of a Holy Society is the belief that the stability of the English kingdom depends on the morality of the English people: just as the people's sins will lead inevitably to their destruction, so their sincere repentance will bring salvation. As Wulfstan preached in the sermon *On Various Misfortunes* (Napier 35, translated below, pp. 130–2),

175 Gatch 1977: 114; Prideaux-Collins 2003: 295–6; and Lionarons 2010: 47.

176 Cf. Lionarons 2004a: 427–8.

177 See below, pp. 152–3.

178 Lionarons 2004a: 428.

> If it comes about that a great misfortune befalls the realm because of the people's deeds – war or hunger, fire or bloodshed, crop failure or bad weather, the death of men or cattle from a sudden plague – then amends always is to be made to God himself. Foremost among all things is that one is to ... yield to righteousness and renounce sin, and then afterwards do just as David did along with many others: call upon Christ with a remorseful spirit.[179]

Wulfstan then goes on to compare the English to the Ninevites, who 'had wholly descended into sin but, as was necessary for themselves, they turned to righteousness, engaged in fasting, and prayed sincerely with a remorseful spirit'.[180] Wulfstan here characterises repentance as more than just a matter of individual contrition; rather, collective penance becomes the cornerstone of civic life.[181] Emphasising the civic importance of penance, not only in his sermons but in his law-codes, allows Wulfstan to align the moral character of the community with that of the individual Christian soul. As Allen Frantzen points out, it is in Wulfstan's laws that 'penitential discipline penetrated more deeply into secular legislation than before'.[182] These laws distil the moral exhortations of homilies such as *On Various Misfortunes* into specific penitential prescriptions designed to achieve justice on earth while simultaneously saving the souls of lawbreakers in the afterlife.[183] In the words of II Cnut, 'the [criminal] is to be punished, but the soul preserved'.[184] This penitential component of secular justice placed priests and their bishops at the centre of the legal process. As outlined in the *Canons of Edgar* and the *Handbook for a Confessor*, the obligation to hear confession and assign penance was no less instrumental in the establishment of a virtuous society than it was in the salvation of the individual soul.[185] Likewise, the penitent's obligation to seek confession was no less a part of his

---

179 *On Various Misfortunes*, below, p. 131.

180 *On Various Misfortunes*, below, p. 131.

181 Simon Keynes provides a vivid example of the way in which Wulfstan's vision of penance may have played out in reality. He conjures a picture of England following the promulgation of VII Æthelred, 'in which 'for three days in late September 1009 ordinary people throughout Æthelred's kingdom were to be seen processing barefoot through their parishes, with cross and relics, crying out again and again to Christ, and invoking the *Agnus Dei* in the desperate hope that the Lamb, i.e. Christ, would take away the sins of the world and bring them peace. It must have been an extraordinary scene; and anyone wishing to understand the impact of the Viking raids in the early eleventh century would do well, in their historical imaginations, to join the procession'. Keynes 2007: 188.

182 Frantzen 1983: 146. See also Hough 2000: 136–7; and Cubitt 2007: 154.

183 Cf. O'Keeffe 1998: 216–17 and Marafioti 2008: 53.

184 II Cn. 30.5.

185 Cf. Fowler 1965: 11–12.

civic duty than his promise to 'truly keep [his] oath and pledge'.[186] Penance thus becomes the essential building block of the Holy Society, the means by which the redemption of the individual came to be linked to the regeneration of the community as a whole.

The order of society

The centrepiece of Wulfstan's political thought is his vision of the properly ordered society. Just as the breakdown of communal bonds reflects the people's sins and anticipates the coming of the Antichrist, the restoration of those bonds through prayer and repentance results in a kingdom characterised by social stability and just governance. Wulfstan sets out this vision most clearly in the series of short chapters referred to by modern editors as the *Institutes of Polity*. Begun sometime around 1010, the final version of *Polity* dates from approximately 1020 and may have been composed in tandem with the law-codes I–II Cnut. It is here that Wulfstan provides one of the earliest accounts of what would become the medieval doctrine of the Three Orders of Society:[187]

> Every just throne that stands fully as it should stands on three pillars: first, *those who pray*; second, *those who labour*; and third, *those who fight* … If any of them weaken, immediately the throne will tremble; and if any of them fracture, then the throne will crumble to pieces, and that will bring that people all to ruin. Therefore, they are to be diligently steadied, strengthened, and reinforced with God's wise teachings and with just worldly law.[188]

Wulfstan did not originate the tripartite division of society – earlier instances appear in the writings of both Ælfric and Alfred the Great[189] – yet his account provides the trope's most detailed elaboration up to that time as well as the first attempt to situate it within a broader conception of Christian law and moral governance. The 'three pillars' passage is the last in a series of similar metaphors beginning in *Polity*'s previous chapter.[190] Wulfstan first lists the 'eight columns that firmly support just kingship', a metaphor taken from Sedulius Scottus' *Book of Christian Rulers*, and afterwards recounts the 'seven things appropriate for a righteous king', this drawn from the *Collectio canonum Hibernensis*.[191]

---

186 *Polity* XXXVI.

187 Bethurum Loomis 1971: 129–30; Duby 1982; and Wormald 1999d: 459–60.

188 *Polity* IV.

189 See *Polity*, n. 15 below. The history of the Three Orders trope in Anglo-Saxon literature has been discussed at length in Powell 1994.

190 Cf. Loyn 1975: 101 and Wormald 1999d: 458.

191 See *Polity* III.

Only then does Wulfstan offer his account of *those who fight* (*bellatores*), *those who labour* (*laboratores*), and *those who pray* (*oratores*). The 'three pillars' thus serve as the culmination of a metaphorical programme that integrates British and continental sources in order to present a comprehensive description of an ordered society.[192] Grouping these metaphors together emphasises the extent to which the functional division of society into three distinct yet interdependent orders rests upon an ideological foundation of just kingship and Christian governance. The picture of chaos Wulfstan evokes when visualising society's fall into sin and corruption thus resolves into a vision of the balance and stability that comes with a virtuous Christian community.[193] In the realisation of this vision, Wulfstan suggests, lies the fulfilment of the Holy Society.

Wulfstan's afterlife

The century following Wulfstan's death in 1023 witnessed the circulation of both his works and his ideas, though often in ways which disguised their association with the archbishop.[194] Although the laws composed by Wulfstan for Cnut are the last surviving examples of Old English legislation, they provided crucial source material for other types of legal documents produced after the archbishop's death, most notably Cnut's proclamation of 1027.[195] Either shortly before Wulfstan's death or not long thereafter, modified versions of his regulations for clerical behaviour came to form the basis for a series of short tracts likely produced by members of his circle at York. The texts – *Rectitudines Singularum Personarum*, *Gerefa*, and the *Northumbrian Priests' Law* – have each been credited to Wulfstan by various modern scholars, though such attributions have been shown to be spurious. The *Northumbrian Priests' Law* bears a particularly close resemblance to Wulfstan's other work, though its more pedestrian style and divergence from the archbishop's policies on matters such as clerical marriage make an attribution to Ælfric Puttoc, Wulfstan's successor at York, far more likely.[196] The archbishop's influence can also be felt in the so-called 'Sunday Letters' of the early eleventh century, which quote freely (though without attribution) from

192 On the insular and continental context for this image, see Bethurum Loomis 1971: 130–2; Powell 1994: 105–10; and Wormald 1999d: 460–1.

193 Cf. Wormald 1999a: 244–6 and Richards 2002: 46.

194 More detailed accounts of early uses of Wulfstan's work can be found in Scragg 1977: 197–211; Cross 1991: 203–20; Wilcox 1992: 199–217; Morrison 1996: 229–34; Wilcox 2000b: 83–97; and Orchard 2007: 316–17.

195 Liebermann 1903–1916: v. III, pp. 189–92 and Robertson 1925: 345–7.

196 On these texts, see Harvey 1993: 1–22 and Wormald 1999: 247–51.

Wulfstan's political writings, including I Cnut, *Polity*, and the sermon translated below as *On Tithes and Tithing* (pp. 165–7).[197] More broadly, passages from Wulfstan's homilies recur in the works of other late Old English liturgists and homilists, often as source material but sometimes as part of what may have been a conscious effort at imitation.[198] The extent to which such uses of Wulfstan's work reflect a comprehensive awareness of or engagement with the archbishop's canon remains unknown; however, they do reflect the traction of Wulfstan's works in later Anglo-Saxon England and suggest that his writings circulated far more widely than the current manuscript evidence indicates.

Of knowledge of Wulfstan's writings on the continent during this period there is very little that can be said. Insufficient evidence of either manuscript copies or unambiguous citations of his works survives to indicate the extent (or even the existence) of continental familiarity with the archbishop's canon. Nonetheless, the appearance of similar visions of divine kingship and social order – especially the 'Three Estates' theory – in the works of such mid-eleventh century bishops as Gerard of Cambrai and Adalbero of Laon, has led some to raise the possibility that Wulfstan's writings may have reached a few readers in Carolingian Francia.[199] Barring the discovery of new evidence, though, a firm answer to the question of Wulfstan's continental readership must remain elusive.

After 1066, Wulfstan's political writings played a crucial role in the Anglo-Norman appropriation of pre-Conquest law. In the years following the Conquest, Norman legislators engaged in a concerted attempt to reformulate the laws of Anglo-Saxon England as ideological instruments of the new regime. This reformulation took place through the production of Latin compilations such as *Quadripartitus*, legal forgeries such as the *Leges Edwardi* (the 'Laws of Edward the Confessor') and the *Instituta Cnuti* ('Institutes of Cnut'), and the great manuscript anthologies of Anglo-Saxon law such as *Textus Roffensis* and C.C.C.C. 383.[200] Those responsible for producing such documents revised, reorganised, and rewrote the Old English laws in order to cast the conquerors as the rightful heirs of their Anglo-Saxon predecessors

---

197 Haines 2010: 81–2, 91–3.

198 Cf. Scragg 1977: 197–8; Wilcox 1992: 206–17; Jones 1998b: 700–1; Scragg 1998: 8–15; Ogawa 2002: 389–90; and Orchard 2002: 313.

199 Abels 1988b: 294 and Wormald 1999d: 459–60.

200 O'Brien 1999: 8–30; Wormald 1999d; Wormald 1999b: 115–38; Wormald 1999e: 81–114; and Greenberg 2010: 273–300.

and to characterise earlier legislation as a precursor to the policies of the new Anglo-Norman ruling class. As Bruce O'Brien points out, 'kings saw in the affirmation of such *laga* a way to assure their subjects that they would rule wisely. The affirmation became a stage on the path to political stability'.[201] Wulfstan's political writings were particularly useful for a project of this sort: his emphasis on strong, centralised governance, the necessity of social order, the royal right to a portion of compensatory payments, and the divine aspects of kingship reflected the legislative agenda of the new dynasty, thus making the archbishop's works prime candidates for appropriation. The authors of such texts as the *Leges Henrici Primi* borrowed clauses or sets of clauses from Wulfstan's political and legislative writings and added to them or set them within new legal frameworks in order to remake the archbishop's policies as their own.[202] Likewise, the compositors of manuscripts such as *Textus Roffensis* did not distinguish between Wulfstan's royal laws and his political tracts (if they were even aware of the difference), but treated both as prescriptive legislation. The compositors also broke up such carefully assembled textual groupings as the 'Compilation on Status' and rearranged or rewrote the component texts in an unconscious imitation of Wulfstan's own procedure in assembling such groupings.[203] As was the case with Wulfstan's own legal compilations and forgeries, the compositors' goal was to remake the Anglo-Saxon legal past in their own image. Indeed, from a modern perspective, the fates of both Wulfstan's writings and the legal inheritance of Anglo-Saxon England during this period are fraught with irony: even as Wulfstan himself was slowly being forgotten or dismissed as 'reprobus' by historians such as William of Malmesbury, his political writings were circulating more widely than ever. More broadly, in erasing and rewriting Old English legal history for their own ends, the Anglo-Norman compilers of texts such as *Quadripartitus* and manuscripts such as *Textus Roffensis* produced the very documents in which the majority of pre-Conquest legal texts would come to be preserved.[204]

The historical and legal developments of the eleventh and twelfth centuries left Wulfstan and his contributions to English political

---

201 O'Brien 1999: 7.

202 See, for instance, the *Leges Henrici Primi* 11.15–16a. Downer 1972: 114; and Hudson 2010: 229–30. See also Downer 1972: 28–30.

203 See Richards 1986: 176–86; Richards 1988: 43–60; Richards 1997: 53–6; Wormald 1999b: 115–38; Wormald 1999d: 224–52; and Hough 2006: 114–31.

204 O'Brien 1999: 133–4.

thought largely forgotten. By the end of the thirteenth century, the emergence of Common Law and the accompanying changes in the understanding of legal reasoning and expertise caused the Anglo-Saxon legal inheritance itself likewise to fade from memory.[205] It was not until the early eighteenth century that scholars finally began to rediscover Wulfstan and his works. Although the literary and historical signifi-·cance of the 1014 *Sermo Lupi* had been recognised as early as 1572, when Archbishop Matthew Parker provided a Latin summary of the text in his *De antiquitate Britannicae ecclesiae*, Wulfstan was not identi-fied as the author until the antiquarian Humphrey Wanley included it in his 1705 catalogue of Anglo-Saxon manuscripts.[206] The first scholar to attribute authorship to Wulfstan based on evidence of style, Wanley credited the archbishop with fifty-three homilies and several shorter ecclesiastical texts.[207] Wanley's list was expanded to sixty-two texts by Arthur Napier in his 1883 dissertation, in which he provided the first modern edition of Wulfstan's works. Important as Napier's work is, however, it suffers from a number of significant shortcomings: not only does it lack an introduction and notes – Napier had intended to provide these in a second volume which was never published – but many of his attributions have not held up under further scrutiny and several of his editorial decisions concerning choice of manuscript witnesses and the divisions between texts have been severely criticised.[208]

The recovery of Wulfstan's legislation and political tracts has been similarly complex.[209] William Lambarde's 1568 *Archaionomia*, the earliest printed edition of Anglo-Saxon legislation, contained several of Wulfstan's works, including the *Laws of Edward and Guthrum*, the three central texts of the 'Compilation on Status', and I–II Cnut.[210] Wulfstan's authorship of these texts had not yet been recognised, however, nor had the fact that *Edward-Guthrum* was an eleventh-century forgery. More problematic was Lambarde's inclusion of texts translated into Latin and then re-translated into Old English by his friend Laurence Nowell. The confusion caused by Nowell's linguistic experiment led historians

---

205 On this point, see Hudson 2010: 220ff.

206 Bethurum 1957: 24–6; Graham 2000: 84; and Wormald 2004: 10.

207 Bethurum 1957: 25.

208 See, for instance, Lionarons 2004b: 165–6 and Lionarons 2010: 22.

209 A complete history of the editing of Old English law can be found in Wormald 1999d: 3–28.

210 Lambarde 1568. On Lambarde's edition, see Dunkel 1965; Grant 1996; and Brack-mann 2012.

to believe that he had access to a lost manuscript of Old English law, a misconception that persisted until 1923.[211] Later editions of Old English law – most notably those by Reinhold Schmid (1832, 2nd edn 1858) and Benjamin Thorpe (1840) – filled out the Anglo-Saxon legal corpus while also providing the first editions of major Wulfstanian texts such as the *Institutes of Polity* (the title of which comes from Thorpe) and the *Canons of Edgar.*[212] Finally, between 1898 and 1916, Felix Liebermann published his three-volume *Gesetze der Angelsachsen,* a monumental work of scholarship which remains the standard edition of the early English laws.[213] To produce his edition, Liebermann consulted approximately 180 manuscripts and spent more than fifteen years preparing his texts. Magisterial as the *Gesetze* is, however, its treatment of texts produced in the early eleventh century shares many of the limitations of its predecessors.[214] Many of the texts now known to have been composed by Wulfstan are misdated and misattributed. Moreover, legal fictions such as *Edward-Guthrum* are taken at face value (though Liebermann did have his suspicions), Nowell's 'back-translations' into Old English are treated as independent manuscript witnesses, and little distinction is drawn between private political tract and public prescriptive legislation. The reliability of Liebermann's edition thus suffers considerably from the fact that its publication predated recognition of the full extent of Wulfstan's involvement in the legal and political life of eleventh-century England.

The relatively small role attributed to Wulfstan in the editions of Schmid, Thorpe, and Liebermann finds its parallel in accounts of the archbishop's career in early histories of English law. The most influential of such histories, Pollock and Maitland's *History of English Law Before the Time of Edward I* (1895, 2nd edn 1898), notes only that Wulfstan 'probably took an active part in the legislation of Æthelred'.[215]

211 Sisam 1953 and Wormald 1999c.

212 Thorpe 1840 and Schmid 1858.

213 Liebermann 1903–1916. Liebermann began publishing his editions in instalments in 1898. These editions were gathered together into the first volume of the *Gesetze,* published in 1903. The second volume was published in two instalments, the *Wörterbuch* in 1912 and the *Rechts- und Sachglossar* in 1912. The final volume, containing Liebermann's introduction and notes, was published in 1916. On Liebermann and the *Gesetze,* see Rabin 2010b: 1–8.

214 On the shortcomings of Liebermann's edition, see Dammery 1994: 251–61 and Schwyter 2010: 43–58.

215 Pollock and Maitland 1968: 40. Wulfstan is similarly absent from other major histories of Old English law. See Adams 1876; Stubbs 1887; Chadwick 1905; and Richardson and Sayles 1966.

It was not until the mid-twentieth century that Wulfstan's career finally came to be recovered, primarily through the work of Dorothy Whitelock in England, Dorothy Bethurum in the United States, and Karl Jost in Germany. In a series of articles published between 1937 and 1966, Whitelock not only established the range of Wulfstan's activities as 'homilist and statesman', but she also demonstrated his authorship of a variety of texts, most notably *Edward-Guthrum* and I–II Cnut.[216] For his part, Jost added two major texts to Wulfstan's corpus, the *Canons of Edgar* and the Old English *Regula Canonicorum*.[217] He also produced the first modern edition of *Polity*, in which he determined the order of the text's successive versions and offered a detailed account of the coherence of its chapters.[218] Equally important is Jost's study of Wulfstan's homilies which, despite his persistent refusal to accept several of Whitelock's attributions, remains among the most complete discussions of the texts, their sources, and their connections to later Anglo-Saxon political thought.[219] Bethurum's research likewise contributed to a more rounded sense of Wulfstan's career, both through the further attribution of texts, most significantly the Status tracts and *On Sanctuary* (*Grið*), and through her identification of the manuscripts of the archbishop's 'commonplace book' (though the term itself has been subject to criticism).[220] Bethurum's most influential contribution, however, has been her edition of Wulfstan's homilies.[221] Although more limited than Napier's edition – she only edits twenty-one homilies, in contrast to his sixty-two – Bethurum's was the first to provide complete texts and apparatus for a significant cross-section of Wulfstan's homiletic corpus. That said, her edition has been criticised by a number of recent scholars, both because of her practice of combining manuscript witnesses to produce a 'best' text and because of the exclusive criteria which led her to omit many of Wulfstan's most important works. The most problematic of these omissions is that of the political homilies which, due to their legal content, she viewed as insufficiently homiletic, a perspective more reflective of modern generic

---

216 Whitelock 1937; Whitelock 1937–45; Whitelock 1941; Whitelock 1942; Whitelock 1948; Whitelock 1955; Whitelock 1959; Whitelock 1965; and Whitelock 1966.

217 Jost 1932: 265–315.

218 Jost 1959.

219 Jost 1950.

220 Bethurum 1942; Bethurum 1950; Bethurum 1957; Bethurum 1966; and Bethurum Loomis 1971.

221 Bethurum 1957.

conventions than the practices of Wulfstan's own time.[222] It is easy to overstate such criticisms, though, and Bethurum's edition still must be characterised as one of the high points of Wulfstan studies.[223]

Whitelock, Jost, and Bethurum established the parameters within which Wulfstan's career is still understood. Recent scholarship has focused on filling out Wulfstan's corpus, developing a better understanding of his relationship with his sources, and demonstrating the depth and complexity of his political thought. Although a comprehensive edition of his writings is still lacking, among modern scholars he nonetheless has come to be recognised as perhaps the most important social theorist of later Anglo-Saxon England.

Note on the translations

Translation is particularly treasonous when it comes to Wulfstan. Many of the aural and rhetorical techniques he used to such great effect have no parallel in modern English. Likewise, while his repetition of key words and phrases contributed to the incantatory power of his prose, in modern English such repetition can make his writing seem tedious and his thought appear stagnant. Accordingly, I have attempted to follow the model of Alfred the Great in rendering the texts 'sometimes word for word and sometimes sense for sense' ('hwilum word be worde, hwilum andgit of andgite'). As a result, a word like *georne*, among the most frequently used words in Wulfstan's corpus, can be translated as 'eagerly', 'zealously', 'assiduously', 'earnestly', or 'urgently'. Similarly, *riht* and its related forms, words fraught with meaning for Wulfstan, may be rendered as 'law', 'right', 'righteousness', 'justice', 'virtue', or 'fairness', depending upon the context. My goal throughout has been to remain faithful to Wulfstan's original text, while also trying to convey some sense of the fluency and vigour of his prose.

The translations are divided into three categories. The first consists of Wulfstan's political tracts, those texts the archbishop composed either for public circulation or as private memoranda with the purpose of articulating or advocating for some aspect of his social vision. Although several of these texts resemble royal legislation and may reflect actual

---

222 For critiques of Bethurum's edition see Wilcox 1991: 8n. 31; Orchard 2004: 63–5; and Lionarons 2010: 23–4.

223 An eloquent defense of Bethurum's edition has recently been mounted in Gatch 2012: 253–4.

legal practices, there is no evidence that any ever functioned formally as prescriptive and enforceable secular law. The second section contains those homilies and homiletic fragments most closely related to Wulfstan's political writings. In some cases, the homilies draw upon the same sources as the political tracts, others are constructed piecemeal out of excerpts from the political tracts, and several are direct adaptations of individual political tracts for homiletic delivery. In *Polity*, Wulfstan writes that the bishops are to be 'messengers and teachers of God's law, and they must proclaim justice and forbid injustice' ('bydelas 7 Godes lage lareowas, 7 hi sculan riht bodian 7 unriht forbeodan'). The homilies offer a useful illustration of what Wulfstan understood this role to entail and how he sought to fulfil his joint legal and episcopal obligations. The themes and passages from his other writings incorporated into these sermons illuminate those aspects of his political thought Wulfstan believed to be most important for a broad audience. The final category includes sources and analogues of Wulfstan's political writings, such as other instances of his homiletic prose, examples of formal royal legislation produced under his supervision, and texts showing his influence.

The introductions and notes to the translations are intended to provide context for Wulfstan's writings as well as an indication of his sources. Although unquestionably well-read, Wulfstan was also an inveterate re-user and reviser of his own works. As such, the notes also indicate those passages Wulfstan recycled from his other texts. Political tracts and legislation are cited by clause or canon number and *Polity* by chapter number. Lacking clausal divisions, homilies translated in this volume are cross-referenced by footnote. Homilies authored by or attributed to Wulfstan which do not appear in this volume are cited according to the editions of Bethurum or Napier. Passages from the Bible are cited according the Vulgate and translated following the Douay-Rheims version.

Except for the surviving text of the law-code VII Æthelred, all texts translated here were composed almost entirely in Old English. Words or passages that originally appeared in Latin are indicated by *italics*. In several instances, passages have been inserted from manuscript witnesses other than that used as the primary source. These are designated by square brackets and the reasons for the insertion discussed in the notes. The two exceptions to this rule are the translation of the homily *On Various Misfortunes*, in which the brackets designate revisions to the text by a later scribe, and the translation of *Northumbrian Church Sanctuary*, in which the brackets indicate passages reconstructed due to manuscript damage (see pp. 82–4 and 130–2 below).

I
POLITICAL TRACTS

1. *THE LAWS OF EDWARD AND GUTHRUM*

The text referred to as the *Laws of Edward and Guthrum* survives in two twelfth-century manuscripts: Cambridge, Corpus Christi College 383 and Strood, Medway Archive and Local Studies Centre, MS. DRc/R1 (*Textus Roffensis*). Both manuscripts treat the text as an authentic example of early tenth-century Anglo-Saxon royal legislation, a belief which persisted until 1941, when Dorothy Whitelock demonstrated that it was really an eleventh-century forgery from the pen of Archbishop Wulfstan.[1] Perhaps the earliest of his political writings, it likely dates to between 1002 and 1004, the period just after Wulfstan ascended to the York see.[2] Although the circumstances surrounding its composition are unclear, it may have been intended as a companion to the late ninth-century *Treaty of Alfred and Guthrum*, perhaps as a way of adapting the earlier text's legislation concerning Viking-English relations for the heavily Danish north.[3] Though a forgery, it is unclear whether Wulfstan ever intended *Edward-Guthrum* – or, indeed, any of his other 'forgeries', such as *The Canons of Edgar* – to fool anyone. Although the text's opening clauses explicitly locate its provisions in the distant past, the prescriptions themselves reflect the influence of the late tenth- and early eleventh-century Reform movement more than the concerns of early Viking-age England.[4] As Whitelock pointed out, it is more likely that Wulfstan, confronted with the heterodox practices of his new minster, composed these regulations and added a historical preface in order to claim an authoritative precedent and avoid accusations of innovation.[5] Whether such was the case or not, the text does reveal that many of Wulfstan's greatest preoccupations – his interest in legal history, emphasis on Christian orthodoxy, and advocacy for the rights of the Church – were already present even in the earliest stages of his career.

---

1 Whitelock 1941. Although Whitelock's essay is now almost seventy-five years old, scholars are still sometimes fooled into thinking the text to be authentic. See, for instance, Thomas 1985: 492.

2 Wormald 2004: 26 and Pons-Sanz 2007: 25.

3 Wormald 1999d: 390–1.

4 Whitelock 1941: 14–17.

5 Whitelock 1941: 18–19.

TRANSLATION[1]

THESE ARE THE MEASURES AGREED UPON BY KING ALFRED AND KING GUTHRUM:[2]

And this also is the decree which King Alfred and King Guthrum, and later King Edward and King Guthrum, agreed upon and proclaimed when the English and the Danes fully resolved on peace and friendship.[3] And the councillors too, who met afterwards, often and frequently renewed it and strengthened it with improvements.

[**Prol. 1**] This is foremost among those things which they agreed upon: that they would love the one God and wholeheartedly reject every heathen practice.[4]

[**Prol. 2**] And they also established secular penalties, for they knew that otherwise they could not govern many people, nor would many men otherwise comply with Church discipline as they should;[5] and then they decreed that secular compensation will be shared by Christ and king wherever anyone refused to submit properly to Church penance at the order of the bishops.[6]

1 This translation is based on the text in Liebermann 1903–16: v. I, pp. 128–35 with reference to those in Attenborough 1922:102–110 and Whitelock 1981: 302–13.

2 C.C.C.C. 383: 'Next, that of Guthrum and Edward'.

3 King Alfred of Wessex (849–899) defeated the Viking king Guthrum (d. 890) at the battle of *Ethandun* (identified as Edington in Wiltshire) in May 878. Although the initial treaty signed after the battle does not survive, a subsequent treaty (the so-called *Treaty of Alfred and Guthrum*, c. 878x890) is preserved in C.C.C.C. 383 as the text immediately preceding this one. It seems likely that Wulfstan composed *EGu.* as a companion piece to *AGu.* – possibly as a way of extending the provisions of the earlier treaty to encompass northern England as well as southern – and intended the two to circulate together.

4 Cf. V Atr. 1, 34; VI Atr. 1.6; VIII Atr. 44; IX Atr. *explicit*; X Atr. 1; *NPL* 47, 67; *Polity* XXXV; *On Justice* n. 50; *Canons* 16; and *On the Proper Support* n. 4.

5 This clause is the earliest example of a theme that will reoccur frequently in Wulfstan's political writings. Cf. *Clerical Compensation* 11, *Sanctuary* 24, *Evil Rulers*, n. 11, and VIII Atr. 36. The joint authority of church and king is referenced also in *Concerning the Ranks of People and the Law* 8 and *NPL* 54.1 and 59. Bethurum suggests that its appearance here may have been influenced by Wulfstan's reading of c. 49.7 of the Mosaic preface to Alfred's laws: 'then many synods throughout middle earth were convened, and also among the English people, and then they accepted the faith of Christ, of the holy bishops, and also of the illustrious wise men. Then, on account of that mercy which Christ taught, they established that for almost every misdeed the secular lord could, by their leave, without sin, at the first transgression, take that monetary compensation which they had established'. On this clause, see Bethurum 1950: 455.

6 Wormald points to this clause as evidence of Wulfstan's intention for this text. He

[1] This is afterwards foremost among those things which they agreed upon: that ecclesiastical sanctuary within church walls and protection received from the king's hand shall remain equally inviolable.[7]

[2] And if anyone violates Christian practice or shows reverence for heathenism by word or deed, he must pay either his wergild or a penalty or *lahslit*, according to the nature of the deed.[8]

[3] And if a man in orders steals or fights or commits perjury or adultery, he shall atone according to the nature of the deed either with his wergild or with a penalty or with *lahslit*; and indeed, he must do penance before God as the canon decrees and either find a surety or submit to imprisonment.

[3.1] And if a priest misleads the people concerning a holy day or a fast, he must pay thirty shillings among the English or three half-marks among the Danes.[9]

[3.2] If a priest does not fetch the holy oil on the proper day[10] or denies baptism to one who needs it, he must pay a penalty among the English and *lahslit* of twelve ores among the Danes.[11]

[4] And in cases of incest[12] the councillors ruled that the king shall

---

writes that the newly appointed archbishop aimed 'to create a more satisfactory situation in the northern province, in the name of those who first codified the relationships between native and newcomer. This, then was essentially a "forgery". It is revealing in more ways than one that security for the Church, vested by Carolingian scholars in a mighty series of bogus papal decretals, could be sought by an English archbishop from a fictitious agreement between kings'. Wormald 1999d: 391.

7   Cf. *Sanctuary* 2, VI Atr. 14, I Cn. 2.2, *On the Laws of God* n. 15, *On Justice* n. 6, and *Polity* ch. XXXV.

8   Cf. V Atr. 31, VI Atr. 51, and *On Heathen Practices* n. 4. On this clause, see Barlow 1979: 149–50; Meaney 2004: 475. *Lahslit*, for which there is no adequate modern English equivalent, is a term of Old Norse derivation used by Wulfstan to denote the Danish analogue to Old English wergild payments. Its appearance here reflects Wulfstan's attempt to balance the legal traditions of the southern West Saxon kingdom and the northern Danelaw. A partial sense of the values attached to *lahslit* can be gleaned from the prescriptions in *NPL* 51–4.

9   Cf. *Canons* 48, *NPL* 11.

10   Maundy Thursday (the Thursday before Easter). See also n. to *Canons* 6.

11   Cf. *NPL* 8–9. Liebermann argues that the injunction regarding baptism in this clause must refer to an adult heathen. As Whitelock shows, however, the baptism of a sickly infant is far more likely. Liebermann 1903–1916: III.90 and Whitelock 1941: 14–15.

12   The term for incest used here, *sibleger*, occurs exclusively in Wulfstan's writings. Cf. Napier 27, p. 130, ll. 4–5; Bethurum 20.1, l. 94; Bethurum 20.3, l. 137; II Cn. 51; and *Cn. 1020* 15. The source for Wulfstan's language remains unknown as incest is not mentioned in other Anglo-Saxon law-codes and *sibleger* is not among the terms used for incest in the Old English penitentials. On this point, see Whitelock 1941: 8.

have jurisdiction over the upper and the bishop the lower,[13] unless penance is performed before God and the world, as the bishop decrees according to the nature of the deed.

[4.1] If two brothers or two close relatives lie with the same woman, they must atone most fervently, just as it may be allowed, with a penalty or with *lahslit*, according to the nature of the deed.

[4.2] If a man in orders compromises himself with a capital crime, he is to be arrested and held for the bishop's judgment.[14]

[5] And if a man sentenced to death desires confession, it shall never be denied to him.[15]

[5.1] And all God's dues shall be rendered assiduously for God's mercy and because of the penalties which the councillors assigned.[16]

[6] If anyone withholds his tithe, he shall pay *lahslit* among the Danes and a penalty among the English.[17]

[6.1] If anyone withholds the dues owed to Rome, he shall pay *lahslit* among the Danes, a penalty among the English.[18]

[6.2] If anyone does not pay the dues for the lighting of the church, he shall pay *lahslit* among the Danes, a penalty among the English.[19]

[6.3] If anyone does not pay his plough-dues, he shall pay *lahslit* among the Danes, a penalty among the English.[20]

[6.4] If anyone withholds his Church dues, he shall pay *lahslit* among the Danes, a penalty among the English.[21]

---

13 That is, the male offender shall be punished by the king and the female by the bishop. Cf. II Cn. 51–51.1.

14 Cf. II Cn 43. A more specific penalty for clerics guilty of homicide is recorded in VIII Atr. 26.

15 Cf. II Cn. 44.

16 Cf. V Atr. 12.2, VI Atr. 21.1, VIII Atr. 14, I Cn. 14, *On Justice* n. 47, and *On Christian Practices* n. 14.

17 Cf. II Eg. 3.1, VIII Atr. 8, I Cn. 8.2, *NPL* 60, and Napier 43 l. 177.

18 Cf. I Cn. 9, *Canons* 54, *On Justice* n. 44, and *On Christian Practices* n. 6. The source for this clause is II Eg. 4, though it should be noted that the penalty set forth in the earlier clause has been significantly reduced. See Bethurum Loomis 1971: 134.

19 This is the earliest example of legislation concerning *leohtgesceot* ('dues for the lighting of the church'). See Whitelock 1941: 9 and Chaney 1963: 274.

20 Analogues to the penalty for withholding plough-dues occur in VII Atr. 7, VIII Atr. 12, and I Cn. 8.2.

21 Cf. II Cn. 48. For this and the next three clauses, see also V Atr. 31–31.1 and VI Atr. 38. For a discussion of the similarities and differences between *EGu.* 5.1–6.4 and *Canons* 54, see Wormald 1999d: 338–41.

[**6.5**] And if he fights and wounds anyone, he will be liable for his wergild.[22]

[**6.6**] If he causes anyone's death, then he will become an outlaw and be hunted with enmity by all those who wish for justice.[23]

[**6.7**] And if he acts in such a way as to cause his own death through resistance to God's justice or the king's, and if that is shown to be true, no compensation need be paid for him.[24]

[**7**] If anyone does business on a Sunday, he shall forfeit his purchases and twelve ores among the Danes and thirty shillings among the English.[25]

[**7.1**] If a freeman works on a holy day, he shall forfeit his freedom, or pay a penalty or *lahslit*. A slave will receive a whipping or pay to redeem himself.[26]

[**7.2**] If a lord compels his slave to work on a holy day, he must pay *lahslit* within the Danelaw and a penalty among the English.[27]

[**8**] If a freeman breaks a legally mandated fast, he must pay a penalty or *lahslit*. If a slave does so, he shall receive a whipping or pay to redeem himself.[28]

[**9**] Ordeals and oaths are prohibited on holy days and legally mandated fast days; and one who violates that shall pay *lahslit* among the Danes, a penalty among the English.[29]

[**9.1**] If it can be managed, no one sentenced to death should ever be executed on a Sunday festival, but he is to be arrested and held until the holy day has ended.[30]

22 Cf. II Cn. 48.1.

23 Cf. II Cn. 48.2.

24 Cf. V Atr. 31.1 and II Cn. 48.3.

25 Cf. II As 24.1, VI As. 10; VI Atr. 22.1 and 44; I Cn. 15; *Canons* 19; *Cn. 1020* 18; *NPL* 55; Napier 43 l. 94; *On Tithes* n. 5; *On Justice* n. 45; and *On the Duties of the Laity* n. 16.

26 Cf. Wi. 11, Ine 3.2, II Cn. 45.1–2, and *NPL* 57. Significantly, although clearly based on this clause, the analogous clauses in II Cn. and *NPL* omit the loss of freedom as a penalty for working on a holy day.

27 Cf. Ine 3.1 and II Cn. 45.3. Prohibitions against Sunday labour reach back as far as the eighth-century *Lex Baiuvariorum*. On the place of such prohibitions in Wulfstan's writings, especially as they relate to his understanding of slavery, see Pelteret 1995: 93.

28 Cf. Wi. 14–15, II Cn. 46–46.2, and *NPL* 57.

29 Cf. V Atr. 18, VI Atr. 25, I Cn. 17, *Canons* 24, Napier 43 l. 104, and *On Tithes* n. 8.

30 Cf. II Cn. 45. Although legal proceedings had been banned on Sundays as early as the Theodosian Code, clauses 9–9.1 are the first instance in Anglo-Saxon law of a

[10] If a mutilated man, who might have been executed, comes to be abandoned and he survives for three nights: afterwards, with the bishop's permission, anyone who wishes to heal his injuries and his soul might help him.

[11] If magicians or wizards, perjurers or murderers[31] or foul, corrupted, notorious prostitutes come to be discovered anywhere in the land, then they must be expelled from the country and the realm cleansed, or they must be utterly wiped out unless they desist and repent most deeply.[32]

[12] If a man in orders or a foreigner is, by any means, cheated of his goods or his life, then the king – or the lord of that land – and bishop of that people shall act as kinsman and protector, unless he has another; and fitting compensation must readily be paid to Christ and the king according to the nature of the deed; or he who is king of that people must punish the crime most harshly.[33]

---

specific prohibition on oaths, ordeals, and executions. Although Wulfstan's source for the ban on oaths and ordeals remains unknown (if he had one at all), the ban on executions is likely of Carolingian origin, as similar injunctions are found in the acts of the Synod of Mainz as well as in the works of Regino of Prüm and Burchard of Worms. See Haines 2010: 23–4.

31 The pairing of 'perjurers or murderers' ('mansworan oððe morðwyrhtan') bears a striking resemblance to the phrase 'men perjured and wolfish murderers' ('men meinsvara ok morðvarga') in the Old Norse *Vǫluspá*, though the similarity likely results only from the two authors drawing on a shared stock of conventional formulae. See North 2006: 218–19.

32 Cf. VI Atr. 7, II Cn. 4a, *Cn. 1020* 15, and *On Heathen Practices* n. 6. On the injunction to cleanse the realm, see also *Polity* II, VIII Atr. 40, II Cn. 4 and 7.1, and *On Justice*, n. 39. On this clause, see Meaney 2004: 480.

33 Cf. VIII Atr. 33–4, II Cn. 40–40.1, and *On Ranks* 8.

2. CONCERNING EPISCOPAL DUTIES (*EPISCOPUS*)

This short text, interposed after *Polity* VI in Oxford, Bodleian Library, Junius 121, is among Wulfstan's earliest statements on bishops' roles and responsibilities.[1] Sara Pons-Sanz assigns it to the period just after Wulfstan's appointment to York (1002x1008), postdating *Edward-Guthrum*, and contemporaneous with his homilies on baptism (Bethurum 8a and 8b).[2] If so, then it would also be among the archbishop's first forays into legal composition. The extent to which this text exemplifies Wulfstan's early thought is indicated by the many similarities between injunctions included here and clauses found in V and VI Æthelred. Wormald characterises this text as only 'putatively legal', yet this judgment is somewhat unfair.[3] Not only does the text concern itself with the range of episcopal jurisdiction in both religious and secular affairs – especially in its opening clause, which Bethurum suggests 'sounds like a call to battle of the late eleventh century'[4] – but it also incorporates injunctions on a number of other matters that will recur frequently in Wulfstan's legal writings, most notably the legal status of slaves, the importance of accurate weights and measures, and the necessity of just judgments in secular disputes. Perhaps most significantly, this text provides some of the earliest evidence for the use of the parish as a jurisdictional unit and for a distinction between the rights of town and country.[5] As such, although it is unclear whether the text was intended to carry any prescriptive force, it nonetheless testifies to Wulfstan's early thought on issues that would influence his work over the rest of his career. Moreover, that it later came to be incorporated into the manuscript of *Polity* as well as translated into Latin and included in *Quadripartitus* (where it is paired with the Compilation on Status and mistakenly included among the laws of Æthelstan) suggests that later readers likewise understood it at the very least as a significant statement of legal principles.

---

1 Although the text's single Old English manuscript witness incorporates it into *Polity*, there is no evidence that Wulfstan composed it for this purpose, or even that he intended it to be used in this way. See Liebermann 1903–1916: v. III, p. 270 and Jost 1959: 23–4. Wormald plausibly suggests that the text may owe its inclusion in Junius 121 to the interest of the manuscript's late eleventh-century Worcester scribe in the writings of the monastery's former abbot. Wormald 1999d: 392n. 584.

2 Pons-Sanz 2007: 25. Liebermann simply dates the text between 1000 and 1050. Cf. Liebermann 1903–1916: Vol. I, p. 477.

3 Wormald 1999d: 392n. 584.

4 Bethurum Loomis 1971: 142.

5 Loyn 1971a: 122; Hill 1978: 213; Blair 2005: 497; and Baxter 2007: 94–5.

TRANSLATION[1]

VII. ITEM[2]

[1] It is proper for a bishop to offer guidance in all things,[3] both in religious and secular matters.[4]

[2] He must first oversee men in orders, so that each of them may know what is rightly appropriate for him to do and also what they should preach to laymen.

[3] He must always be concerned with reconciliation and peace as fervently as he can.

[4] He must readily resolve disputes and make peace along with those secular judges who love justice.[5]

[5] He must oversee the exculpation in response to an accusation, so that no one might inflict harm on another through an oath or an ordeal.

[6] He must not permit any injustice, not an incorrect measurement nor a false weight; but it is proper that every law – both law in the town and law in the country[6] – undergo his review and consent. And every town measurement and every weigh-scale is to be properly adjusted under his supervision, lest any man defraud another and thereby sin all too greatly.[7]

---

1 This translation is based on the text in Liebermann 1903–16: v. I, pp. 477–9 with reference to that in Whitelock 1981: 417–22.

2 This is the only rubric given to the text in the manuscript, where it follows ch. VI of *Polity*. The title *Episcopus* was given to it by Liebermann. Cf. Liebermann 1903–1916: v. I, p. 477.

3 Lit. 'Every guidance'.

4 The pairing 'religious and secular' ('godcundan ... woruldcundan') recurs frequently in Wulfstan's writing. See, for instance, VI Atr. 50 and 52; II Cn. 38.2 and 68.1c; *Evil Rulers* n. 6; and *Polity* XXII. On this clause, see Bethurum Loomis 1971: 142–3.

5 Cf. VI Atr. 1. The bishop's role in secular dispute resolution had been established in English law at least as early as III Eg. 5.3.

6 'Of first importance [to the development of towns in later Anglo-Saxon England] was perhaps the growth of a clearer idea of a borough-right which was separate and distinct from simple land-right. The early-eleventh-century tract *Episcopus* gives the most precise statement when it divides all legal right into the two elements of land-right and borough-right. The distinction it makes, however, is implicit throughout the period, in relation to trading regulations, the rights of *burhwaru* to take action against men who infringe a truce, rights of exculpation, or in the simple phrase "within or without the borough", which becomes enshrined in the common form of many medieval charters.' Loyn 1971a: 122. On this point, see also Hill 1978: 213; Baxter 2007: 94–5.

7 Cf. V Atr. 24, VI Atr. 28.2 and 32.2, II Cn. 9, Bethurum 10c l. 88, and *On Justice* n. 42. See also Bethurum Loomis 1971: 143; Hagen 1995: 283.

[7] He must always shield Christian men against each of those things which are sinful; and thus he must devote himself the more deeply in all matters so that he might know the more truly how the flock fares which he must tend on God's behalf,[8] so that the devil may not inflict harm too greatly thereon nor sow too much of his falseness among them.[9]

[8] Nor will the people's ways ever be well-reasoned or well-protected by God in that land where ill-gotten gains and the greatest falsehoods are held dear. Thus, God's friends must quell each injustice and encourage what is right and never permit men to ruin themselves too greatly through falsehood and ill-gotten gains before the righteous God who despises all injustice.[10]

[9] It is proper for all Christians to love righteousness and hate injustice;[11] and indeed, men in orders must always support what is right and reject what is wrong; thus, bishops must pronounce sentences[12] with secular judges so that they do not permit, if it is in their power, any injustice to spring up there.[13]

[10] And it is likewise proper for priests in their parishes that they readily assist each person to obtain justice and never permit, if they can correct it, any Christian to inflict injury on another all too greatly, neither the strong on the weak, nor the higher on the lower, nor the shire official on his inferior, nor the lord on his men, nor even his slaves.[14]

[11] It is rightly proper that slaves work for their lords according to the guidance of the confessor and under his own supervision throughout the entire shire in which he hears confession.

[12] And it is right that there not be any measuring stick longer than another, but all are to be standardised according to the confessor's measure; and each measure in his parish and each weight is to be

---

8 Cf. VI Atr. 2, I Cn. 26.1–3, *Polity* VI, and Bethurum 16b l. 27f.

9 Cf. *Matthew* 13:39.

10 Cf. *Deuteronomy* 25:16.

11 Cf. II Cn. 7.1; *Polity* II; *Cn. 1020* 15; Bethurum 11, l. 127; Bethurum 13, l. 103; Bethurum 21, ll. 26–7; and *On Justice*, n. 13.

12 The phrase used here is 'domas dihtan', a collocation which does not appear in the laws. Whitelock suggests that it may be a specialised term used to describe the handing down of sentences in secular courts. See Whitelock 1981: 420n. 424.

13 See above, n. 5. This clause marks one of the most significant points of conflict between Wulfstan and Ælfric, who strongly opposed cooperation between ecclesiastics and secular judges. Whitelock 1981: 418.

14 Cf. *Polity* VI.

standardised very precisely according to his direction; and if anything there is disputed, the bishop will judge.

[**13**][15] It is the responsibility of every lord to protect his slaves[16] as best he can, for they are loved by God as much as those who are free, and he bought us all for the same price.

[**14**] We are all God's own slaves, and he judges us just as we judge those over whom we hold power here on earth.[17]

[**15**] Accordingly, we have an obligation to protect those compelled to serve us; then we may experience a greater protection at God's own judgment.

---

15 The final three clauses of *Episc.* also occur in Napier 58, ll. 3f. The seeming lack of influence of Bethurum 8b on these clauses led Whitelock to suggest that *Episc.* must predate that text. Whitelock 1981: 418.

16 *nidþeowum*, lit. 'slaves by compulsion', that is, those who have entered slavery because of poverty or starvation. Pelteret 1995: 95. This term also appears in the next clause.

17 On clauses 13 and 14, see Pelteret 1995: 90, 95.

3. THE 'COMPILATION ON STATUS' (*GEÞYNCÐU, NORÐLEODA LAGA, MIRCNA LAGA, AÐ,* AND *HADBOT*)

Likely begun between 1006 and 1008, the 'Compilation on Status' represents Wulfstan's most elaborate early attempt to develop a comprehensive vision of an ordered Christian society. In this sense, it serves as a crucial precursor to the more sophisticated models of Christian social order in the *Institutes of Polity* and I–II Cnut. Unfortunately, however, the 'Compilation's complex transmission history has complicated modern efforts to understand both Wulfstan's purposes in conceiving of such a collection and his methods in assembling it. As Wormald has memorably observed, the texts of the 'Compilation' 'form a group and were clearly meant to, but it is a group with an amoebic tendency to divide and multiply'.[1] The 'Compilation' consists of a core of ninth-century texts – the first half of *Norðleoda laga, Mircna Laga,* and the first clause of *Að* (here translated as *Concerning Wergild, Concerning the Law of the Mercians,* and *Concerning the Mercian Oath*[2]) – to which Wulfstan added an introductory text (*Geþyncðu,* here translated as *Concerning the Ranks of People and Law*), the second half of *Norðleoda laga,* a second clause to *Að,* and a concluding text (*Hadbot,* here translated as *Concerning Priests' Oaths and Clerical Compensation*).[3] Old English versions of the 'Compilation' survive in three manuscripts: Cambridge, Corpus Christi College 190; Cambridge, Corpus Christi College 201; and Strood, Medway Archive and Local Studies Centre, MS. DRc/R1 (*Textus Roffensis*). An additional Old English version, long thought to be a transcription from a lost manuscript, occurs in William Lambarde's 1568 *editio princeps* of Anglo-Saxon law, *Archaionomia*; however, this version has been shown to be spurious, the result of an attempt by Laurence Nowell to 'back-translate' the Latin of *Quadripartitus* into Old English.[4]

Of the authentic versions, only C.C.C.C. 201 preserves the entire 'Compilation' in what has come to be accepted as its proper order.[5] In contrast, C.C.C.C. 190 contains only *Mircna Laga, Að,* and *Hadbot,* perhaps because these texts would

---

1 Wormald 1999d: 391.

2 The titles of the translations reflect the texts' rubrics in their manuscripts. See the notes to the translations below.

3 The coherence of these texts as a compilation and Wulfstan's responsibility for their assemblage was first demonstrated in Bethurum 1950: 449–63. Further evidence for Wulfstan's methods in compiling these texts can be found in Whitelock 1979: 468–71; Wormald 1999d: 391–4; Rabin 2010a: 43–52; and Rabin forthcoming.

4 Sisam 1953 and Wormald 1999c. See also above, pp. 47–8.

5 A longer, more detailed version of the discussion which follows can be found in Rabin forthcoming.

have been more relevant to the manuscript's Worcester origin and emphasis.[6] All five texts do occur in *Textus Roffensis*, yet here the similarities to the
earlier versions end. The twelfth-century scribe has not only disarticulated
the 'Compilation' and redistributed its contents across the manuscript, but
he omits the concluding clause of *Hadbot* and inverts the two clauses of *Að*,
adding one as a final clause to the oath formulary *Swerian* and appending the
other to *Mircna Laga*. Although the earlier date of C.C.C.C. 190 and complete-
ness of C.C.C.C. 201 have long led scholars to favour these versions over
that in *Textus Roffensis*, there is reason to suspect that the twelfth-century
manuscript may actually preserve a more finished version of the 'Compilation'
than its eleventh-century predecessors.[7] Variations of vocabulary and content
in *Textus Roffensis* (particularly the inclusion of clauses 5 and 6 of *Geþyncðu*,
omitted from the earlier manuscripts) suggest that the scribe worked from
a different exemplar, possibly one of Canterbury origin, than that used for
C.C.C.C. 190 and 201.[8] Furthermore, the unique presence of Wulfstanian
collocations in *Textus* indicates that the versions of the 'Compilation' texts
in the Rochester scribe's source reflect alternate versions attributable to the
archbishop himself, rather than simply corrupted renderings of the texts
found in C.C.C.C. 201 and 190. Examples of these collocations include 'on
engla lagum' ('in the laws of the English'), 'þegenrihtes weorðe' ('worthy of
a thegn's rights'), 'inne mid englum on folcriht' ('according to the folk-law
of the English people'), and 'friðan 7 griþian' ('preserve and protect').[9] It
may be significant that most of the texts in which these collocations occur
are thought to have been composed later in the archbishop's career than
the texts of the 'Compilation'. Although the 'Compilation' traditionally has
been dated to *ca.* 1006–1008, the *Textus* collocations are more typical of texts
composed between 1010 and 1016. Accordingly, while we cannot date the
Textus variants with certainty, it seems reasonable to conclude that Wulfstan
composed an earlier version of the 'Compilation' preserved in C.C.C.C. 201
and 190 between 1006 and 1008, which he then revised several years later to
produce the version used by the Rochester scribe. The likelihood thus exists
that the texts, if not the arrangement, of the 'Compilation' in *Textus Roffensis*
more closely resembles Wulfstan's final vision for his collection. The translations below are based primarily on the texts in *Textus Roffensis*, with variants
from C.C.C.C. 190 and 201 identified in the notes.[10]

---

6 Wormald 1999d: 223.

7 For discussions of manuscript precedence, see Whitelock 1979: 468; Wormald
   1999d: 392; and Rabin 2010a: 44–6.

8 On the arguments for and against a possible Canterbury source, see Sawyer 1957: 14
   and Wormald 1999b: 130ff.

9 *On Ranks* 1, *Mercian Oath* 2 and *On Ranks* 6, *On Wergild* 1, and *Clerical Compensation*
   1.1.

10 The C.C.C.C. 201 version has been translated in Whitelock 1979: 468–71.

Ascertaining Wulfstan's intent in assembling the 'Compilation' is no less complex a problem than determining its manuscript history. The texts share an interest in rank and social status, yet many of the practices they record do not conform to those found in more mainstream royal legislation. While some have argued that the 'Compilation' should nonetheless be treated as an accurate depiction of later Anglo-Saxon legal customs, more recent scholarship has shown that many of the practices it describes are unsupported by contemporary evidence.[11] Dorothy Bethurum proposed that the 'Compilation' might be better understood as an exercise in Wulfstanian political philosophy than practical legislation. In her words, 'they are another chapter in the orderly arrangement of society with which he was occupied from the time when he wrote the *Laws of Edward and Guthrum* to the composition of the *Institutes of Polity*'.[12] Understanding the texts of the 'Compilation' in this way helps make sense of such features as *Geþyncðu*'s nostalgic tone and nearly exclusive use of verbs in the past tense, the substitution of national for regionally specific terminology in the ninth-century core texts, and the general movement of the 'Compilation' from secular to ecclesiastical concerns.[13] The 'Compilation' does not so much record defunct regional legal practices as it conjures a nostalgic image of an idealised past characterised by 'wise ... councillors who ... venerated the sacraments and holy orders for the love of God, and greatly honoured God's houses and God's servants'.[14] In this sense, the 'Compilation' serves as one of Wulfstan's earliest attempts to imagine a legal polity that would fulfil his vision for a holy society. It thus marks a first step towards the more far-reaching vision present in such texts as the *Institutes of Polity* and I–II Cnut.

11 See, for instance, Brown 1969: 141; Abels 1988a: 108–11; Lawson 1993: 60; and Hadley 2000: 74–5.

12 Bethurum 1950: 461.

13 See below, notes 4 and 15.

14 *On Clerical Compensation* 11.

TRANSLATION[1]

Concerning the Ranks of People and Law[2]

[1] In the laws of the English,[3] it once was that people and law were ordered by status;[4] and the people's councillors were treated with dignity, each according to his rank, noble and layman, thegn[5] and lord.

[2] And if a layman prospered so that he had fully five hides[6] of his own property with a church and kitchen, a bell-house and fortified gate,[7] a

---

1 These translations are based on the texts in Liebermann 1903–16: v. I, pp. 456–69.

2 In C.C.C.C. 201, the text is titled, 'Concerning wergilds and ranks'.

3 This phrase omitted from C.C.C.C. 201.

4 Lit. 'people and law went by rank'. The word *geþincðu* lacks a direct modern English equivalent and previous scholars have translated it variously as 'rank', 'status', 'dignity', and 'honour'. In this clause, Wulfstan appears to be using it to conflate notions of social status and moral worth in order to invoke a nostalgic picture of a properly organised society. Historians disagree over whether the prescriptions recorded in *Ranks* possessed the force of formal legislation; however, the text's retrospective tone and nearly exclusive use of the preterite verb tense – rhetorical features unique in the surviving corpus of Anglo-Saxon law – suggest that any legal force the text's prescriptions may once have possessed had faded by Wulfstan's day.

5 A landowner lower in status than a lord with military obligations to his superior. The thegn roughly corresponds to the post-Conquest knight. On the specific use of the term in this passage, see Abels 1988a: 142.

6 One hide is equivalent to the amount of land a single ploughman could till in one day. During the Old English period, depending on region, one hide could equate to an area ranging from 60 to 180 acres, though it was standardised following the Conquest to roughly 120 acres. The five-hide unit seems to have been a common standard of measurement in Old English law and may have indicated the threshold above which a landowner owed military obligations to the king. The laws of Ine also decree that a Welshman who acquires five hides of land may have his wergild raised to six hundred shillings (Ine 24.2). The extent to which such clauses were observed in practice remains disputed, however. Not only is there no surviving evidence of a layman (*ceorl*) actually advancing to the status of thegn based on his acquisition of five hides of property, but extant property records do not indicate the sort of flexibility in land tenure needed to make social mobility on these grounds a regular practice. It seems more likely here that Wulfstan is conjuring an idealised legal past rather than accurately recording a legal present. This claim remains controversial, however. For perspectives on the historical accuracy of this clause, see Brown 1969: 141; Stenton 1970: 382–93; Abels 1988a: 108–11; Lawson 1993: 60; Hadley 2000: 74–5; Campbell 2009: 29–30; Rabin 2010a: 50–2; and Rabin forthcoming.

7 C.C.C.C. 201: '... fully five hides of his own property, a bell and fortified gate ...'. The stipulation that a would-be thegn had to possess a bell (or bell-house) and fortified gate has given rise to considerable critical head-scratching. Although *burh* is often translated as 'town', it seems more likely that Wulfstan is here using the word in its more traditional sense, a fortified or defensible location. Noting a similar reference to a 'belle et burgiet' in a charter of the mid- twelfth century, Maitland argued that the gate may have served as 'some outward and visible sign of jurisdiction or lordly

seat and an appointed role in the king's hall, then he was worthy of a thegn's rights ever after.[8]

[3] And if a thegn prospered so that he waited upon the king and rode on his business among his retinue; then, if he had a thegn who followed him, who had five hides for the king's service, and had waited upon his lord in the king's hall, and had gone three times on his business to the king, then [his thegn] afterwards might represent his lord in various obligations with his initial oath and handle his litigation, wherever he must.[9]

[4] And he who did not have such a worthy representative swore for himself to his rights or forfeited his case.[10]

[5] And if a thegn prospered so that he became a noble, he was afterwards worthy of a noble's rights.

[6] And if a merchant prospered, so that he fared three times over the wide sea by his own means, he was afterwards worthy of a thegn's rights.[11]

[7] And if a student prospered by his learning, so that he took orders and served Christ, he was afterwards worthy of such respect and protection as was fitting thereto, unless he should sin so that he could not practice his ministry.[12]

[8] And if it so happened anywhere that someone injured one in orders or a stranger by word or deed, then it was the responsibility of the king and the bishop[13] to remedy it as swiftly as they could.[14]

---

power'. More recently, scholars have suggested that the 'bell-house and fortified gate' may instead refer to the possession of a fortified homestead, possibly a precursor to the post-Conquest castle or manor house. See Maitland 1898: 209–10; Davison 1967: 202–11; Brown 1969: 141; Loyn 1971a: 119–20; and Williams 2003b: 27–9.

8 See below, *Concerning wergild*, 9. For other criteria used to deem someone worthy of a thegn's rights in Wulfstan's writings, see V Atr. 9.1, VI Atr. 6.3, and *On Justice*, n. 30.

9 That is, the thegn might serve as his lord's agent in minor legal matters and financial transactions.

10 Clauses 3 and 4 deal with the use of advocates in the transaction of business and the settling of legal disputes. For a more detailed discussion of advocacy in Anglo-Saxon law, see Rabin 2007: 223–55.

11 Clauses 5 and 6 are omitted from C.C.C.C. 201.

12 The final phrase of this clause ('unless … ministry') is omitted from C.C.C.C. 201.

13 The positions of king and bishop are reversed in C.C.C.C. 201. On the possible significance of this reversal, see Bethurum 1950: 458 and Bethurum Loomis 1971: 136.

14 This, of course, will be the subject of the concluding text in the 'Compilation',

Concerning Wergild[15]

[1] According to the folk-law of the English people,[16] a king's wergild[17] is thirty-thousand *thrymsas*.[18] fifteen thousand *thrymsas* are for the man and fifteen thousand *thrymsas* are for the kingship.[19] The personal wergild belongs to his kinsmen and the royal compensation belongs to the people.[20]

[2] A nobleman's wergild is fifteen thousand *thrymsas*.

[3] Bishops and ealdormen, eight thousand *thrymsas*.

[4] A Danish nobleman and a high-reeve, four thousand *thrymsas*.[21]

[5] A mass-priest and a secular thegn, two thousand *thrymsas*.[22]

[6] A layman's wergild is two-hundred and sixty-six *thrymsas*,[23] that is, two hundred shillings according to the law of the Mercians.[24]

Concerning priests' oaths and clerical compensation. For more detailed versions of this clause, see *EGu.* 12 (on which this clause is likely based) and II Cn. 42. The king's jurisdiction over assaults on clerics and foreigners also occurs in VIII Atr. 33 and II Cn. 40.

15 C.C.C.C. 201: 'The Law of the Northern People', that is, Northumbria. The revision of this text – most likely by Wulfstan himself – to diminish its regional specificity should not be taken as a sign that the wergild values listed here necessarily applied south of the Humber. Cf. Chadwick 1905: 167.

16 Omitted from C.C.C.C. 201.

17 C.C.C.C. 201: 'The wergild of a king of the northern people'.

18 The term *thrymsa* was used both as a general term for coins and more specifically to the equivalent of one-third of a shilling, about four pennies. It is the latter meaning which most likely applies here. See Grierson and Blackburn 1986: 157.

19 *Mercian Law* below, 3.1.

20 See *Mercian Law* below, 4.

21 On the equivalence between the wergilds of Danish and English nobility, see *AGu* 2.

22 The wergild value for a thegn appears to be fairly typical. Compare, for instance, the value listed in the will of the reeve Abba (S 1482), l. 22, ed. in Harmer 1914: pp. 3–5.

23 On this clause and its analogues in insular (especially Scottish) law, see Chadwick 1905: 104.

24 Cf. Ine 70, *Concerning the Mercian oath* 1 (below), and *Concerning the Law of the Mercians* 1 (below). This is the final clause of the text's 'original' section, which likely dates from the ninth century but may have been composed as early as the mid-seventh century. The clauses that follow (nos 7–12) are all composed by Archbishop Wulfstan. On the ninth-century dating, see Wormald 1999d: 393. On the arguments for an earlier date, see Fulk 2010: 66–7. Chadwick pointed out that the wergilds enumerated in these clauses correspond with those found in the nearly contemporary Scottish text, the *Leges inter Brettos et Scottos*, an observation which led Wormald to suggest the possibility either of a shared source or of some sort of direct connection between Wulfstan's York and the Scotland of Malcolm II. Chadwick 1905: 28, 104; and Wormald 2009: 195–6.

⟦7⟧ And if a Welshman prospers so that he possess a hide of land and can pay the king's tribute,²⁵ then his wergild shall be two hundred and twenty shillings.²⁶

⟦7.1⟧ And if he does not prosper to more than half of a hide, then his wergild will be eighty shillings.

⟦8⟧ And if he does not have any land but is still free, then compensation for him shall be seventy shillings.

⟦9⟧ And if a layman prospers so that he possesses five hides of land for his obligations to the king and anyone kills him, compensation for him shall be two thousand *thrymsas*.²⁷

⟦10⟧ Yet even if he prospers so that he possesses a helmet and a coat of mail and a gold-plated sword, if he does not possess the land he will still be a layman.

⟦11⟧ And if his son and his son's son prosper so that they have sufficient land, then the offspring will be of the rank of *gesith* at two thousand *thrymsas*.

⟦12⟧ And if they do not have it and cannot acquire enough, their compensation will be that of a layman.

⟦Concerning the Law of the Mercians⟧²⁸

⟦1⟧ According to the law of the Mercians, a layman's wergild is two hundred shillings.²⁹

⟦1.1⟧ The wergild of a thegn is six times as much, that is, twelve hundred shillings.³⁰

⟦2⟧ According to the law of the Mercians, then, the king's individual wergild is the wergild of six thegns, that is, thirty thousand *sceattas*,

---

25 OE *gafol*. This word can also refer taxation in a more general sense.

26 Cf. Ine 23.3, 24.2, 32.

27 The wergild here equates to that of a thegn in clause 5, thus bringing the clauses on social promotion in this text in line with those in *Concerning the ranks of people and law* above, esp. clause 2.

28 The title is omitted from *Textus Roffensis*.

29 See above, *Concerning wergild*, 6.

30 See below, *Concerning the Mercian Oath* 1. A similar stipulation is also found in clause 1.1 of a mid-tenth century law-code promulgated under either Edmund or Edgar and referred to as *Wergild* by Liebermann. This law-code should not be confused with the text of nearly the same name in the 'Compilation on Status' (though both do occur with nearly identical rubrics in *Textus Roffensis*).

which is one hundred and twenty pounds in all.[31]

[**3**] So much is wergild in the folk law of the people, according to the law of the Mercians.

[**3.1**] And for the kingship there is a second compensation owed equal to that for the king.[32]

[**4**] The wergild belongs to his kinsmen and the royal compensation to the people.[33]

[Concerning the Mercian Oath][34]

[**1**] The oath of a man with a wergild of twelve hundred shillings equals the oath of six laymen: therefore, if a man with a wergild of twelve hundred shillings must be avenged, he will be fully avenged on six laymen; furthermore, his wergild will be the wergilds of six laymen.[35]

[Concerning Priests' Oaths and Clerical Compensation][36]

[**1**] A mass-priest's oath and a secular thegn's are considered equal in English law because of the seven Church degrees that the mass-priest has acquired through the grace of God.[37] Sevenfold are the gifts

---

31 Cf. the ratios between layman, thegn, and king in *Concerning Wergild* 1, 5, and 6. On this clause, see Chadwick 1905: 28 and Scammel 1993: 614–15.

32 See above, *Concerning Wergild*, 1.

33 See above, *Concerning Wergild*, 1.

34 Title omitted from *Textus Roffensis*. This text and the one following it in the 'Compilation', *Concerning Priests' Oaths and Clerical Compensation*, were significantly reworked by the *Textus* scribe: the single clause of *Concerning the Mercian Oath* and the first sentence of *Concerning clerical compensation* were extracted from their context in the 'Compilation', inverted, and appended as the twelfth and thirteenth clauses of the Old English oath compilation *Swerian*. The treatment of these texts in *Textus Roffensis* led Thorpe to treat this text simply as part of *Swerian*, and its subsequent editors, Schmid and Liebermann, to combine *Concerning the Mercian Oath* and the first sentence of *Concerning Clerical Oaths* into a single, bi-clausal text, an editorial creation known as *Að*. However, the fact that C.C.C.C. 190 and 201 as well as the twelfth-century compilers of *Quadripartitus* and the *Instituta Cnuti* construe the texts in the manner in which they are treated above – the first clause of Liebermann's *Að* as an individual text entitled *Concerning the Mercian Oath* and the second clause as the first sentence of a longer text entitled *Concerning Clerical Oaths and Priests' Compensation* – indicates that the arrangement in *Textus Roffensis* should be understood simply as a scribal variation. On this point, see also Whitelock 1979: 470.

35 See , *Concerning the Law of the Mercians* 1.1. See Clauses 1–1.1 of the Old English legal text *Wergild* (not to be confused with *On Wergild*, translated above).

36 Title omitted from *Textus Roffensis*.

37 Cf. VIII Atr. 28, *Canons* 68b, I Cn. 6a.2a., and *On Justice*, n. 30. On this clause, see Bethurum 1950: 459; Bethurum Loomis 1971: 140; and Rabin 2010a: 43–52.

of the Holy Spirit; and seven are the steps of ecclesiastical ranks and holy orders; and seven times daily should God's servants praise God in church and diligently advocate for all Christian people.[38]

[1.1] And very rightly, it is proper for all friends of God that they love God's Church and venerate it, and preserve and protect God's servants.[39]

[1.2] And he who injures them by word or deed must diligently remedy it with sevenfold compensation, according to the deed and according to the order, if he wishes to earn God's favour.[40]

[1.3] For one must always – for fear of God – diligently honour the sanctity, orders, and house of God.[41]

[2] And as compensation for one in orders if loss of life occurs, one must make amends for the first rank with one pound in addition to the standard wergild, and he must diligently plead for proper reconciliation.[42]

38 *Isaiah* 11:2–3 lists the seven gifts of the Holy Spirit as Wisdom (*sapientia*), Understanding (*intellectus*), Counsel (*consilium*), Fortitude (*fortitudo*), Knowledge (*scientia*), Godliness (*pietas*), and Fear of the Lord (*timor Domini*). Wulfstan provided an earlier commentary on this passage in his homily, *De Septiformi Spiritu* (Bethurum IX, esp. ll. 19–31), though any consideration of clerical hierarchy or compensation is absent from the earlier text. The concept of a correspondence between the seven ecclesiastical grades and the seven gifts of the Holy Spirit evolved over the seventh and eighth centuries, possibly originating with the text *On the VII Ecclesiastical Ranks* (*De vii ordinibus ecclesiae*), falsely attributed to Jerome. Wulfstan's immediate source for this passage is unclear, though similar comparisons appear in the *Collectio canonum Hibernensis* (at 42.22), Ælfric's letter to Bishop Wulfsige (also a major source for *The Institutes of Polity*), as well as in pontificals associated with Archbishop Dunstan and the churches of Durham and Canterbury. On possible sources for this passage, see Reynolds 1978: 86–8; Reynolds 1979: 669–84; Jones 1998b: 684. On the duty of the clergy to 'diligently advocate for all Christian people', see V Atr. 4.1, I Cn. 6a, *Canons* 1, *Polity* XVII and XXXV, *On the Duties of the Laity* n. 5, and Napier 37, p. 179, l. 9.

39 See VI Atr. 45. C.C.C.C. 190 and 201 read 'preserve and save [friðian 7 nerian] God's servants'. Calls to 'preserve and protect' ('friðian 7 griðian') the people or goods of the Church occur frequently in Wulfstan's writings. See also Napier 30, l. 2; Napier 37, l. 24; VI Atr. 42.3; I Cn. 2 and 4; and, in this volume, the homilies *On the Duties of the Laity* and God's *Threat to a Sinning Israel.*

40 A translation of §70 in the B recension of Wulfstan's Canon Law Collection. Cross and Hamer 1999: 133–4. See also II Cn. 49.

41 Wormald suggests that clauses 1.1 and 1.3 may serve as the source for I Cn. 4's injunction concerning the necessity to revere the clergy and clerical foundations. The similarities between these clauses and those in I Cn. are so general, however, that the connection may be more thematic than direct. See Wormald 1999d: 356 and Richards 2010: 142.

42 Clauses 2–8 enumerate the compensation to be paid to members of each of the seven grades in the ecclesiastical hierarchy. These are: door-keeper (*ostiarius*), reader (*lector*),

[**3**] And as compensation for one in orders if loss of life occurs, one must make amends for the second rank with two pounds in addition to the standard wergild, and he must diligently plead for divine penance.

[**4**] And as compensation for one in orders if a full breach of the peace occurs,[43] one must make amends for the third rank with three pounds in addition to the standard wergild, and he must diligently plead for divine penance.

[**5**] And as compensation for one in orders if a full breach of the peace occurs, one must make amends for the fourth rank with four pounds in addition to the standard wergild, [and with divine penance].[44]

[**6**] And as compensation for one in orders if a full breach of the peace occurs, one must make amends for the fifth rank with five pounds in addition to the standard wergild, and with divine penance.

[**7**] And as compensation for one in orders if a full breach of the peace occurs, one must make amends for the sixth rank with six pounds in addition to the standard wergild, and with divine penance.

[**8**] And as compensation for one in orders if a full breach of the peace occurs, one must make amends for the seventh rank with seven pounds in addition to the standard wergild, and with divine penance.

[**9**] And as compensation for one in orders if a partial violation occurs,[45] one must diligently make amends according to the deed.

[**9.1**] And one part of the compensation for one in orders rightly shall go to the bishop, a second part to the altar, and a third part to the community.

[**10**] One must always pass a judgment appropriate for the deed and set a penalty appropriate[46] for the rank in matters divine and secular.

[**11**][47] [And wise were the councillors who added these laws to the

---

exorcist (*exorcista*), acolyte (*acolitus*), sub-deacon (*subdiaconus*), deacon (*diaconus*), and priest (*presbiter*).

43 A 'full breach of the peace' is here equivalent to the 'loss of life' specified in the previous clause.

44 The end of this clause is omitted in *Textus Roffensis*, likely inadvertently, but present in C.C.C.C. 190 and 201.

45 That is, if the victim is only injured but not killed.

46 C.C.C.C. 190 reads 'merciful'.

47 *Textus Roffensis* inverts clauses 9.1 and 10 and omits clause 11 entirely. This is in keeping with the scribe's treatment of the 'Compilation on Status' generally, which he disarticulates and re-edits in order to reformulate the component texts for a twelfth-

ecclesiastical canons for the guidance of the people, and who venerated the sacraments and holy orders for the love of God, and greatly
honoured God's houses and God's servants.]⁴⁸

century readership and fit them into the manuscript's organisational programme.
The preterite verb tenses of this clause recall those of *On Ranks*, thus providing a
neat bookend to the 'Compilation'.

48 Cf. *EGu.* Pr.2, *Sanctuary* 24, *Evil Rulers*, n. 11, and VIII Atr. 36.

4. *CONCERNING SANCTUARY* (*GRIÐ*)

This text, to which the manuscript gives the title *Concerning Sanctuary and Protection*, survives only in London, British Library, Cotton Nero A.i. Although paired in the manuscript with a selection of similarly-themed clauses from VIII Æthelred, *Sanctuary*'s nostalgia for an idealised legal past, interest in social mobility, and praise for the 'wise ... councillors of former days' have led to suggestions that it was composed in tandem with the Compilation on Status, perhaps between 1006 and 1008.[1] Further support for this supposition may be found in *Sanctuary*'s association with the Status group in the twelfth-century Latin compilation *Instituta Cnuti*, which might indicate that they circulated together at some point in their early history as well.[2]

The text consists of three parts: an initial statement of principles (clauses 1–2); an extended catalogue of past and present sanctuary laws (clauses 3–19); and a homiletic conclusion (clauses 20–31). The care Wulfstan took in composing *Sanctuary* is evident in detailed research underlying the legal catalogue of clauses 3–19: not only does he record the variations in regional sanctuary practices, but this section also contains the most sustained discussion in any of his surviving writings of the Kentish and West Saxon laws of the seventh and eighth centuries. Perhaps the most important feature of the text, however, is the way in which it illustrates Wulfstan's evolving sense of the relationship between secular and ecclesiastical authority. Many of *Sanctuary*'s clauses characterise ecclesiastical protection as either equal or superior to royal power, while the revisions introduced into earlier laws often appear designed to raise the status of Church officers over that of their counterparts in secular administration.[3] If the 1006x1008 date is correct, *Sanctuary* thereby offers useful insight into Wulfstan's mindset just at the moment when he was beginning to exercise influence over the composition of royal legislation.

---

1 See clauses 1–5, 21–2, and 24. For a more extended discussion of the similarities between the texts and their chronology, see Bethurum 1950: 449–63; Wormald 1999d: 394–5; and Wormald 2004: 17–18.

2 Wormald 1999d: 394.

3 Bethurum Loomis 1971: 140 and Shoemaker 2010: 89.

TRANSLATION[1]

CONCERNING SANCTUARY AND PROTECTION

[1] Of all forms of sanctuary, God's sanctuary[2] is the best to deserve and the most diligently to be held, and next to that, the king's.[3]

[2] Therefore, it is right that the sanctuary within the walls of God's church and the sanctuary received from the hand of a Christian king remain equally inviolable.[4]

[3] And it once was that capital cities and those of high rank were entitled to greater privileges and to offer protection and sanctuary to those who needed it and sought it there, always in keeping with the privileges that belonged thereto.[5]

[4] And it so stood in those days among the English that if a condemned man sought the king, the archbishop, or a nobleman, then he had nine nights' sanctuary in which to save his life, unless the king wished to grant him more time.[6]

[5] And if he appealed to a suffragan bishop or an ealdorman or an important capital city, then he had sanctuary for seven nights, unless he was granted more.[7]

[6] And in Kentish law, the king and archbishop are owed an equal and likewise costly penalty for the violation of their protection.[8]

---

1 This translation is based on the text in Liebermann 1903–16: v. I, pp. 470–3.

2 'God's sanctuary' ('Godes grið') is a favorite phrase of Wulfstan's and survives almost exclusively in his writings. Cf. V Atr. 10.1, 21; VI Atr. 13, 26; I Cn. 2.1; Polity XXXV; Bethurum 20.3 l. 80; and On Justice, n. 6.

3 Cf. I Cn. 2.1. The extent of the king's sanctuary is defined in the short tenth-century legal tract Pax, which reads in its entirety, 'Thus far shall be the king's sanctuary from where he is sitting in four directions, that is three miles and three furlongs and three lineal acres and nine feet and nine hand-spans and nine barleycorns'.

4 Cf. EGu. 1, I Cn. 2.2, VI Atr. 14, On the Laws of God n. 15, On Justice n. 6, and Polity ch. XXXV. Earlier versions of this injunction occur in II Eg. 5.3 and III Atr. 1.

5 The nostalgic tone of clauses 3–5 recalls the similar evocation of an idealised past in the opening clauses of On Ranks, a text likely composed at roughly the same time as this one. It also highlights the present-day deterioration in ecclesiastical status which made necessary the injunctions that follow.

6 Cf. Af. 2, 5, and IV As. 6.1.

7 Cf. IV As. 6.2.

8 Similar injunctions occur in VIII Atr. 3 and I Cn. 2.5. The closest analogue is I Cn. 3a.2. See Bethurum Loomis 1971: 140.

[7] And according to those laws, elevenfold compensation is due for the archbishop's property and ninefold for the king's.[9]

[8] And the penalty for violating the protection of Christ's church is that same as that [for violating the protection] of the king.[10]

[9] And according to southern English law, the law of sanctuary stands thus: if anyone fights in church or in the king's house, then he is to forfeit all that he owns and it is the king's judgment whether he lives or dies.[11]

[10] And if anyone fights within the minster close outside a church, he is to compensate for all with the full penalty to which it is entitled, according to the status of the church.

[11] And if anyone otherwise violates the king's protection, he is to compensate for that with five pounds according to English law; violation of an archbishop's and nobleman's protection with three pounds; another bishop's and ealdorman's with two pounds.[12]

[12] And if anyone starts a fight in the presence of a nobleman or archbishop, he is to compensate with one hundred and fifty shillings; if this occurs in the presence of another bishop or ealdorman, he is to compensate with one hundred shillings.[13]

[13] And it stands in northern English law that anyone who slays a man within church walls is to be condemned to death.[14]

[13.1] And anyone who wounds shall lose his hand.[15]

[13.2] And anyone who slays a man within the church doors is to give to that church one hundred and twenty shillings according to northern English law.[16]

---

9 Cf. Abt. 1. This is the only surviving clause in Old English law to echo the first clause of Æthelberht's legislation, though it is significant that Wulfstan assigns compensation to the archbishop, rather than to a bishop as in the earlier text. Moreover, Æthelberht's laws do not mention the king, implying that the purpose of this clause is, in Bethurum's words, 'to elevate the status of the upper clergy'. Bethurum Loomis 1971: 140. See also Oliver 2002: 84–5 and Wormald 1999d: 132.

10 Cf. Wi. 2, VIII Atr. 2, and I Cn. 2.3–4.

11 Cf. Ine 6, Af. 7, II Cn. 59, and clause 15 below.

12 Cf. Af. 3.

13 Cf. Ine 6, Af. 15 and 38.

14 Cf. VIII Atr. 1.1.

15 This is the only instance of the loss of a hand serving as a penalty for assault.

16 Cf. Ine 6.1.

[**14**] And a freeman who injures a living person under protection is to give thirty shillings.

[**15**] And anyone who fights or steals in the king's compound or in his vicinity is to be condemned to death, unless the king permits that he may be redeemed with his wergild.[17]

[**16**] And if a condemned man seeks sanctuary[18] and thereby saves his life, then unless greater mercy is shown, he is to receive one of three [penalties] in exchange for his life: wergild, perpetual enslavement, [or] imprisonment.[19]

[**17**] And whichever of these three it is – whether he pays, serves, or suffers – he is to arrange for security if he can; and if he cannot, then he is to swear that he will never commit robbery nor steal livestock nor avenge his punishment.[20]

[**18**] And if he breaks any of these [oaths], he may not go anywhere in his life or take flight.[21]

[**19**] The security and ecclesiastical privileges of the sanctuary[22] are always to be observed most assiduously according to the law, and God's laws are to be followed and teachers are to be heeded, as is appropriate to them.[23]

[**19.1**] Bishops are the messengers and teachers of God's law and they must fervently call to Christ often and frequently and readily intervene on behalf of all Christian people; and they must preach and diligently set an example for the spiritual benefit of the Christian people.[24]

---

17 See above, clause 9.

18 This clause employs *friðstol* as a general term for sanctuary, although the word originated as the name for a specific 'peace-seat' for sanctuary-seekers to use when claiming refuge. Such seats were present in the churches at York, Southwell, Hexham, and Beverly, the latter two of which still survive. Notably, York and Beverly are two of the three foundations whose privileges are set forth in the in the first clause of *Northumbrian Church-Sanctuary*. On the *friðstol*, see Blair 2005: 223.

19 The term used here for imprisonment, *hengenwitnung*, is a *hapax legomenon* (a term with only a single surviving attestation). On this clause, see Pelteret 1995: 94.

20 Cf. VI As. 12.2.

21 This clause mitigates the more severe punishment of execution decreed for those guilty of second offenses in VI As. 12.2.

22 'Hælnesgrið 7 hadgrið': both *hapax legomena*.

23 Cf. VI Atr. 42.2; II Cn. 84.1; *On the Duties of the Laity* n. 3; *Polity* VI; Napier 37, p. 179, ll. 21–3; Bethurum 5, ll. 113–18; and Bethurum 20.3, ll. 192–4.

24 Cf. I Cn. 26, *Polity* V, and Bethurum 17 l. 36.

[20] Anyone who rejects that which he hears from them must settle his dispute with God himself.[25]

[21] But there are some men who, because of their pride and also their birth, refuse to heed their spiritual betters, just as they ought to do if they desired virtue;[26] and they often start into blame that which they should praise, and judge to be inferior because of their humble birth those whose ancestors were not in the world either wealthy or made proud through their worldly finery or in this transitory life prosperous or powerful.

[21.1] Indeed, they are not wise nor entirely perceptive who will neither obey God nor better understand how often he has raise from insignificance to greatness those who obeyed him and pleased him rightly.

[21.2] We know that, through God's grace, a slave can become a thegn and a layman become a nobleman, a performer become a priest and a scholar become a bishop.[27]

[22] And it once came to pass, just as God decreed, that a shepherd became a king and he was exceedingly great; it also came to pass, just as God decreed, a fisherman became a bishop, and he was greatly beloved and pleasing to Christ.

[23] Such are the gifts of God, who can easily raise from insignificance to greatness all that he himself wishes, just as the psalmist truly said when he sang thus: *Who is as our Lord, etc. raising up the needy from the earth, and lifting up the poor out of the dunghill: That he may place him with princes, with the princes of his people.*[28]

[23.1] This is understood by those who have a fear of God and heed wisdom.[29]

---

25 Cf. I Cn. 26.4, *Polity* V, and Bethurum 17 l. 39.

26 Cf. Napier 37 p. 178, ll. 19–20.

27 Cf. Bethurum 20.3 (*Sermo Lupi ad Anglos*), l. 117. Bethurum cites this clause as evidence that Wulfstan may have been a scribe prior to his appointment as bishop as London; however, in the absence of any corroborating evidence or examples of comparable promotions, it seems more likely that this clause offers simply another example of Wulfstanian hyperbole. Bethurum 1957: 58.

28 *Psalm* 112:5, 7–8: 'quis sicut Dominus Deus noster ... suscitans a terra inopem et de stercore erigens pauperem ut conlocet eum cum principibus cum principibus populi sui'.

29 *Proverbs* 1: 7: 'Timor Domini principium sapientiæ' ('The fear of the Lord is the beginning of wisdom'). This phrase or variations on it also appears in *Proverbs* 9:10, *Job* 28:28, and *Psalm* 110.

[24] And also wise were the councillors in former days who first added secular laws to the just ecclesiastical canons for bishops and holy assemblies, and venerated sanctity and the holy orders for the love of God, and steadfastly protected God's house and God's servants.[30]

[25] And indeed, where can anyone ever worship God better than in churches and in sanctuaries, and then in the high holy orders?

[26] And lo, how, indeed, can anyone ever think that he may pray fervently in church and bow willingly to God's altars, but before or after, within or without, pillage the church and destroy or damage that which belongs to the church?[31]

[27] Or how can anyone ever think in his mind that he may bow his head to the priests, desire their blessings, attend their masses in church, and kiss their hand during the procession with the host, yet then immediately thereafter injure or abuse them by word or deed?

[28] But holiness and the holy orders and the hallowed house of God shall always be fervently venerated for fear of God, and God always be loved with inward heart.

[29] And it is also a great necessity for every man to offer others the justice he wishes to be given to him, just as is his due.[32]

[30] We all have one heavenly father and one spiritual mother, who is named *Ecclesia*, that is, God's Church; and therefore we are brothers.[33]

[31] And then it is also right that each of us treat the other with justice, and that every church be ever in the protection of God almighty and of all Christian people.[34]

> [31.1] Therefore, every church sanctuary is Christ's own sanctuary, and every Christian has a fundamental responsibility to hold that sanctuary in great reverence.

---

30 Cf. *EGu.* Pr.2, *On Clerical Compensation* 11, *Evil Rulers*, n. 11, and VIII Atr. 36.

31 Cf. *Polity* XXXV, Bethurum 10c, ll. 45–51, and Napier 30, p. 143, ll. 15–19.

32 *Matthew* 7:12: 'All things therefore whatsoever you would that men should do to you, do you also to them' ('Omnia ergo quæcumque vultis ut faciant vobis homines, et vos facite illis'). Cf. VI Atr. 49; I Cn. 18.2; Bethurum 7 ll. 169–70; Bethurum 8b, ll. 78–80; Bethurum 8c ll. 112–13; Bethurum 10c ll. 136–7; Bethurum 13 ll. 55–6; Bethurum 18 ll. 142–3; Napier 30, p. 144, ll. 1–2; Napier 37, p. 179, ll. 27–9; *On the Laws of God* n. 4; *On the Proper Support* n. 3; and *On the Duties of the Laity* n. 17.

33 Cf. *Polity* XXXV, Bethurum 10b, l. 118, and Bethurum 10c ll. 41–2.

34 Cf. VIII Atr. 1.

5. *NORTHUMBRIAN CHURCH-SANCTUARY* (*NORÐHYMBRA CYRICGRIÐ*)

This puzzling document, which Liebermann (its first editor) alternately labelled *Northumbrian Church-Peace* and *Northumbrian Church-Sanctuary* (*Norðhymbra Cyricfrið* and *Norðhymbra Cyricgrið*), survives only in a single manuscript, Cotton Nero A.i. Inevitably, its brevity means that the text's attribution to Wulfstan must be tentative at best; nonetheless, the verbal and thematic similarities to VIII Æthelred, I Cnut, and the *Canons of Edgar*, as well as the use of source material drawn from Wulfstan's Canon Law Collection, make it difficult to imagine another author. The text's nine lines have been interposed immediately after VIII Æthelred 5.2, a clause setting out the penalties for a 'violation of sanctuary' ('griðbryce') at a 'principal church' ('heafodmynstre'), the same topic discussed in more specific terms by *Northumbrian Church-Sanctuary*. The theme and placement of the text in the manuscript have given rise to the supposition that it may have been composed as part of a now-lost alternate version of VIII Æthelred.[1] Equally likely, however, is Patrick Wormald's suggestion that it may have been intended to stand alone 'as a local application of Wulfstan principles'.[2] A third possibility is that its composition reflects the same interest in regional legal practices that informs Wulfstan's other writings of this period, most notably the three central texts of the Composition on Status. Unfortunately, though, future work on *Northumbrian Church-Sanctuary* will be significantly limited by the deteriorated state of the manuscript: in an unfortunate attempt to clarify a difficult-to-read passage, Liebermann recommended a treatment with a solution of sulphuric acid, the effect of which was to leave much of the page entirely illegible.[3]

Despite its difficulties, *Northumbrian Church-Sanctuary* provides important evidence for northern Anglo-Saxon sanctuary practices and for the development of Wulfstan's thought. Regarding the former, it confirms the special status accorded to the churches at York, Ripon, and Beverly and indicates that the special sanctuary privileges first granted to these churches by King Æthelstan were still recognised nearly a century later.[4] For students of Wulfstan, it offers, in Richard Dammery's words, 'further evidence of [the archbishop's] penchant

---

1 Dammery 1994: 257. In particular, Dammery notes that the scribe begins the text in the same manner as he does other clauses in VIII Atr. – with a shaded tironian *et* – rather than with an independent rubric of the sort used to distinguish between separate texts elsewhere in the manuscript.

2 Wormald 1999d: 395.

3 Liebermann 1903–1916: Vol. I, p. 473n. a.

4 Blair 2005: 223.

for redrafting the law-codes he composed' and reflects his attempt to extend to northern churches the same status and protections that VIII Æthelred guarantees to southern foundations.[5]

5 Dammery 1994: 257 and Wormald 1999d: 395.

TRANSLATION[1]

[1] And according to Northumbrian law, the compensation owed for a violation of [church][2]-sanctuary at Saint Peter's, Saint Wilfrid's, and within the walls of Saint [John]'s[3] is three [hundr]ed if the man is alive, but it [cannot be compensated] for if he is dead.

[2] And the sanctuary protection of other locations is less [in scale] always according to the status of the site.[4]

[3] And [a priest] is forbidden from attending church with women or weapons.[5]

[4] And church-sanctuary is to be respected everywhere according to its degree over the entire kingdom.[6]

1 This translation is based on the text in Liebermann 1903–16: v. I, p. 473.

2 Words in brackets are those which have now been rendered completely illegible due to Liebermann's experimental use of a sulfuric acid solution to enhance the faded ink of the manuscript.

3 That is, at the churches of York, Ripon, and Beverly.

4 Cf. VIII Atr. 4.1, I Cn. 3–3a.2.

5 A similar prohibition against the carrying of weapons by clergy occurs in Ansegisus' *Admonitio generalis* (§70) and was later copied by Wulfstan into the B recension of his canon law collection (§159). See Cross and Hamer 1999: 167. This clause is likely based on *Canons* 44 and 46. See Wormald 1999d: 395n. 603.

6 Cf. VIII Atr. 4–4.1, I Cn. 3–3a, and *NPL* 19.

6. THE CANONS OF EDGAR

Wulfstan's *Canons of Edgar* offers a synthesis of Church doctrine on pastoral care and clerical behaviour for use by diocesan priests. Along with the *Institutes of Polity*, it provides perhaps Wulfstan's most detailed account of the Church's role in English society. Its importance in the development of the archbishop's thought is indicated by the extent to which he continued to revise it over the course of his career: begun sometime between 1004 and 1006, possibly as either a manual for the wayward clergy of York Minster or an ecclesiastical counterpart to the secular decrees of *Edward-Guthrum*, *Canons* only reached what appears to be its final form in 1017 or 1018.[1] Versions of the text survive in four manuscripts: Cambridge, Corpus Christi College 201; Oxford, Bodleian Library, Junius 121; Cambridge, University Library, Additional 3206; and Brussels, Bibliothèque Royale, 8558–63. The most complete texts are those in C.C.C.C. 201 and Junius 121, the former of which likely represents an earlier version of *Canons* (designated '*Canons* I' by modern editors) while the latter preserves a later revision ('*Canons* II', the basis for the translation below). The Junius 121 version was the basis for the text in C.U.L. Additional 3206, though only a four-page fragment of this manuscript now remains. The version in Brussels, Bibliothèque Royale, 8558–63 is not, *strictu sensu*, a text of *Canons* itself, but rather a homiletic fragment of uncertain authorship based primarily on canons 2, 12, 13, and 68b.[2]

Canons' title, which comes from the rubric to the version in C.C.C.C. 201, suggests that Wulfstan may have originally composed the text as a historical forgery in a vein similar to *Edward-Guthrum*. Wulfstan emphasises the importance of Edgar's reign as a legal and moral precedent elsewhere in his writings, and his practice in his earlier works of evoking an idealised – and sometimes fictional – legal past may be on display here also.[3] It may well be a sign of his maturation as an author or growing confidence as a legislator that later versions of *Canons* replace the false attribution to Edgar with the more general rubric, 'Synodal Decrees'. Whatever the initial intent behind the rubric may have been, however, it did lead many of the text's earliest editors to accept the attribution as accurate. It was not until Liebermann suggested that the

---

1 Wormald 2004: 15–16, 26–7.

2 A complete account of the manuscript history of *Canons* can be found in Fowler 1972: xi–xx.

3 On this point, see the note to *Cn 1020* 13 below, as well as Whitelock 1948: 442–3; Whitelock 1955: 82–3; and Wormald 1999d: 132–3. For the most detailed discussion of the rubric, see Fowler 1972: 22.

text ought to be attributed to an independent canonist and Jost recognised the distinctive signs of Wulfstan's style that the archbishop's authorship was finally realised.[4]

In composing *Canons*, Wulfstan relied more heavily on his source material than he did in any other surviving work. That he did so is not surprising, given the nature of the text as a compilation of Church law. The sources he drew upon, however, reveal much about his intentions for the text and expectations for his audience. The majority of the material in *Canons* comes from either the pastoral letters of Ælfric, the *Capitula* of Theodulf of Orléans, or the collection of canon law excerpts and fragments Wulfstan himself compiled, perhaps in preparation for this work. Other sources include the *Homilia* of Pope Leo IV, the *Regula canonicorum* of Amalarius of Metz, the *Penitential of Pseudo-Theodore*, and *The Old English Penitential* (also known as the *Penitential of Pseudo-Ecgbert*).[5] This list of sources reflects Wulfstan's preference for relatively contemporary, rather than classical or patristic, source material as well as his affinity for thinkers in the Carolingian and English reformist traditions. Perhaps more importantly, these texts share an interest (though by no means an exclusive one) in the duty and behaviour of the secular clergy. In drawing upon these sources, Wulfstan is not, as some have suggested, revealing his ignorance of classical Church thought and doctrine; rather, he carefully selects those works most useful for the adaptation of Church doctrine for use by those clergy tasked with ministering to a lay flock. *Canons* thus fills a crucial role in Wulfstan's reformist programme: as a synthesis of canon law, it asserts the moral obligations of the Church to the secular community, and as a handbook for pastoral clergy, it provides practical guidance for the fulfilment of those obligations. Though evidence for the reception of *Canons* is slight, its influence on the *Northumbrian Priests' Law*, for which it served as the primary source, suggests that Wulfstan's efforts were seen as a success.

---

4 Thorpe 1840: 395; Wasserschleben 1851: 49–50; Liebermann 1903–16: Vol. I, p. L, v. 2, pp. 618–19, 'Pönitenz'; Oakley 1923: 135; and Jost 1932: 265–315. See also Fowler 1972: xxvi–xxxiv.

5 A complete discussion of the sources can be found in Fowler 1972: xxxiv–xlv.

TRANSLATION[1]

XX ITEM: SYNODAL DECREES[2]

[1] It is right that priests willingly obey and serve God and pray for all Christian people;[3] and that they all be faithful and obedient to their lord, and all single-minded for the common need; and that each be supportive and helpful to others in both spiritual and secular matters; and that they also be faithful and true to their secular lords, in keeping with God's law.[4]

[2] And it is right that each respect the other; and the younger willingly obey their elders, and the elders willingly love and instruct the younger.[5]

[[3] And we instruct that at each yearly synod they are to have books and robes for the holy service, and ink and parchment for their decrees,[6] and provisions for three days.[7]

[4] And we instruct that each priest at the synod is to have his clerk and a well-mannered man as an attendant, and no one ignorant who

1 This translation is based on the text in Oxford, Bodleian Library, Junius 121, ed. in Fowler 1972: 1–19, with reference to the other versions edited in Jost 1959:178–209 and Whitelock 1981: 313–38.

2 C.C.C.C. 201 reads instead: 'Here now are the practices fitting for those in orders according to the decrees of Edgar'.

3 Cf. V Atr. 4.1, I Cn. 6a, *Clerical Compensation* 1, *Polity* XVII *and* XXXV, *On the Duties of the Laity* n. 5, and Napier 37, p. 179, l. 9.

4 Cf. Bethurum 10c, ll. 165–6 and *On Baptism*, n. 3. Wulfstan's phrasing here also recalls the pledge of loyalty preserved as the first item in the Old English oath compilation, *Swerian*: 'By the Lord, before whom this relic is holy, I will be faithful and true to N, and love all that he loves and despise all that he despises, according to the law of God and the custom of the world' ('On ðone Drihten, þe ðes haligdom is fore halig, ic wille beon N hold 7 getriwe 7 eal lufian ðæt he lufað 7 eal ascunian ðæt he ascunað, æfter Godes rihte 7 æfter woroldgerysnum').

5 Cf. Bethurum 10c, ll. 176–8. The ultimate source for this passage appears to be ch. 145 of the *Regula canonicorum* of Amalarius of Metz.

6 Canons 3, 4, 10, 11, 12, 34, 51, and 65 all provide evidence for the nature of priestly literacy during this period; however, as Wormald notes, there is reason to question whether such injunctions ever translated into actual practice. See Wormald 1977: 108–9.

7 This clause and the one following are based on c. IV of the *Capitula* of Theodulf of Orléans. Both are omitted from C.C.C.C. 201. Ann Hagen points out that this canon is one of many injunctions surviving from the early Middle Ages to deal with the perennial problem of provisioning episcopal synods and other large gatherings. It is one of the few, however, to place the onus of providing food on the meeting's attendees, a stipulation she describes as 'eminently practical ... from the organisers' point of view'. Hagen 1995: 330–1.

loves foolishness; but all are to proceed with decorum and with fear of almighty God. [8]]

[5] And it is right that priests make known at a synod if anyone injures them and if anyone has seriously abused them. Let them receive it just as if it had been done to them all and assist so that it can be rectified just as the bishop directs.[9]

[6] And it is right that every priest make known at the synod if he knows of anyone in his parish disobedient to God or plunged by evil into mortal sin whom he cannot sway to repentance or dare not because of their power in the world.[10]

[7] And it is right that no dispute between priests is to be submitted to the adjudication of laymen, but their own colleagues are to judge and make peace or submit it to the bishop if one must.[11]

[8] And it is right that no priest abandon the Church into which he was ordained because of his own willfulness, but he is to keep it as his lawful wife.[12]

---

8 The stipulation that a priest is to be accompanied by his clerk may provide some insight into the circumstances in which Wulfstan composed his works. Whitelock points out that evidence survives showing that both Bishop Ælfsige of Chester-le-Street and the later Bishop of Worcester, St. Wulfstan, frequently travelled in the company of scribes. It would thus make sense to conclude that an administrator as busy as Archbishop Wulfstan would also keep one or more scribes as part of his permanent retinue. Whitelock 1965: 215.

9 Cf. *NPL* 1 and §4 in 'Injunctions on the Behaviour of Bishops'. See Whitelock 1981: 409. The fact that injunctions regarding synodal participation occur only in texts associated with Wulfstan has led some scholars to suggest that they may be more aspirational than anything else. As John Blair writes, 'it is only in Wulfstan-associated texts that the obligation of priests to collect the episcopal chrism at the proper time [*EGu.* 3.2, *Canons* 70, and *NPL* 9], to obey the bishop's or archdeacon's summonses, and to attend synods [*Canons* 3–6, *NPL* 3, 4, 6, 7, 44–5] are even enunciated. One wonders how far rural clergy did bother to attend synods, except in the aspirations of the greatest English ideologue of the age'. Blair 2005: 495–6.

10 Cf. Theodulf, *Capitula* c. XXVIII. See also *NPL* 42. Particularly distinctive in this canon is the use of the Wulfstanism *scriftscire* (also used in canons 9 and 15; translated here as 'parish', but which might be more literally rendered as 'confessional district'), indicating the administrative function of penance in late Anglo-Saxon pastoral practice. On this canon, as well as the use of this term elsewhere in Wulfstan's writings, see Cubitt 2006: 44–5. Sarah Hamilton also links canons 5 and 6 to the legislation on excommunication in the laws of Æthelred and Cnut. See Hamilton 2005: 99.

11 Cf. VI Atr. 1, *NPL* 5, and §10 in 'Injunctions on the Behaviour of Bishops' (See Whitelock 1981: 411). The principal source for this canon is c. 9 of the Council of Chalcedon.

12 In Junius 121, a marginal note adds 'as long as his life lasts' to the end of this clause. For likely sources of this passage, see Ælfric's first Latin pastoral letter to Wulfstan, §194–5, and §14 in the B Recension of Wulfstan's Canon Law Collection. See also Bethurum 10a, ll. 12–13, *NPL* 28, and *Polity* XXII.

[9] And it is right that no priest deprive another of any of those things which belong to him, neither in his church, nor in his parish, nor in his guild, nor in any of those things which belong to him.[13]

[10] And it is right that a priest not receive another's student without the consent of him he followed previously.[14]

[11] And it is right that every priest study a handicraft as well as his scholarship.[15]

[12] And it is right that a learned priest not insult someone poorly taught, but correct him if he knows better.[16]

[13] And it is right that a highborn priest not disparage those of lower birth, for if one understands it properly, then all men are of equal birth.[17]

[14] And it is right that every priest support himself properly and not be any sort of corrupt dealer or grasping merchant.[18]

[15] And it is right that every priest consent to baptism and confession as soon as anyone requests it; and he is to instruct that each child throughout his parish is to be baptised within seven nights and that one is not to remain unconfirmed for too long.[19]

[16] And it is right that every priest ardently preach the Christian faith and fully wipe out every heathen practice;[20] and forbid the worship of wells and the raising of the dead, and divination and sorcery, [and the worship of trees and stones, and that devil's trick which is performed when children are drawn through the earth,][21] and the deception

13 Cf. Theodulf, *Capitula* c. XIV, *NPL* 2.

14 Cf. Theodulf, *Capitula* c. XV.

15 Cf. §163 in the B Recension of Wulfstan's Canon Law Collection, *Polity* VII and VIII, and Bethurum 10a, l. 52. The context for this clause has been discussed in Smith et al. 2001: 572.

16 Cf. Bethurum 10a, l. 45, *NPL* 29. This canon and the one following it both appear in a corrupt version of the *Canons* preserved in Brussels Bibliothèque Royale MS. 8558–63 (2498).

17 Cf. Bethurum 10a, l. 46, and *NPL* 29.

18 Cf. Ælfric's first Old English pastoral letter for Bishop Wulfsige, §77.

19 Although injunctions concerning the early baptism of children are relatively common in canon law, the prescribed time limit tends to vary, with a range between seven and thirty days being the most common. Cf. Ine 2, Ælfric's first Old English pastoral letter for Bishop Wulfsige, §71, *EGu.* 3.2, and *NPL* 10. See Fowler 1972: 26 and Lynch 1998: 101n. 108.

20 Cf. *EGu.* Pr.1; V Atr 1, 34; VI Atr. 1.6; VIII Atr. 44; IX Atr. *explicit*; X Atr. 1; *NPL* 47, 67; *Polity* XXXV; *On Justice* n. 50; and *On the Proper Support* n. 4.

21 C.C.C.C. 201 omits this phrase and substitutes '7 manweorþunga', a phrase meaning

performed [on New Year's night][22] in various magical practices, and in
heathen refuges, and in elder-trees, and in the many diverse superstitions in which men do much that they should not.[23]

[17] And it is right that every Christian readily tutor his children in
Christianity and teach them the paternoster and the creed.[24]

[18] And it is right that on holy days one refrain from heathenish
songs and devil's games.[25]

[19] And it is right that one refrain from trade on a Sunday.[26]

[20] And it is right that one refrain from frivolous clothing and
thoughtless elegance and shameful hairstyles.[27]

[[21] And we instruct that one refrain from fornication with a concu-
bine and love one's lawful wife.][28]

---

either 'and the worshipping of human beings' or 'and the worshipping of evil'. The
practice referred to here seems to be one described in ch. xxvii.16 of the *Penitential of
Pseudo-Theodore*, whereby a sick child is drawn through a pit, hole, or trench in order
to transfer his or her illness to the earth. References to this practice occur in the
works of Ælfric, the *Penitential of Pseudo-Theodore*, the *Old English Penitential* (also
known as the *Penitential of Pseudo-Ecgbert*), and the *Penitential of Halitgar*, among
others. For a discussion of the possible sources of this passage, see Grendon 1909:
129–31; Fowler 1972: 27–8; Whitelock 1981: 320; and Meaney 2004: 491–5. Audrey
Meaney raises the possibility that the revisions to this passage may not be Wulfstan's
own. See Meaney 2004: 476–8.

22 Omitted in C.C.C.C. 201.

23 Though this clause is more detailed than most, passages inveighing against heathen
practices occur frequently in Wulfstan's writings. Wulfstan does not appear to have
drawn on a single, identifiable source for this particular canon; however, it does share
a number of common elements with the much longer ch. xxvii of the *Penitential of
Pseudo-Theodore*. See Blair 2005: 481–3.

24 Cf. Bethurum 8c ll. 142–3 and 10c ll. 170–1, as well as canon 22 below. Both this
canon and canon 22 are based on c. 22 of Theodulf's *Capitula*. On these canons and
their source, see Lynch 1998: 186–7.

25 An abridged version of ch. xxxviii.9 of the *Penitential of Pseudo-Theodore*. It is likely
that this canon was intended as a general prohibition against lewd songs or games,
rather than a specific injunction against activities with pagan content. See Meaney
2004: 471.

26 Cf. *EGu*. 7; VI As. 10; VI Atr. 22.1 and 44; I Cn. 15; Cnut 1020 18; *NPL* 55; Napier 43
l. 94; *On Tithes* n. 5; *On Justice* n. 45; and *On the Duties of the Laity* n. 16. The source
for this clause is ch. xxxviii.8 of the *Penitential of Pseudo-Theodore*. On this canon, see
Haines 2010: 24.

27 Cf. §158 in the B Recension of Wulfstan's Canon Law Collection, §115 in Ælfric's
first Old English Pastoral Letter, §206 in Ælfric's second Old English Pastoral
Letter, and *NPL* 34.

28 Cf. II Cn. 54.1, *Polity* XXII, and *The Old English Penitential*, II.9. This canon omitted
from C.C.C.C. 201. While it is doubtful that Wulfstan intended this canon to serve as

[22] And it is right that every man study so that he learns his pater-noster and creed if he wishes to lie in a consecrated grave or be worthy to receive the sacrament; for he is not truly a Christian who will not learn it, nor may he who does not know it lawfully sponsor another at baptism or confirmation until he learns it.[29]

[23] And it is right that on holy days and legally designated fast-days there be no conflict between men.[30]

[24] And it is right that one forgo oaths and ordeals on holy days and legally designated fast-days.[31]

[25] And it is right that every man forgo his wife during holy times and legally designated fast-times.[32]

[26] And it is right that priests, with all reverence, preserve churches for holy observances and pure service and for no other use; nor are they to permit any foolishness inside nor in the vicinity; neither idle speech, nor idle deeds, nor thoughtless actions, nor any idleness ever; nor that any dog nor horse come within the church precincts, much less a pig if one can control it.[33]

[27] And it is right that one bring nothing into church that is inappro-priate to it.[34]

[28] And it is right that one be very sober at church vigils, and pray fervently, and not engage in any drinking nor foolishness there.[35]

---

political commentary, it is worth noting that the crime described here is one of which Cnut himself was famously guilty. See Lawson 1993: 132.

29 The source for this canon is Theodulf, *Capitula* XXII. For analogous passages in Wulfstan's works, see *On the Duties of the Laity* n. 9. For a more distant echo, see Bethurum 8c, ll. 1–6.

30 Cf. V Atr. 19, VI Atr. 25.1, and I Cn. 17.2. The source for this canon is Theodulf, *Capitula*, XLII.

31 Cf. *EGu.* 9, V Atr. 18, VI Atr. 25, I Cn. 17, Napier 43 l. 104, *Polity* XXI, and *On Tithes* n. 8. See also Theodulf, *Capitula*, XXIV.

32 Cf. Theodulf, *Capitula* XLIII and *Polity* XXI. See also the *Penitential of Pseudo-Theodore*, ch. xvii.3 and §117 in the B recension of Wulfstan's Canon Law Collection.

33 The most likely source for this canon is Ælfric's Pastoral Letter to Bishop Wulfsige, §48, though earlier occurrences of these prohibitions can be found in Theodulf's *Capitula*, c. X and c. 71 of the *Admonitio generalis* (789). See also *Polity* VIII and XII, the *Admonition to Bishops* 3 and 6, and *NPL* 25. See below, *Canons* 28.

34 Cf. Ælfric's second Latin Pastoral Letter to Archbishop Wulfstan, §72, and his second Old English Pastoral Letter to Archbishop Wulfstan, §115. See also Theodulf, *Capitula*, c. VIII and the first sentence of §41 in the B recension of Wulfstan's Canon Law Collection. For a later occurrence, see *NPL* 26.

35 Cf. Ælfric's Pastoral Letter to Bishop Wulfsige, §107–110. A similar passage also occurs in second Latin Pastoral Letter to Archbishop Wulfstan, §25. Cf. *Canons* 26.

[29] And it is right that no one be buried inside the church unless it is known that he pleased God so well in his life that he is therefore believed to be worthy of that burial place.[36]

[30] And it is right that a priest not celebrate mass in any building except a consecrated church, except in the case of someone's extreme sickness.[37]

[31] And it is right that a priest never celebrate mass except on a consecrated altar.[38]

[32] And it is right that a priest never celebrate mass without the book; but the canon is to be before his eyes. He may consult it if he wishes, so as not to make a mistake.[39]

[33] And it is right that every priest have a corporal when he celebrates mass and an amice under his alb, and all the mass-vestments in a worthy state.[40]

[34] And it is right that every priest strive conscientiously to have good and, likewise, correct books.[41]

[35] And it is right that a mass-priest not celebrate mass alone so that he has no one to answer him.[42]

36 Cf. Theodulf, *Capitula*, c. IX. See also *On Tithes*, n. 10, *On Christian Practices* n. 13, and *NPL* 63.1.

37 The Council of Laodicea (364) ruled that priests may not celebrate mass in unconsecrated dwellings, a decree included in both the A (§25) and B (§60) recensions of Wulfstan's Canon Law Collection. Similar prohibitions also occur in c. XI of Theodulf's *Capitula*, §70 of Ælfric's Pastoral Letter to Bishop Wulfsige, and *NPL* 13, though Ælfric's letter is the only source to make an exception in cases of illness. Cf. Ælfric's Pastoral Letter to Bishop Wulfsige, §69–70, Theodulf, *Capitula* XI

38 Cf. Ælfric's first Latin Pastoral Letter to Archbishop Wulfstan, §142 and *NPL* 14.

39 A list of books that a priest is to have occurs in Ælfric's first Old English Pastoral Letter to Archbishop Wulfstan, §157 and Ælfric's first Latin Pastoral Letter to Archbishop Wulfstan, §137; however, advice offered in the second sentence appears to be Wulfstan's own addition. See also c. LXXVII of the Old English *Rule of Chrodegang*.

40 This canon is based on c. V of the *Homiliae* of Pope Leo IV (*PL* cxv.675). Cf. Ælfric's Pastoral Letter to Bishop Wulfsige, §55–6, Ælfric's first Latin Pastoral Letter to Archbishop Wulfstan, §140, and Ælfric's first Old English Pastoral Letter to Archbishop Wulfstan, §159. The alb and the amice are both vestments worn by the priest during the mass, while the corporal is the small cloth upon which the chalice and host rest on the altar.

41 See above, *Canons 32.*

42 This canon is based on c. XII of the *Homiliae* of Pope Leo IV (*PL* cxv.675) and c. VII of the *Capitula* of Theodulf. See also c. LXXV of the Old English *Rule of Chrodegang* and Ælfric's second Old English Pastoral Letter to Archbishop Wulfstan, §84.

[36] And it is right that no one receive the sacrament without fasting, except in the case of extreme sickness.[43]

[37] And it is right that a priest not celebrate mass more often than three times in one day at most.[44]

[38][45] And it is right that a priest always have the host prepared for those who need it, and that he carefully keep it in a pure condition, and be sure that it does not decay.[46] Then, if it is not cared for, so that one cannot use it, it is to be burnt in a clean fire and the ashes placed under the altar, and he who neglects it is to atone sincerely to God.[47]

[39] And it is right that a priest not presume to celebrate mass unless he has all that is necessary for the sacrament: that is, a pure wafer and pure wine and pure water. Woe to him who commences the mass unless he has each of these, and woe to him who puts anything foul in there; for he does then just as the Jews did when they mixed vinegar and gall together and afterwards gave it in mockery to Christ.[48]

[40] And it is right that a priest should never celebrate mass and fail to receive the host, nor should he consecrate the Eucharist after it has

---

43 Injunctions against receiving the sacrament without fasting occur in c. IV of the *Homiliae* of Pope Leo IV (*PL* cxv.675) and ch. xxxix.12 of the *Penitential of Pseudo-Theodore*; however, neither of these makes an exception for the sick. Such an exception is found in a variant version Theodulf's *Capitula* (*PL* cv.208) but this variant survives only in Paris, Bibliothèque Nationale, Lat. 3182 (edited in *PL* cv.208). On Wulfstan's use of this MS see Sauer 2000: 373.

44 The limit of three masses likely stems from c. XIX of the Council of Trebur, which forbids priests from celebrating more than three masses per day on a single altar. Notably, Ælfric restricts priests priests to celebrating mass only once per day. Cf. §62 in the B recension of Wulfstan's Canon Law Collection, Ælfric's second Latin Pastoral Letter to Archbishop Wulfstan, §73, Ælfric's second Old English Pastoral Letter to Archbishop Wulfstan, §75, Ælfric's Latin Pastoral Letter to Archbishop Wulfstan 2a, §13, and *NPL* 18. Godden 2004: 373.

45 Wulfstan will incorporate variant versions of canons 38, 39, and 43 into ch. 37–9 of his revision of the Old English *De ecclesiasticis gradibus*, also preserved in Junius 121. See Jost 1959: 237.

46 Cf. Ansegisus, *Capitula* I.55, in Boretius 1883: 382–450. See also §109 in the B recension of Wulfstan's Canon Law Collection, the first sentence of which is based on c. V of Theodulf's *Capitula*. For a more distant analogue, see §23 in the B recension of Wulfstan's Canon Law Collection.

47 Cf. *The Penitential of Theodore* I.xii.6, Ælfric's Pastoral Letter to Bishop Wulfsige, §134, Ælfric's second Latin Pastoral Letter to Archbishop Wulfstan, §45, and Ælfric's second Old English Pastoral Letter to Archbishop Wulfstan, §87.

48 Cf. §109 in the B recension of Wulfstan's Canon Law Collection, Theodulf, *Capitula*, c. V. The allusion is to the drink supposedly offered to Jesus on the cross when he complained of thirst. See *Matthew* 27:34.

been consecrated.[49]

[41] And it is right that every chalice in which the host is consecrated be cast of metal,[50] and that it not be consecrated in one made of wood; nor should anyone be baptised more than once.[51]

[42] And it is right that all those things which are near the altar and belong to the church be kept most cleanly and worthily, and that nothing foul come near there; but one is to arrange the hallowed objects very reverently. And a light is always to be burning in church when one sings the mass.[52]

[43] And it is right that nothing consecrated be overlooked: not the holy water, nor the salt, nor the incense, nor the bread, nor the consecrated ashes, nor the consecrated host, nor anything holy. But one is to burn it in a pure fire, unless it can still be used, and the ashes placed under the altar.[53]

[44] And it is right that no woman approach the altar while mass is being celebrated.[54]

[45] And it is right that one ring the hours at the proper time, and then every priest is to attend his service in the church and there, for fear of God, fervently pray and intercede for all people.[55]

---

49 Cf. Ælfric's Latin Pastoral Letter to Archbishop Wulfstan 2a, §11, Ælfric's second Old English Pastoral Letter to Archbishop Wulfstan, §93, and Ælfric's second Latin Pastoral Letter to Archbishop Wulfstan, §68. The final clause of this canon ('nor ... consecrated') appears only in Junius 121, where it is incorrectly moved to the end of canon 41.

50 A marginal note in Junius 121 specifies, 'gold, silver, or tin', a list which echoes that in Ælfric's Pastoral Letter to Bishop Wulfsige, §58.

51 Cf. Ælfric's first Old English Pastoral Letter to Archbishop Wulfstan, §162, and his Pastoral Letter to Bishop Wulfsige, §58. See also NPL 15. In C.C.C.C. 201, the final phrase of this clause occurs instead at the end of Canons 40.

52 See above, Canons 26–7. The final injunction in this canon is based on c. V of the Homiliae of Leo IV: 'No one is to celebrate the mass without light' ('Nullus cantet sine lumine', PL cxv.675).

53 See above, Canons 38–9.

54 The most immediate source for this canon appears to be Theodulf, Capitula, c. VI, though similar prohibitions also occur in Ansegisus, Capitula I.17, Penitential of Pseudo-Theodore, ch. xlvi, and c. VII of the Homiliae of Leo IV (PL cxv.677). It is probable that this canon provided one of the sources for Northumbrian Church-Sanctuary 3.

55 Cf. Ælfric's first Latin Pastoral Letter to Archbishop Wulfstan, §62 and Ælfric's Pastoral Letter to Bishop Wulfsige, §49. See also §29 in the B recension of Wulfstan's Canon Law Collection, Polity VII, and NPL 36.

[46] And it is right that no mass-priest[56] come within the church doors while armed or within the sanctuary without his stole,[57] or indeed to the altar so that he serve without that garment.[58]

[47] And it is right that a man in orders not hide his tonsure, nor permit his hair to be cut improperly, nor keep his beard for any length of time, insofar as he desires to have God's blessing and St. Peter's and ours.[59]

[48] And it is right that all priests be of one mind about holy days and fasts, and all proclaim them in the same way so that they do not mislead the people.[60]

[49] And it is right that every fast be observed with almsgiving, that is, that one should give alms willingly for the grace of God: then his fast will be pleasing to God.[61]

[50] And it is right that priests conduct church services all in the same way, and be equally far along over the course of the year in all church services.[62]

---

56 C.C.C.C. 201 adds 'or minster-priest'.

57 The Old English term used here is *oferslop*, the precise definition of which is unclear. The word is used by Ælfric as a translation of the Latin *colobium* (a sleeveless white shift), though he is not referring to an ecclesiastical vestment. See Clemoes 1997: XXXI.35, p. 440. Elsewhere, it occurs as a gloss on the Latin *camsilis*, further contributing to the impression that the garment referred to is a type of sleeveless tunic. However, in the Lindisfarne Gospels, 'in oferslopum' appears as a gloss on the Latin 'in stolis', though a stole (the band of coloured cloth draped about a priest's neck) is a different sort of garment than a tunic. It seems most likely that Wulfstan is here referring to a stole, a surplice, or, somewhat less likely, an alb. See Fowler 1972: 36 and Whitelock 1981: 329.

58 The three prohibitions in this canon are an amalgam of several different sources. Cf. §75 in the A recension of Wulfstan's Canon Law Collection and §158–9 in the B recension, Ælfric's first Old English Pastoral Letter to Archbishop Wulfstan, §189, Ælfric's first Latin Pastoral Letter to Archbishop Wulfstan, §178, and Ælfric's Pastoral Letter to Bishop Wulfsige, §80. See also *Northumbrian Church-Sanctuary* 3 and *NPL* 37. On Wulfstan's attitude towards clerical arms-bearing, see Powell 1994: 120.

59 Cf. §158 in the B recension of Wulfstan's Canon Law Collection. See also *NPL* 34.

60 An emphasis on uniformity of religious observance had long been a principal concern of English prelates. Most famously, it had been the reason for the Synod of Whitby, described by Bede in III.25 of the *Historia ecclesiastica*, and injunctions similar to this canon occur in the acts of the Council of Hertford (673), §1, and the Council of Clofesho (747), §13. (Haddan and Stubbs 1869–71: Vol. III, pp. 119 and 367.) See also §8 in the A recension of Wulfstan's Canon Law Collection, §43 in the B recension of Wulfstan's Canon Law Collection, *EGu.* 3.1, and *NPL* 11.

61 Cf. Theodulf, *Capitula*, c. XXXVIII.

62 Cf. *NPL* 38.

[**51**] And it is right that priests willingly teach the young, and instruct them in handiwork, so that they may have assistance in church.[63]

[**52**] And it is right that priests preach to the people each Sunday and always set a good example.[64]

[**53**] And it is right that Christians not consume blood.[65]

[**54**] And it is right that priests remind the people of that which they must give to God as dues in the form of tithes and in other ways. And it is right that one reminds them of this at Easter, again at Rogation,[66] and a third time at midsummer when the most people are gathered.[67] First plough-dues fifteen nights after Easter, the tithing of the young animals by Pentecost, the dues to Rome by the mass of St. Peter,[68] the tithe on the fruits of the earth by the mass of All Saints, ecclesiastical dues by Martinmas, and dues for the lighting of the church three times a year: first on Easter eve, a second time on Candlemas eve, and a third time on the eve of the mass of All Saints.[69]

---

63 Cf. Ælfric's second Latin Pastoral Letter to Archbishop Wulfstan, §40 and Ælfric's second Old English Pastoral Letter to Archbishop Wulfstan, §80. See also *Canons* 2, above.

64 This passage has a number of parallels in Ælfric's letters, including his Pastoral Letter to Bishop Wulfsige, §42 and 61, his first Old English Pastoral Letter to Archbishop Wulfstan, §175, and his first Latin Pastoral Letter to Archbishop Wulfstan, §159, and its most likely source, §III in the *Excerptiones pseudo-Egberti*: 'That on all holidays and Sundays, every priest is to proclaim the gospel of Christ to the people' ('Ut omnibus festis et diebus Dominicis unusquisque sacerdos Evangelium Christi praedicet populo'). Gatch suggests that 'by linking *bodigan* ["to preach"] with its alliterative partner *bisnian* ["to set an example"] in this context, Wulfstan actually weakens the force' of the passage in the *Excerptiones*. See Gatch 1977: 45. It has also been observed that this passage possibly draws on c. III of the first capitulary of Bishop Ghaerbald of Liege. See Elliott 2010: 161–5.

65 Cf. Ælfric's Latin Pastoral Letter to Archbishop Wulfstan 2a, §7 and Bethurum 10c, l. 104. The ultimate source of this prohibition is *Acts* 15:20: 'But that we write unto them, that they refrain themselves from the pollutions of idols, and from fornication, and from things strangled, and from blood.' On the history of the prohibitions against the consumption of blood in Anglo-Saxon England, see Hagen 1995: 190.

66 The three days prior to the feast of the Ascension.

67 The feast of St. John the Baptist, 24 June.

68 As important as *romescot* appears to have been to Wulfstan, it is likely that only a small percentage of the monies collected actually reached Rome. See Barlow 1979: 296; Blair 2005: 441n. 466. Cf. I Cn. 9, *EGu.* 6.1, *On Justice* n. 44, and *On Christian Practices* n. 6.

69 Martinmas is celebrated on 11 November and Candlemas on 2 February. Cf. II Eg. 2.3, 3, Bethurum 13, l. 74, *On Tithes*, n. 4, *On Christian Practices*, n. 6, *On the Proper Support*, n. 7. See also the penalties in *EGu.* 6. On this canon, see Wormald 1999d: 338–41.

[**55**] And it is right that priests distribute the people's alms in a manner that both pleases God and accustoms the people to almsgiving.[70]

[**56**] And it is right that one portion be set aside for the priests, a second portion for the church's needs, a third portion for the poor.[71]

[**57**] And it is right that priests sing psalms when they give out alms, and ardently beg the poor that they intercede for the people.

[**58**] And it is right that priests preserve themselves against drunkenness and zealously forbid it in others.[72]

[**59**] And it is right that a priest not be a singer among drunkards, nor himself entertain other men in any way, but he is to act in keeping with his status, wise and respectable.[73]

[**60**] And it is right that priests fervently guard themselves against oaths and also zealously forbid them.[74]

[**62**][75] And it is right that a priest not stand in false witness or be an accessory of thieves.[76]

[**63**] And it is right that a priest never use his oath to validate a questionable ordeal.[77]

[**64**] And it is right that a priest not defend himself against a thegn unless that thegn has sworn an initial oath.[78]

70 Cf. c. V of the first capitulary of Ghaerbald, about which see Elliott 2010: 163. See also Ælfric's Pastoral Letter to Bishop Wulfsige, §68.

71 Cf. Ælfric's Pastoral Letter to Bishop Wulfsige, §68 and VIII Atr. 6.

72 The most likely source for this canon is c. XIII of Theodulf's *Capitula*, though injunctions against priestly intoxication also occur in Ælfric's Pastoral Letter to Bishop Wulfsige, §74, Ælfric's first Old English Pastoral Letter to Archbishop Wulfstan, §186, Ælfric's first Latin Pastoral Letter to Archbishop Wulfstan, §173, and §81 in the B recension of Wulfstan's Canon Law Collection. See also *Admonition* §3 and *NPL* 41.

73 Cf. Ælfric's second Old English Pastoral Letter to Archbishop Wulfstan, §188 and *NPL* 41. On the history of Anglo-Saxon injunctions against clerical drunkenness, see Hagen 1995: 245–9.

74 Cf. Ælfric's Pastoral Letter to Bishop Wulfsige, §82 and his second Old English Pastoral Letter to Archbishop Wulfstan, §186.

75 There is a slight difference here between the ordering of the canons in the text's two recensions: the canon in C.C.C.C. 201 numbered 61 by modern editors occurs instead as canon 68a in the later version of the text preserved in Junius 121.

76 Cf. VIII Atr. 27.

77 Cf. *NPL* 39–40.

78 The meaning of this canon remains unclear. Whitelock speculates that it may be related to the stipulation found in II Cnut 22.2 and *On Ranks* 3–4 permitting thegns to empower chosen subordinates to swear certain kinds of oaths on their behalf.

[65] And it is right that a priest not be a hunter or a hawker or a gambler, but entertain himself with his books in keeping with his status.[79] [The canon says: 'if anyone in orders goes hunting, if he is a cleric he is to abstain from meat for twelve months, a deacon for two years, a mass-priest for three, a bishop for seven.'[80]

[66] And if any bishop or mass-priest or any man in orders knowingly makes himself drunk, either he must cease doing so or lose his status.[81]

[67] And it is right that priests always be ready to perform the rites to which the people are entitled.][82]

[68] And it is right that every priest absolve and assign penance to him who confesses to him, and also guide him to atonement, and administer the sacrament to the sick when they need it, and also anoint them if they desire it, and willingly see to the arrangements after death, and not permit any carelessness around the body, but bury it wisely with fear of God.[83]

[68a] And it is right that a priest not love the company of women all too greatly, but love his lawful wife, that is his church.[84]

[[68b][85] And it is right that if a clergyman who serves at the altar orders his own life properly according to the precepts of the books, then he is worthy of the full status of a thegn, both in life

---

According to Whitelock, Wulfstan may be asserting that an oath must be sworn in person if it involves an accusation against a priest. See Whitelock 1981: 334. Another possible interpretation is that Wulfstan here rules that priests cannot be compelled to mount a defence against an accusation brought by a thegn in a secular court unless that accusation has been levelled through a formal oath-taking ceremony.

79 A similar injunction also appears in Ælfric's first Old English Pastoral Letter to Archbishop Wulfstan, §203. The source of this prohibition is likely a letter of Boniface to Archbishop Cuthbert of Canterbury, composed in 747, in which he writes, 'The servants of God we forbid to hunt and wander in the woods with dogs and to keep hawks and falcons'. Hagen 1995: 145. From here to the end of *Canons* 67 omitted in C.C.C.C. 201.

80 Cf. *The Old English Penitential*, IV.27.

81 Cf. *The Old English Penitential*, IV.28.

82 See below, *Canons* 69.

83 Cf. Ælfric's Pastoral Letter to Bishop Wulfsige, §83–5 and 112–13, Ælfric's first Old English Pastoral Letter to Archbishop Wulfstan, §176 and 178, Ælfric's first Latin Pastoral Letter to Archbishop Wulfstan, §165–7, §94 in the A recension of Wulfstan's Canon Law Collection, and §23 in the B recension of Wulfstan's Canon Law Collection. On this canon, see Hamilton 2005: 85; Cubitt 2006: 52.

84 This canon appears in C.C.C.C. 201 as *Canons* 61. Cf. Bethurum 10a, ll. 34–5 and *Polity* XXII.

85 *Canons* 68b–i in Junius 121 only.

and in death.[86] If he does not order his life properly, his status is to diminish according to his deeds.[87] May he know, if he will, that he is not to involve himself with a wife or with the warfare of this world, if he desires to heed God properly and properly keep God's laws.[88]

[68c] Dunstan ruled that a mass-priest, if he had a wife, was not entitled to clear himself by any means other than that of a layman who was born his equal, if one accused him.[89]

[68d] And it is right that if a clergyman who serves at the altar conducts himself properly, then he is to be entitled to full wergild and honour.

[68e] And if it so happens that a priest who lives according to a rule is charged with an allegation and a claim of wrongful behaviour, and he knows himself to be innocent of that, he may celebrate mass if he dares, and clear himself through the Eucharist against a simple accusation. Against a threefold accusation, he may also, if he dares, clear himself through the Eucharist with two of his rank.[90]

[68f] If a deacon who lives according to a rule is charged with a simple accusation, he may select two of his rank and clear himself with them. And if he is charged with a threefold accusation, he may select six of his rank and clear himself with them, and he himself shall be the seventh.[91]

[68g] And if a charge is brought against a secular mass-priest who does not live according to a rule, he may clear himself in the manner of a deacon who lives according to a rule.[92]

[68h] And if a charge is brought against a clergyman who serves at the altar who lacks friends and supporters for his oath, he is to undergo the ordeal of the consecrated bread, and thereby experience that which God wills, unless he is allowed to clear himself with the Eucharist.[93]

86 Cf. VIII Atr. 28, *Clerical Compensation* 1, I Cn. 6a.2a., and *On Justice*, n. 30. On this canon, see Powell 1994: 123.

87 Cf. *Admonition* 13.

88 Cf. VIII Atr. 28–30.

89 Dunstan served as Archbishop of Canterbury from 960 to 978.

90 Cf. VIII Atr. 19–19.1, I Cn. 5–5a. On the subsequent use of canons 68e–i in I Cn. see Richards 2010: 143.

91 Cf. VIII Atr. 20–20.1, I Cn. 5a.1–1a.

92 Cf. VIII Atr. 21, I Cn. 5a.2.

93 Cf. VIII Atr. 22, I Cn. 5a.2a. The so-called 'ordeal of the consecrated bread' (*corsnæd*)

⸢**68i**⸣ And if a man in orders is charged with feud and it is alleged that he is a murderer, he is to clear himself with his kin, who may either extend the feud or compensate for it.⸣[94]

⸢**69**⸣ And it is right that every priest have both baptismal oil and oil for anointing the sick, and always be prepared to perform the rites to which the people are entitled, and zealously promote Christianity in every way, and both preach well and set a good example. Then almighty God will reward him for that, in the manner most pleasing to him. Amen.[95]

⸢⸢**70**⸣ And we instruct that every priest remembers to announce, when he fetches the chrism, what he has done in his prayers for the king and the bishop.⸣[96]

---

involves the ability to swallow a portion of the Eucharist without choking. This form of ordeal seems to have been reserved for priests and may have been designed to substitute for more physically painful ordeals, such as those of the hot iron or boiling water. See Keefer 1998: 237–55; Niles 2009: 373–5.

94 Cf. VIII Atr. 23, I Cn. 5a.2b.

95 Cf. Ælfric's Pastoral Letter to Bishop Wulfsige, §85. See also above, *Canons* 68.

96 Cf. Ælfric's Pastoral Letter to Bishop Wulfsige, §51 and above, *Canons* 45. This canon is found only in C.C.C.C. 201 where it is likely misplaced. See also n. to canon 6 above.

7. THE INSTITUTES OF POLITY

The *Institutes of Polity* is Wulfstan's most elaborate account of his vision for a Holy Society, yet the text is not nearly as complete and unified as the title (a nineteenth-century coinage) suggests. *Polity* consists of a series of short, quasi-independent chapters, the contents of which vary from manuscript to manuscript.[1] The chapters were first printed by David Wilkins in his 1721 *Leges Anglo-Saxonicae Ecclesiasticae et Civiles* under the title *Liber Constitutionem*; however, they were not understood as part of a single text until edited as such by Benjamin Thorpe in his 1840 *Ancient Laws and Institutes of England*. It was not until 1918 that Karl Jost conclusively demonstrated them to be the work of Archbishop Wulfstan of York.[2] Although scholars agree that the chapters were composed as a unit and intended to be read together, the audience for the work and the extent to which any of the different manuscript versions represent a completed, fully realised draft of the text remain a mystery. *Polity* therefore must be understood, at least in part, as a modern editorial construct that only approximates Wulfstan's original vision for the work.

Wulfstan likely began work on *Polity* sometime between 1008 and 1010, possibly around the same time as he was working on the Compilation on Status, and continued revising it for much of the rest of his career. Jost has shown that the text developed in two stages: an earlier version composed during the waning years of the reign of Æthelred ('*I Polity*') and a later version of *ca.* 1020x1023 ('*II Polity*') reflecting the changed circumstances following the conquest of Cnut.[3] Copies of both *I* and *II Polity* survive in two manuscripts – Cambridge, Corpus Christi College 201 and London, British Library, Cotton Nero A.i – while *II Polity* alone is preserved in a third – Oxford, Bodleian Library, Junius 121. In addition, two homilies based on *II Polity* ch. XVII are included in London, British Library, Cotton Tiberius A.iii and remnants of *II Polity* survive in the fragmentary manuscript Cambridge, University Library, Additional 3206.[4] Of the different versions, that in Junius 121 generally is taken to most closely resemble Wulfstan's final vision for the text; however, as Jost points out, the manuscript's Worcester compiler re-ordered the chapters

1 A useful chart illustrating the different manuscript versions of *Polity* can be found in Trilling 2007: 74–5. For a complete record of the distribution of the chapters of *Polity* across its different manuscripts, see the charts in the Appendix at the end of this volume.

2 Wilkins 1721: 106–18; Thorpe 1840: 422–40; and Jost 1918: 105–12.

3 Jost 1959: 16–34.

4 On the manuscripts of *Polity*, see Jost 1959: 8–15.

and interspersed a number of other texts, only some of which were actually composed by Wulfstan.[5] As such, even though scholars largely accept this version as the 'best' text, they are still forced to confront the limitations of its manuscript witness. The translation below is based on the text in Junius 121, though it follows Jost's edition in the selection and arrangement of chapters.

The hierarchical ordering of *Polity*'s component chapters – present in C.C.C.C. 201, Cotton Nero A.i, and to a lesser extent in Junius 121 – identifies the text as an example of medieval 'estates literature', a genre of text designed to specify the behaviours appropriate to each stratum of society.[6] Drawing extensively on the works of both Carolingian and English reformers (including the writings of his contemporary, Ælfric of Eynsham), Wulfstan used *Polity* to propose a vision of a moral community governed by a Christian monarch and founded on the principle that a just realm emerges from the alliance of three categories of people: those who fight, those who work, and those who pray.[7] When each category fulfils its divinely appointed role, the result is an ordered society populated by virtuous citizens. As Wulfstan points out in *Polity*'s final chapter (pointedly using the first-person plural to include himself in his injunction), fulfilling our social obligations also requires us to 'order our words and deeds rightly, fervently cleanse our inmost thoughts, truly keep our oath and pledge, and frequently reflect on the great judgment to which we all must go'.[8] The properly ordered society here finds its parallel in the properly ordered Christian soul: for Wulfstan, the exterior social world and the interior moral world are inextricably linked.[9] Unlike many of his monastic predecessors, for whom the virtuous life entailed a withdrawal from worldly affairs, Wulfstan's political vision called for secular society to be engaged and remade according to a divine plan. It is this plan which *Polity* provides.

---

5 Jost 1959: 12–15. The texts interspersed include, among others, the *Admonitions to Bishops* and the *Canons of Edgar* (see pp. 85–100 and 180–4). See also the Appendix, below.

6 Bethurum Loomis 1971: 129–30.

7 On the 'Three Estates', see esp. Powell 1994: 115–20. On Wulfstan's sources, see above, pp. 43–4, as well as Jost 1959: 36–8; Bethurum Loomis 1971: 130–4; Wormald 1999d: 456–65; and Hill 2004: 315.

8 *Polity* XXXVI.

9 This point is discussed further in Rabin 2006: 388–414.

TRANSLATION[1]

I. On the Heavenly King[2]

In the name of God. One is the eternal king, lord and maker of all creation. By right, he is king and the glory of kings, and the greatest of all kings who ever were or will be. For him shall there be praise and glory and eternal veneration for all time. Amen.

II. On the Earthly King[3]

It is fitting that the Christian king of a Christian people be, as is proper, a comfort to his people and a just shepherd over a Christian flock.[4] And it is fitting for him that he promote Christianity with all his might and everywhere wholeheartedly encourage and protect God's Church. He shall reconcile and bring peace to all Christian folk with just law, as readily as he can; and in every way he shall embrace righteousness before God and the world. For in this way, he shall himself thrive first and his people likewise if he embraces justice before God and the world. And it is fitting for him to zealously aid those who seek justice and always fiercely restrain those who pursue wickedness.[5] He must punish evil men severely with secular discipline, and he must detest and destroy thieves, robbers, and desecrators of property, and harshly

---

1 This translation is based on the text of *II Polity* found in Oxford, Bodleian Library, Junius 121, and ed. in Jost 1959: 39–164.

2 This section does not occur in *I Polity*. Its addition reflects the emphasis in Wulfstan's later writings on the subordination of royal law to divine authority. On this point, see also the introduction to *Cn. 1020*. See also the discussion of this passage in Trilling 2007: 69.

3 Wulfstan's transformation of his sources in this section has been discussed at length in Bethurum Loomis 1971: 136–9.

4 Cf. VIII Atr. 2.1 and *On Justice*, n. 7. The image of the king as 'a just shepherd over a Christian flock' is one of which Wulfstan was particularly fond. Similar pastoral images are also used in *Polity* to describe bishops, priests, and reeves. See below, sections VI, X, and XVII. On Wulfstan's use of this image elsewhere, see Wilcox 2000a: 395–418; Salvador-Bello 2006: 197. H.R. Loyn characterises the description of earthly kingship in this section and that in cc. 9.10–9.10a of the *Leges Henrici Primi* as bookends that 'illustrate the development in active kingship' and prepare the way for the emergence of the legal nationalism in the eleventh and early twelfth centuries. Loyn 1992: 23–4.

5 Wulfstan's language here recalls that of Sedulius Scottus, ch. II of the *Book on Christian Rulers* (*Liber de rectoribus Christianis*), where he writes that the duties of a king include, 'deterring subjects from wickedness [and] inviting them to virtue' ('subjectos deterrens a malo; invitans ad bona').

repel all of the enemies of God.[6] In the pursuit of justice he must be both merciful and severe: merciful to the good and strict with the evil.[7] This is the king's justice and a royal custom, and it will achieve the most among the people.

Lo, how shall relief and comfort come to God's servants and God's poor except through Christ and a Christian king? Through an unwise king, the people will become miserable – not once, but very often! – because of his foolish counsel; yet through a king's wisdom, the people will become happy, prosperous, and glorious.[8] Accordingly, the wise king must extend and enlarge Christendom and his kingdom, and he must always resist and repress heathenism.

He must study the learning found in books most attentively, and diligently heed God's commandments, and pursue wisdom with his council, if he wishes to obey God faithfully.[9] And if anyone is so rebellious anywhere among the people that he will not obey the law as he should, but flouts the law of God or resists the law of the people, then it must be made known to the king if necessary; and then at once, he will

6 Cf. II Cn. 7; Bethurum 7, l. 131; Bethurum 10a, l. 14; Bethurum 13, l. 95; Bethurum 20.3, l. 165; Napier 42, p. 203, l. 24; Napier 57, p. 298, ll. 15–16; *On Justice*, n. 10; *On the Proper Support*, n. 9; *On Heathen Practices*, n. 8; and below, *Polity* IX.

7 Cf. Sedulius Scottus, ch. II of *Book on Christian Rulers*: a king must be 'a friend of the virtuous, a foe of tyrants, an enemy to criminals, [and] an enemy to their crimes' ('amicus bonorum, inimicus tyrannorum, hostis criminum, hostis viciorum'). Wulfstan's use of Sedulius Scottus in this section has been discussed in Sauer 2000: 369–70.

8 This sentence, the first half of which is absent from I *Polity*, appears to be based on Ælfric's statement in his *Sermon on the Greater Litany* (*Letania maiore* in the Catholic Homilies, second series), 'The people are happy because of a wise king, glorious and prosperous because of a prudent ruler; and they are miserable because of an unwise king, in the many misfortunes from his poor rule'. ('Þæt folc bið gesælig þurh snoterne cyning, sigefæst and gesundful ðurh gesceadwisne reccend; and hi beoð geyrmede ðurh unwisne cyning on manegum ungelimpum for his misræde', ll. 96–9). Jonathan Wilcox suggests that this passage may have had special resonance for Wulfstan's contemporaries, given the circumstances surrounding the expulsion of the '"unwise king', Æthelred *unræd* (whose epithet may be translated as 'the foolish' or 'the badly counselled') in 1014. See Wilcox 2004: 387. While this may be the case, it is unlikely that the term Wulfstan uses here for 'foolish counsel' ('misræd') serves as a specific allusion to Æthelred's unfortunate nickname. Not only would an allusion of this sort have been an uncharacteristically impolitic move by the archbishop, but as the earliest unambiguous reference to Æthelred as *unræd* does not occur until 150 years after his death, it is doubtful that it would have circulated early enough for Wulfstan to have been familiar with it. On the history of Æthelred as *unræd*, see Keynes 1978: 240–1.

9 On this passage and the history of similar exhortations in medieval political thought, see Maddicott 2010: 35.

confer concerning the remedy and, as is his responsibility, zealously subdue him, indeed by force if he cannot do otherwise. And he must do what is necessary for him: purify his people before God and the world if he wishes to earn God's favour, and frequently reflect on what he must do and what avoid according to God's law.[10] And his name and reputation will ever increase both in this life and in the afterlife, insofar as he embraces God's justice, rejects injustice, and diligently heeds divine teaching often and frequently, as he himself requires.[11] For he swiftly becomes feeble who takes too little bodily nourishment, and he who seldom takes spiritual nourishment will soon do great injury to his soul; but he is happy who most often heeds and most zealously obeys divine teachings.[12]

III. On Kingship

There are eight columns that firmly uphold just kingship: honesty, patience, generosity, reasonableness (*truth, patience, largesse, openness to counsel*); fearsomeness, virtuousness, restraint, righteousness (*correction of sins, promotion of virtue, reasonableness in taxation, fairness in judgment*). And seven things are appropriate for a righteous king: first, that he have a very great fear of God; second, that he love righteousness always; third, that he be humble before the virtuous; fourth, that he be stalwart against evil; fifth, that he comfort and feed God's poor; sixth, that he promote and protect God's Church; and seventh, that he rule in righteous judgment for both friend and stranger.[13]

10 The injunction that a king is to 'purify his people' is a common one in Wulfstan's works. Cf. VI Atr. 7, VIII Atr. 40, II Cn. 4 and 7.1, *EGu.* 11, and *On Justice*, n. 39. The final phrase in this sentence, which also appears in Napier 25, p. 123, l. 14, originally derives from ch. CXLV of the *Council of Aachen.*

11 Cf. II Cn. 7.1; *Episc.* 9; *Cn. 1020* 15; Bethurum 11, l. 127; Bethurum 13, l. 103; Bethurum 21, ll. 26–7; and *On Justice*, n. 13. A similar call to embrace justice and reject injustice occurs as the first sentence of the section 'On Men in Orders' in I *Polity*, but is omitted from II *Polity*.

12 Wulfstan here borrows from Ælfric's *Sermon on the Lord's Prayer* (*De Dominica Oratione* in the Catholic Homilies, first series): 'quickly the body weakens and decays if its nourishment is taken from it; so also the soul perishes if it does not have the spiritual nourishment, that is, God's commandments, on which it shall be sustained and enriched' ('hraðe se lichama aswint 7 forweornað gif him bið oftogen his bigleofa; swa eac seo sawul forwyrð gif heo næfð ðone gastlican bigleofan, þæt sind Godes beboda, on þam heo sceal geþeon 7 beon gegodad', ll. 113–16).

13 The eight columns Wulfstan lists here are drawn from Sedulius Scottus's *Book on Christian Rulers*, ch. X. The seven qualities appropriate for a righteous king are taken from the *Collectio canonum Hibernensis*, 25.15.

IV. On the Throne

Every just throne[14] that stands fully as it should stands on three pillars: first, *those who pray*; second, *those who labour*; and third, *those who fight*. *Those who pray* are the clergy, who must serve God and fervently plead for all the people day and night. *Those who labour* are the workers who must toil for that by which the entire community may live. *Those who fight* are the warriors who must protect the land by waging war with weapons.[15] On these three pillars must each throne rightly stand in a Christian polity. If any of them weaken, immediately the throne will tremble; and if any of them fracture, then the throne will crumble to pieces, and that will bring the people all to ruin. Therefore, they are to be diligently steadied, strengthened, and reinforced with God's wise teachings and with just worldly law; in that way they will bring lasting guidance to the people. And what I say is true: if Christian faith weakens, the kingdom will soon fall;[16] and if injustice is exalted anywhere in the

---

14 I *Polity* omits 'just'. The different versions of this chapter have been discussed in Kubouchi 1999: 211–17.

15 This passage, perhaps the most famous in *Polity*, draws on a venerable, if only erratically attested, trope in early English political thought. The earliest surviving division of society into three orders occurs in the Old English translation of Boethius's *Consolation of Philosophy*, attributed to King Alfred. The text describes three 'tools for ruling' ('tol mid to ricsianne'): 'prayer-men and army-men and work-men' ('gebedmen and fyrdmen and weorcmen', 17.11–13). The theme next appears in the work of Ælfric, although variations in his terminology suggest that he (and perhaps Alfred also) was drawing on a now-lost Latin source. Ælfric incorporates variations on the three orders trope into a codicil to his commentary on *Maccabees*, a Latin letter to Wulfstan composed sometime between 1003 and 1005 (edited as number VI in Fehr's edition, at section XIV, ll. 20–1), and his *Book on the Old and New Testament (Libellus de Veteri Testamento et Novo*, also known as the *Letter to Sigeweard*). Wulfstan's discussion of the three orders in *Polity* most likely draws upon the last of these, the relevant text of which reads: 'The throne stands on these three pillars: *those who labour, those who fight, those who pray*. *Those who labour* are those who produce sustenance, farmers and peasants to whom alone that is entrusted. *Those who pray* are those who intercede for us with God and promote Christianity among Christian folk in God's service as a spiritual labour, to whom alone that is entrusted for the benefit of us all. *Those who fight* are those who protect our towns and also our land against the marauding army, fighting with weapons' ('Se cinestol stynt on þisum þrim stelum: *Laboratores, bellatores, oratores. Laboratores* sind þe us bigleofan tiliað, yrðlingas and æhtemen to þam anum betæhte. *Oratores* syndon þe us þingiað to Gode and cristendom fyrðriað on cristenum folcum on Godes þeowdome, to ðam anum betæhte, us eallum to þearfe. *Bellatores* sindon þe us burga healdað and eac urne eard wið þone sigendne here, feohtende mid wæmnum', ll. 868–75). It is noteworthy that Wulfstan alters the order of the three estates as listed by Ælfric, giving priority to *Those who pray* rather than *Those who labour*. On this passage, see Abels 1988a: 132–4; Powell 1994: 115ff.; Wormald 1999d: 458–60; and Wormald 1999a: 244–5.

16 About this sentence, Bethurum notes, 'The language is familiar, and Wulfstan could have got the form of this sentence from one of Alcuin's letters. But he makes a

land or evil customs anywhere too eagerly embraced, then the people will be brought entirely to ruin. Instead, one must do what is needed: suppress injustice and exalt the law of God; that may be of need before God and the world. Amen.

V. On the People's Counsellors[17]

It rightly behooves kings and bishops, nobles and generals, reeves and judges, the learned and the legal counsellors to be of one mind and embrace God's justice before God and the world. And bishops are the messengers and teachers of God's law, and they must proclaim justice and forbid injustice.[18] He who disdains to listen to them may take issue about that with God himself.[19] If bishops fail, in that they do not curb sin or forbid injustice, and they do not make known God's law, but mumble with their mouths when they should shout, woe to them for that silence![20] The prophet spoke of them and thus said harshly: *if thou declare not his wickedness to the wicked, I will require his blood at thy hand.*[21] 'If you will not curb the sins of the sinful', says our lord, 'and forbid injustice and proclaim the wickedness of the wicked, for that soul you shall pay bitterly!' This may be taken to heart by every bishop; let him sincerely reflect upon it for himself, he who will.

He who will not rightly heed God's messengers, nor attend to divine teaching as he should, must listen to his enemies if not to his friends; for he rejects God who rejects God's messenger, as Christ himself in his Gospel clearly said when he spoke thus: *He that heareth you, heareth me;*

---

significant change: the Carolingians make the health of the state depend upon the health of the king, Wulfstan of the church'. Bethurum Loomis 1971: 139.

17 Cotton Nero A.i separates this section from the preceding ones and follows it with a text of the *Sermo Lupi ad Anglos* (Bethurum 20.3). Loyn sees the placement of the text as problematic, writing that it seems 'isolated' from the rest of the *Polity* and 'out of context' in its immediate surroundings. Wilcox, however, argues that the placement is intentional and serves as a means of framing the *Sermo* as a response to this section's concluding injunction against bishops who fail to preach. See Loyn 1971b: 47; Wilcox 2000a: 410; and Rabin 2006: 411–12.

18 Variations on this sentence also occur in I Cn. 26 and *Sanctuary* 19.1. Beginning here, the remainder of this chapter is drawn nearly *verbatim* from Wulfstan's eschatological sermon on *Luke* (*Lectio secundum Lucam*, Bethurum 17, ll. 36ff). On this passage, see Rabin 2006: 413.

19 Cf. Bethurum 16b, ll. 36–7, I Cn. 26.4, and *Sanctuary* 20.

20 A favorite phrase of Wulfstan's, probably influenced by *Isaiah* 58:1. Cf. *Admonition* §1; Bethurum 16b, ll. 17–22; Bethurum 17, ll. 41–3; and Bethurum 20.3 (the *Sermo Lupi ad Anglos*), ll. 180–4.

21 *Ezekiel* 3:18.

and he that despiseth you, despiseth me.[22] He said: 'he who hears you, hears me and he who rejects you, rejects me'.[23]

Alas, onerous is the burden which God's messenger must bear if he will not zealously combat injustice; for although he acts virtuously himself and another person acts wickedly, he himself shall suffer if he does not correct it. And if God's messenger acts wickedly, one should overlook that, but rather heed his teaching if what he teaches is good. One should act just as Christ taught when he thus spoke clearly in his Gospel: *whatsoever they shall say to you, do: but according to their works do ye not.*[24] He said, 'Follow their teachings, and not their sins.' Nor must anyone ever neglect himself because of a bishop's sins, but follow his teaching if he teaches well. And indeed, beloved people, do as I ask and listen to what I say without taking offence: very well do I know myself to be entirely too sinful in word and deed, but for fear of God, I dare not stay wholly silent about many of the things which wound this people.[25]

VI. *Likewise, On Bishops*[26]

Bishops must keep to their books and prayers, and day and night, often and frequently, call upon Christ and fervently intercede for all Christian people. And they must learn and rightly teach and conscientiously watch over the deeds of the people.[27] And they must preach and sincerely exemplify the spiritual commission to a Christian people. And they must not knowingly permit any injustice but readily promote all that is just.[28] They must hold the fear of God in their mind and not grow

---

22 *Luke* 10:16.

23 On Wulfstan's use of this passage from *Luke*, here and elsewhere in his writings, see Heslop 2004: 306–7.

24 *Matthew* 23:3.

25 It is unlikely that Wulfstan intended this statement to be anything more than a conventional expression of humility. Nonetheless, it has given rise to some scholarly speculation over the sorts of sins of which Wulfstan may have considered himself guilty, the most frequently proposed being pride, cupidity, and hypocrisy. See Whitelock 1942: 44–5; Bethurum 1963: 162–70; Cooper 1970: 9–11; and Rabin 2006: 413.

26 The principal source for the following two sections is a short text entitled *De medicamento animarum* (*On the Treatment of Souls*), ed. in Fehr 1914: 251–3. The text appears in London, British Library, Cotton Nero A.i, interposed in the series of short passages identified by modern editors as the B recension of Wulfstan's Canon Law Collection. See Cross and Hamer 1999: 78.

27 On this injunction, see Rabin 2006: 403.

28 Cf. *Episc.* 10.

all too timid for fear of the world.[29] But let those who would do so always
be sure to zealously proclaim the law of God and to forbid injustice;[30]
for the shepherd will be judged weak for the flock who will not defend
the flock that he must protect – even by calling if he can do nothing
else – if any corruptor of the people begins to pillage there.[31] There is
no corruptor as evil as the devil himself. He is always concerned with
one thing: how he might most defile the souls of men. Therefore must
those shepherds who would protect the people against the corruptor be
most watchful and vigorous in their warnings.[32] Those are the bishops
and the mass-priests who must protect and oversee their spiritual flock
with wise teaching, so that the ravenous werewolf does not wound too
greatly nor devour too many of their spiritual flock. And let him who
disdains to listen to them settle that with God himself.[33]

Alas, there are, nonetheless, many of those who lightly regard and little
heed the precepts of the books and the teachings of the bishops; and
also frivolously ignore blessings or curses, and do not understand as
they should what Christ in his Gospel clearly said when he spoke thus:
*He who listens, etc. And likewise: Whatsoever is bound, etc. And likewise:
Whose sins you shall forgive, they are forgiven them, etc. Elsewhere too it is
written: He that blesseth thee, etc. And the psalmist, speaking chillingly, says:
He who would not have the blessing, it shall be put off from him.*[34] This is to
be reflected upon and the wrath of God always to be shielded against.
Now we also strongly enjoin every man to heed God's teachings and
his laws;[35] then he will secure for himself eternal joy.[36]

29 Cf. I Cn. 25; Bethurum 10c, ll. 149–51; Napier 37, p. 179, ll. 13–16; and *On the Duties of the Laity,* n. 14.

30 Cf. Bethurum 17, ll. 14–15 and *Admonition* §1.

31 Cf. Cf. VI Atr. 2, I Cn. 26.1–3, *Episc.* 7, and Bethurum 16b l. 27f. The ultimate source for this passage is *Matthew* 13:39.

32 Cf. Ælfric's *Sermon on the Nativity of the Lord* (*Nativitas Domini*, in the Catholic Homilies, first series): 'It befits a teacher to be watchful always over God's flock, so that the invisible wolf does not scatter God's sheep' ('þam lareowe gedafenað þæt he symle wacol sy ofer godes eowede. Þæt se ungesewenenlica wulf godes shep ne tostence', ll. 109–11).

33 Cf. *Episc.* 7, VI Atr. 2, I Cn. 26.1–3, and Bethurum 16b l. 27.

34 *Luke* 10:16, *Matthew* 16:19, *John* 20:23, *Numbers* 24:9, and *Psalms* 108:18.

35 Cf. VI Atr. 42.2; II Cn. 84.1; *Sanctuary* 19; *On the Duties of the Laity* n. 3; Napier 37, p. 179, ll. 21–3; Bethurum 5, ll. 113–8; and Bethurum 20.3, ll. 192–4.

36 In Junius 121, this section is followed by the legal compilation *Concerning Episcopal Duties* (*Episcopus*), numbered VII by the scribe. In Cotton Nero A.i, it is followed by a short Latin text on tonsure and ecclesiastical garb, a series on injunctions on episcopal behavior headed 'Incipit de synodo', and the text translated in this volume as *An Admonition to Bishops* (below, pp. 180–4).

VII. *LIKEWISE*

The proper daily work of a bishop is: first his prayers and then his studies, reading or writing, teaching or learning; and his canonical hours at the right times, always along with those things which are relevant thereto;[37] and cleansing the feet of the needy and the distribution of alms and the supervision of works where it is necessary.[38] Good handicrafts are also suitable for him, and that those in his service practice crafts, so that indeed no one too idle remain there.[39] And it is also fully appropriate for him, when he is at a meeting, to relate the divine teachings often and frequently to those people with whom he then is.

VIII. *LIKEWISE*[40]

For bishops, wisdom and discretion are always appropriate, and those that practice them – and also that learn a special craft[41] – have praiseworthy ways.[42] Nothing useless is ever appropriate for bishops, neither thoughtlessness nor foolishness nor drunkenness nor childishness in speech nor idle frivolousness of any kind, neither at home nor on a journey nor in any place.[43] But wisdom and discretion suit their status and dignity befits those who follow them.[44]

---

37 Cf. Ælfric's first Latin Pastoral Letter to Archbishop Wulfstan, §62 and Ælfric's Pastoral Letter to Bishop Wulfsige, §49. See also §29 in the B recension of Wulfstan's Canon Law Collection, *Canons* 45, and *NPL* 36.

38 Cf. *On Various Misfortunes* n. 9.

39 Cf. §163 in the B Recension of Wulfstan's Canon Law Collection, *Canons* 11, and Bethurum 10a, l. 52.

40 In *I Polity*, this section occurs between sections IV and V.

41 Cf. §163 in the B Recension of Wulfstan's Canon Law Collection, *Canons* 11, and Bethurum 10a, l. 52.

42 I Timothy 3:2.

43 Cf. Ælfric's Pastoral Letter to Bishop Wulfsige, §48, though earlier occurrences of these prohibitions can be found in Theodulf's *Capitula*, c. X and c. 71 of the *Admonitio generalis* (789). See also *Canons* 26 and *Admonition* 3, 6, and 14.

44 In Junius 121, this section is followed by a collection of canons entitled *Incipit de synodo* and numbered VIII by the scribe. See Jost 1959: 210–16.

IX. On Nobles[45]

Nobles, generals, secular judges, and also reeves have the obligation to embrace justice before God and the world; and never through foolishness, nor out of bribery or friendship, neglect their wisdom so that they twist injustice into justice or pronounce unjust rulings harmful to the poor.[46] But they must always venerate and protect the Church over all other things, and they must console the widow and the orphan, aid the poor, and defend the helpless slaves, if they wish to fulfil God's will rightly. They must abhor thieves and villains, and they must suppress robbers and criminals, unless they cease [their crimes].[47] And they must always greatly detest injustice. For it is the truth that I speak, believe it who will: woe unto that person who pursues injustice all too long, unless he turn aside![48] He will certainly sink, bereft of help, into Hell's dark and deep abyss.[49] Too few, however, are those who understand that as one should; but may God correct that! But each friend shall do as is most necessary: warn and protect himself so as not to anger God all too greatly, but instead please his Lord with righteous deeds.

X. On Reeves

It is right that reeves toil assiduously and always provide for their lord properly. But now since Edgar died, just as God willed, it has come to pass all too much that there are more thieves than righteous people, and it is a terrible thing that they are thieves who should be the shepherds of the Christian people.[50] At times, they steal from those who are poor

45 This chapter and the following one are a significant expansion of a short passage entitled 'Concerning Injustice' ('Be unlagum', ll. 175–80) in Wulfstan's homily, 'On the Vision of the Prophet Isaiah' (*De visione Isaie Prophete*, edited as number 11 in Bethurum's edition). For specific verbal parallels, see the notes below.

46 Cf. Bethurum 11, ll. 176–7: 'Woe to him … who elevates injustice to justice and pronounces unjust judgments for the harm of the poor' ('Wa þam … þe ræreð unriht to rihte 7 undom demeð earmum to hynðe'). The context for the passage in *Polity* has been discussed in Baxter 2007: 109, 116.

47 Cf. II Cn. 4.2 and *Cn. 1020* 10.

48 Cf. *On Justice*, n. 35.

49 Cf. Bethurum 11, ll. 178–9: 'for he shall sink into the dark and deep abyss of Hell, bereft of help' ('forðam he sceal drefan dimme 7 deopne helleswites grund, helps bedæled').

50 The sudden death of King Edgar (r. 959–75) and the subsequent succession crisis initiated a crisis in ecclesiastical authority that still resonated with Wulfstan more than twenty-five years later. The years between 975 and 978 witnessed a series of legal challenges to ecclesiastical power and violent attacks on monastic institutions against which the under-aged King Edward (later referred to as 'the Martyr' following his assassination, possibly at the instigation of his step-mother, Queen

through no fault of their own and torment the flock which they should protect, and abuse the unfortunate with evil slander, and promote unjust laws in every way to exploit the needy and rob widows again and again.[51] But formerly, these men were chosen wisely as shepherds for the people and they dared not behave dishonestly nor obtain anything unjustly because of worldly shame and the fear of God; instead, they acquired things properly. Yet afterwards, this has been pursued most eagerly of all by those who understood how to cheat and swindle most cruelly, and to harm the unfortunate with deceit, and to extract money from the innocent most swiftly. Since then, God has been provoked again and again. And woe unto that man who has acquired most of his wealth through injustice, unless he turn aside and repent all the more deeply before God and the world.[52]

XVII. On Priests[53]

Priests in their parishes must wisely and sensibly lead and instruct the spiritual flock which they are to protect. They must both preach well and set a good example for others; and at God's judgment, they must render into God's hand an account both of their own deeds and of those people they are to oversee.[54] And if they shall have done anything, they may not hesitate, neither out of fear nor love of any person, to proclaim justice and forbid injustice.[55] The shepherd will be of little use

Ælfthryth) could offer no protection. For Wulfstan and his contemporaries, Edgar's death signalled the end of the golden age of Monastic Reform and the beginning of a new age of national and ecclesiastical instability. See Rabin 2013: 228–30. Other references by Wulfstan to Edgar's death are discussed in Keynes 1991: 74 and Lawson 1993: 40–3.

51 Cf. Bethurum 11, ll. 176–8: 'Woe to him ... who elevates injustice to justice ... for the harm of the poor and the widow ... most often afflicts' ('Wa þam ... þe ræreð unriht to rihte ... earmum to hynðe 7 wudewan ... oftost ahwæneð').

52 Cf. Bethurum 11, ll. 122–3: 'And woe to the one who has acquired most of his wealth ...' ('7 wa þæs gestreones þam þe his mæst hafaþ ...'). This phrase is drawn from a section of the homily entitled, 'Concerning Robbery' ('Be Reaflacum'). See also *Admonition* §7.

53 Excerpts from this section circulated independently as the homilies *On the Duties of the Clergy* and *On the Sins of the Clergy*. Preceding this section in Junius 121 is the text translated below as *On the Duties of the Laity*.

54 Cf. Theodulf, *Capitula*, ch. I: 'Truly, you should know and always remember that we, to whom the care of souls has been entrusted, must render an account for those which are lost through our negligence' ('Veraciter nosse debetis et semper meminisse, quia nos, quibus animarum cura commissa est, pro his, qui nostra negligentia pereunt, rationem reddituri sunt').

55 Cf. *The Old English Penitential* (also known as the *Penitential of Pseudo-Ecgbert*), III.15: 'The holy apostle Paul instructed every mass-priest who is appointed as a

to the fold who will not protect the flock, which he must defend with an outcry if he can do nothing else, if the corruptor of the people begins to raid. There is no corruptor as evil as the devil himself. He is concerned with thing always: how he might most defile the souls of men. Therefore must those shepherds who would protect the people against the corruptor be most watchful and vigorous in their warnings. Those are the bishops and the mass-priests who must protect and oversee their spiritual flock with wise teaching.[56] Thus if he would protect himself he must not hesitate either out of love or fear to say to men that which is most just. Nor may he hesitate before either the humble or the mighty, for he does not do as he ought if he grows timid or ashamed to proclaim what is right.[57] He will fare miserably if, through his weakness, the flock which he must protect should perish, and he himself with it.[58] Should any of our shepherds overlook even one sheep, we will require that he pay for it.[59] And then how will those shepherds fare at God's fearful judgment, who cannot protect the spiritual flocks which Christ purchased with his own life, and which they must protect if they can?[60] Because of their lack of learning, they cannot lead nor teach nor tend them properly. With what can we expect them to pay for them then? Woe unto them, then, that they ever received that which they could not protect. Indeed, how can a blind man lead another? How can an

---

teacher of God's people that none of them should hesitate, either out of fear of any person or out of love or out of shame or because of any payment, so that they not proclaim to all men what is to be done by them and what is to be refrained from, if they wish to protect themselves on the Day of Judgment before God himself' ('Se halga apostol Paulus læreð ælcum mæssepreoste þe godes folce to lare bið gesett. þæt heora nan ne wandige for nanes mannes ege ne for lufe ne for sceame ne for nanum sceatte. þæt hy ne bodian ælcon men hwæt him sy to donne and hwæt to gif hy sylfe wyllað þæt heom beo geborhgen on domesdæg beforan gode sylfum').

56 Cf. I Cn. 26.1–3.

57 Cf. *The Old English Penitential* I.1: '[A priest] should never hesitate before either the humble or the mighty to proscribe correctly …' ('na ne for ricum ne for heanum þæt he him riht tæce …').

58 The final phrase of this sentence appears to be taken from Ælfric's homily, *Of the Eight Faults and Twelve Abuses* (*De viii vitiis et xii abusivis*). See the edition in Morris 1868: 293–304. The relevant passage occurs on p. 303 at l. 30–1.

59 Gareth Mann notes that Wulfstan's use of this image closely resembles a passage in a letter of Alcuin's to Abbot Æthelbald of Wearmouth-Jarrow, though he stops short of claiming the letter as a source. See Mann 2004: 247.

60 Jost suggests that Wulfstan's source here is c. XII of the *Consilium Rispacense*; however, both the image and the phrasing in which it is couched occur with sufficient frequency – similar passages appear, among other places, in the writings of Gregory and the Benedictine Rule – to suggest that Wulfstan may simply have been drawing on a common trope. The ultimate source for this image is *Ezekiel* 34:10. See Jost 1959: 92.

ignorant judge instruct another?[61] Truly, woe unto them who receive a
spiritual flock and can neither tend to themselves nor to the flock which
they must protect, and worse are those who can and will not.

Alas, alas, there are many of those who, as it may seem, seek the priesthood wrongfully, most for idle glory and worldly wealth, and they do
not know that which they should know.[62] About them the prophet spoke
and said thus: *Woe unto the priests who eat the sins of the people, etc.* That
is, in English: Woe to the priests, he said, who devour and consume the
people's sins.[63] Those are the ones who will not or cannot or dare not
warn the people against sins and punish sins, but nonetheless desire
their money in the form of tithes and all Church dues;[64] yet they neither
lead them well with examples, nor teach them well with preaching, nor
heal them well with penances, nor intercede for them with prayer;[65]
instead, they scavenge people's possessions for whatever they can grab,
just as gluttonous ravens do from a carcass wherever they can.[66] It is all
the worse, once they have it all: then they do not treat it at all as they
should, but they decorate their women with that which should be on
the altars;[67] and they exploit for their own worldly pride and idle vanity

61 Cf. *Matthew* 15:14 and *Luke* 6:39. This image also occurs in Ælfric's *Sermon on the
    Greater Litany* (*Letania maiore* in the Catholic Homilies, second series): 'How can
    the ignorant exercise a teacher's authority and preach properly to laypeople? The
    Saviour spoke about this to his disciples: 'If a blind man be a guide to another blind
    man, then both will fall into a blind pit' ('Hu mæg se ungelæreda lareowdom healdan.
    and læwedum folce fægre bodian. þe ðan cwæð se hælend to his discipulum. gif se
    blinda man bið oðres blindan latteow. þonne befeallað hi begen. on sumum blindum
    seaðe', ll. 107–11).

62 Cf. the prologue to the *Penitential of Ecgbert*: 'And indeed, there are truly some …
    blind to divine wisdom, who seek the priesthood, not for the sake of God, but out of
    a desire for earthly glory' ('Et item sunt nonnulli … qui ad sacerdotium vehuntur,
    qui non propter Deum sed plus propter honorem terrenum inhiantes, ceci divina
    sapientia'). This passage occurs in Haddan and Stubbs 1869–71: p. 416 (not p. 426,
    as cited by Jost).

63 Cf. *Hosea* 4:8 and *Ezekiel* 44:29. The *Ezekiel* passage is also cited in the prologue to
    the *Penitential of Ecgbert*, Haddan and Stubbs 1869–71: p. 417.

64 Cf. the prologue to the *Penitential of Ecgbert*: 'that is, taking from their victims and
    not praying for them, preying upon their victims and not warning them' ('Hoc est
    sibi eorum sumentes victimas et non orantes pro eis, comedentes hostias et non
    corripientes', Haddan and Stubbs 1869–71: p. 417.). Cf. Bethurum 16b, ll. 18–19.

65 Cf. V Atr. 4.1, I Cn. 6a, *Clerical Compensation* 1, *Canons* 1, *Polity* XXXV, *On the Duties
    of the Laity* n. 5, and Napier 37, p. 179, l. 9.

66 Cf. *Matthew* 24:28. See also Ælfric's first Old English Pastoral Letter to Archbishop
    Wulfstan, §182.

67 Pauline Stafford points to this injunction as a crux in Wulfstan's understanding of
    the relationship between women and the clergy as well as in the development of the
    role of gender in reformist theology more generally. She writes, 'As far as gender

that which they should put towards the worship of God in Church affairs or towards assistance to the needy or towards the ransoming of captives[68] or towards some matters which might be of enduring benefit both to themselves and to those who give to them their goods for the love of God. There is great need, then, that he who erred beforehand readily repent for it henceforth.

Therefore, let him understand who can: great and wondrous is that which priest must do for the benefit of the people, if he wishes to please his lord properly. Great is the exorcism and wondrous is the blessing which expels devils and puts them to flight, just as often as a person is baptised or the host is consecrated. And angels hover there and oversee those deeds and, through God's might, aid those priests just as long as they serve Christ properly. Thus they do always, as often as they fervently call upon Christ with their innermost heart and readily inter-cede for the needs of the people. Accordingly, for fear of God, the ranks of holy orders must be understood with discernment.[69]

Indeed, beloved, it is solemnly commanded to us that we must fervently admonish and teach that every man is to submit to God and refrain from sins. That decree is most fearsome, which God spoke through his prophet concerning those who must preach righteousness to God's people, namely the bishops and the priests. Concerning them, he said, *Cry, cease not; like a trumpet, etc.* 'Cry loudly, and raise up your voice as loudly as a trumpet, and preach to my people so that they refrain from sins.'[70] Yet if you do not do that, but pass over it in silence, and will not make known to the people its obligation, then you must render an account at Judgment Day for all those souls which are lost because they lack the teaching and the admonition that they require.[71] Let this decree be most remembered by all those who are entrusted to preach

---

definitions were concerned, reform both reinforced and threatened to redraw them. "Woman" symbolised all that the male cleric was to reject. For Archbishop Wulfstan of York, writing in the early eleventh century, the choice for a priest was between his altar and a wife: he must not bedeck a woman with the ornaments and goods which belonged to his altar; his marriage was to his church. The concern with sexual purity readily aligned "woman" with all the notions of impurity and, specifically, with those which were coming to be seen as markers of the laity'. Stafford 1999: 8–9.

68 These three actions – worshipping God, assisting the needy, and ransoming captives – are those deemed appropriate for a charitable man in the *Old English Penitential*, IV.57. The pairing of worldly pride and idle vanity also occurs in *Admonition* §3.

69 Cf. I. Cn. 4.1–3. On this passage, see Bethurum Loomis 1971: 141–2.

70 Cf. *Isaiah* 58:1. On this passage, see Rabin 2006: 396.

71 Cf. *Ezekiel* 33:8.

righteousness. And the people also have a great need to be mindful of the decree delivered after this one. The prophet said after that: 'If you proclaim righteousness to the people yet you cannot bend them to righteousness, then you will save your own soul nonetheless';[72] and he who pursues wickedness and will not cease, he shall have eternal punishment; that is, they must then travel to hell in soul and body and dwell with the devil in infernal suffering. Woe to him who must dwell there in suffering: better it would have been for him to have never become a man in this world than to have become one. There is no one alive who can recount all of the sorrows which must be endured by one who falls entirely into that suffering; and it is all the worse, in that an end never will come to it for all eternity.[73]

XXII. On Men in Orders[74]

All forms of purity are appropriate for men in orders, for they must forbid all forms of impurity to other men.[75] And if they do what is right, they must themselves most assiduously become an example of every form of purity. Accordingly, it is exceedingly dreadful that of those who must preach righteousness to all Christians and also set a good example, some have become an example of damnation rather than duty. That is, those adulterers who accepted marriage to the Church through their holy orders and later violated it. No clergyman who serves at the altar is permitted to have a wife;[76] rather, it is forbidden

---

72 Cf. *Ezekiel* 33:9. See also, Bethurum 6, ll. 3–20. On Wulfstan's use of these verses from *Ezekiel*, see Hall 2004: 102–3.

73 Cf. Bethurum 6, ll. 120–8.

74 In Junius 121, this section is preceded by two short, non-Wulfstanian texts (numbered XVIII and XIX by the scribe), the *Canons of Edgar* (numbered XX), and *Polity* XXI ('On Laymen'). I follow Jost in restoring it to the position it occupied in *I Polity*. See Jost 1959: 13.

75 In *I Polity*, this section opens with the injunction, 'It is proper for all Christian men that they love righteousness and hate injustice; and indeed, for men in orders there is a great obligation to both preach well and set a good example for others'. Cf. II Cn. 7.1; *Episc.* 9; *Polity* II; *Cn. 1020* 15; Bethurum 11, l. 127; Bethurum 13, l. 103; Bethurum 21, ll. 26–7; and *On Justice*, n. 13.

76 Cf. Ælfric's *Sermon on Sexagisma Sunday* (*Dominica in sexagisma* in the Catholic Homilies, second series): 'Truly, to the others who serve at God's altar – namely, to the mass-priests and the deacons – all sexual intercourse is entirely forbidden' ('Witodlice ðam oðrum þe æt godes weofode þeniað þæt is mæssepreostum. and diaconum. is eallunge forboden ælc hæmed', ll. 144–6). In Cotton Nero A.1, a later hand (probably of the late eleventh century) has crossed out this sentence and replaced it with 'It is right that a priest love a pure woman as his bed-fellow' ('Riht is þæt preost him lufie clænlicne wimman to gebeddan'). Whitelock 1965: 220.

to each. Now, however, there are all too many who commit adultery or have committed it, yet for the love of God, I command and solemnly decree that this is to cease. To a layman is every woman forbidden save his lawful spouse;[77] and there are some in orders so deceived by the devil that they take a wife unlawfully and destroy themselves through the adultery in which they abide.[78] But I urgently command that they cease straightaway from this mortal sin. The priest's wife is the Church, [and by the law he has no other; for neither a wife nor the warfare of this world are fitting for a priest in any way, if he wishes to obey God properly and heed God's law in a manner appropriate to his status.][79]

Constantine, the great emperor, convened a very important synod in the city of Nicea for the affirmation of the true faith.[80] Gathered at that synod were three hundred and eighteen bishops from many peoples, and there they proclaimed the true faith; and then, as an affirmation of this, they established the mass-creed which is sung widely, and they arranged the church services appropriately, and many other matters concerning both God's servants and God himself. They decreed there, entirely unanimously, that if a clergyman who serves at the altar – that is, a bishop or mass-priest or deacon[81] – took a wife, it were right that he forfeit forever[82] his order and be excommunicated, unless he desist and repent the more sincerely. Four synods were convened concerning the true faith in the Holy Trinity and concerning Christ's humanity: the first was in Nicea[83] and the second was in Constantinople, where there were one hundred and fifty bishops; the third was in Ephesus of two hundred bishops[84] and the fourth was in Chalcedon, of many bishops together.[85] And they were all of one mind about all of those matters which were first decided at Nicea, and they forbade entirely and forever

77 Cf. II Cn. 54.1, *Canons* 21, and the *Old English Penitential* II.9. See also n. to *Canons* 21.

78 Cf. §136 in the B Recension of Wulfstan's Canon Law Collection.

79 The text in Junius 121 is incomplete here. This passage is taken from C.C.C.C. 201. Cf. Bethurum 10a, ll. 34–5 and *Canons* 68a. The remainder of this section is a paraphrase of Ælfric's Pastoral Letter to Bishop Wulfsige, esp. §5–6, 12–13, and 93–101, and his first Old English Pastoral Letter to Archbishop Wulfstan, §61–3.

80 C.C.C.C. 201: 'It befell that Constantine, the great emperor, convened a very important synod, as we earlier stated, in the city which is called Nicea for the confirmation of the true faith'. Cf. the discussion of early Church synods in *On Justice*.

81 C.C.C.C. 201 omits the reference to deacons.

82 C.C.C.C. 201 adds, 'thenceforth'.

83 C.C.C.C. 201 adds, 'just as we stated'.

84 Omitted from C.C.C.C. 201.

85 C.C.C.C. 201 adds, 'gathered from all over'.

all fornication by those who serve at the altar. Let them now reflect, those who are so arrogant that they neglect God and the judgment of so many holy men such as were gathered at these synods and everywhere afterwards, what reward they can expect for themselves; and indeed, they need not expect but know with certainty that they must receive an evil reward[86] and the wrath of God fearsomely because they so enrage God in that they live all of their lives in filth.[87] I entreat those clergymen who serve at the altar that they examine themselves and refrain from all corruption.[88] Moreover, may those who beforehand engaged in the sinful practice of decorating their women with that which should be on the altars, end that sinful practice and decorate their churches as best they can,[89] so that they command for themselves both spiritual wisdom and earthly honour.[90] Nor is a priest's mistress[91] anything other than a snare of the devil, and he who is thus trapped will be caught fast by the devil from then on until his end and, furthermore, he must fall then into the hand of fiends and perish entirely.[92] But let everyone eagerly help himself while he may and can, and let each person turn away from sin to righteousness; then will he be redeemed from eternal torment. And indeed, he who persists in good deeds from then on until his end shall receive eternal reward as recompense.[93] To you, now, has the truth been spoken: understand yourself thereby, you who will. May God strengthen you to your own advantage, and protect us all as his will may be. Amen.[94]

XI. On Abbots

It is right that abbots and, in particular, abbesses remain perpetually secure in their monasteries and always conscientiously oversee their flocks, and ever set a good example for them and preach rightly; and

---

86 C.C.C.C. 201 adds, 'unless they desist'.

87 Instead of 'filth', C.C.C.C. 201 reads 'wrongfulness'.

88 Instead of 'filth', C.C.C.C. 201 reads 'uncleanness'.

89 C.C.C.C. 201 adds, 'and preserve their purity'.

90 Cf. V Atr. 9.1. See also n. to *Episc.* 1.

91 Instead of 'a priest's mistress', C.C.C.C. 201 reads 'foul lustfulness'.

92 For the final clause of this sentence, C.C.C.C. 201 substitutes 'he will fare worse than he needed to'.

93 C.C.C.C. 201 adds 'in the heavenly kingdom'.

94 C.C.C.C. 201 follows this with a quotation from *Psalm* 112:2: 'Blessed be the name of the Lord, from henceforth now and forever, etc.' ('Sit nomen Domini benedictum ex hoc nunc et usque in saeculum et reliqua').

they are never to be concerned too greatly nor all too frequently with worldly cares or idle vanity, but they are to occupy themselves most often with spiritual needs.[95] This is fitting for abbots and men in orders.

XII. On Monks[96]

It is right that monks always reflect upon God in their innermost heart by day and night and sincerely pray and live according to the rule with all humility; and they always are to sever themselves from secular occupations as diligently as they can, and they are to fulfil that which is their obligation: to consider always how they might best please God and perform all that they promised when they took orders: to adhere diligently to their books and prayers, to learn and teach as best they can, and to entirely reject every arrogance and idle vanity and private property and frivolous deed and foolish speech.[97] Thus is fitting for monks. But it is an evil truth, as one might suspect, that some are too arrogant and entirely too proud and too susceptible to straying and too worthless and entirely too lazy for any good deed and too corrupted by hidden lusts; inwardly slack and outwardly strict. Some even are apostates who could, if they wished, be God's champions in their monasteries, especially those[98] who have rejected their orders and dwell sinfully amidst worldly things.

All too commonly do all things fare badly. So much does it worsen widely among men that those in orders who, through fear of God, once were the most useful and industrious in divine service and scholarship, are now indeed everywhere the most useless and never work seriously to any benefit for God or the world; instead, they act wholly for pleasure and ease, and they love gluttony and idle pleasure, they meander and stray and waste the entire day, they gossip and play and accomplish nothing of any significance. It is a loathsome life that they have thus created; and it is the worse in that their elders do not correct it, but they themselves do not behave as well as they should. Yet we have need to correct it as urgently as we can, and become dedicated to the common good before God and the world.

---

95 Cf. *Admonition* 11.

96 On this section, see Mann 2004: 276–8.

97 Cf. *Canons* 26.

98 Jost inserts 'earman' ('wretches') here from Cotton Nero A.i, though the word is omitted in Junius 121.

XIII. On Women Monastics[99]

It is right that women in orders act in a monastic fashion, even as we have said before about monks, and not consort with men of the world nor have all too much familiarity with them, but they are to live always according to the rule and to sever themselves from worldly occupations as best they can.[100]

XIV. On Priests and Nuns

It is right that priests and even nuns also live according to the rule and preserve their chastity if they desire to live in a monastery or earn respect in the world.[101]

XXI. On Laymen[102]

It is right that men in orders instruct the laypeople how they should best keep their marital vows. That life is virtuous in which a young man remains an adolescent until he weds a maiden properly, and afterwards has her and no other for as long as she lives.[103] Then, if her death occurs, it is most fitting that he remains a widower thenceforth. By the Apostle's consent, though, a layman can marry a second time if necessary; however, the canons forbid the blessings thereto which are reserved for a first marriage and a penance is fixed for such men to perform.[104] Moreover,

---

99 Wulfstan here refers to *mynecenan*, a specific category of female monastics that emerged as part of the tenth-century reform. See V Atr. 4 and VI Atr. 2. For a more extended discussion of this terms, see Clayton 1994: 225–7; Stafford 1999: 10; Cubitt 2000: 9–10. On the adaptation of the Benedictine Rule for female monastic communities, see Jayatilaka 2003: 147–87.

100 Possible sources for this short section include the *Regularis Concordia*, Pr.7, the *Regula Sanctimonialium* of Amalarius of Metz, c. VIII, and the Council of Nantes, c. XIX. By the beginning of the eleventh century, the strict enclosure of female monastics had come to be rigorously enforced in English foundations. On this point, see Schulenburg 1984: 51–86; Schulenburg 1998: 115–16; Foot 2000: v. I, pp. 67–8; Horner 2001.

101 Cf. *Regularis Concordia*, Pr.7, VI Atr. 4 and 5.4.

102 I have followed Jost in returning this section to the position it occupies in *I Polity*. In C.C.C.C. 201, this section is titled, 'To Men in Orders and Laymen'.

103 A similar injunction occurs in Ælfric's sermon, 'Concerning Holy Purity' ('Be þære halgan clænnysse', edited as number II in Assman 1889): 'It is very proper for a virtuous life, that a young man hold himself pure until he weds, just as he would have a clean maiden when they come together' ('Hit wære swyþe rihtlic æfter rihtum life, þæt se cniht heolde hine sylfne clæne, oð þæt he wifode, swa swa he wyle habban clæne mæden, þonne hi cumað togæderes', ll. 147–50).

104 Wulfstan here quotes Ælfric's letter to Bishop Wulfsige: 'The layman may, nevertheless, by the Apostle's consent, wed a second time if his wife abandons him, but the

a priest is forbidden from presiding in the way that he did previously at a marriage at which a man weds a second time, nor may he perform the blessing specified for a first wedding. By that, one may know that it is not entirely proper that a man take a wife or a woman take a husband after the first time. And indeed it is too many if it should happen a third time, and wholly wrong if it happens more often. And though a wife is permitted to laymen, it is still necessary that they understand how it is permitted. On festivals and in fasting-times, laymen may not consort with their wives in fornication, any more than those in orders may do that thing at any time.[105]

XV. On the Widow[106]

It is right that widows readily abide by the example of Anna: she remained in the temple day and night in heartfelt service.[107] She fasted very rigorously and kept to her prayers and called on Christ with a sorrowful spirit and handed out alms very frequently; and she always pleased God as much as she could with words and deeds; and now as a reward, she has heavenly bliss. In this way shall a good widow heed her Lord.

XXXV. On the Church

It is right that Christians fervently adhere rightly to the Christian faith and readily honour and uphold the Christian Church every-where. We all have one heavenly father and one spiritual mother: she is named *Ecclesia*, that is, God's Church which we must always love and

---

canons forbid the blessings thereto and assign a penance for such men to perform' ('Se læwede mot swa-þeah be þæs apostoles leafe oðre siðe wifigan gyf his wif him ætfylð, ac þa canones forbeodað þa bletsunga þær-to and gesetton dædbote swylcum mannum to donne', §28).

105 Cf. Theodulf, *Capitula* XLIII and *Canons* 25. This prohibition is an abbreviated version of a broader injunction against marital sex on a lengthy list of holy days, including Sundays. Cf. Napier 58, p. 305, ll. 17–26. Haines 2010: 32n. 74.

106 Junius 121 locates this section in the midst of a series of short, non-Wulfstanian texts interposed between chapters X ('On Reeves', 'Be gerefan') and XVII ('On Priests', 'Be sacerdum'). I follow Jost in restoring it to the same place in the order of chapters that it occupied in *I Polity*.

107 Wulfstan here refers to Anna the Prophetess (not to be confused with Anna, mother of Mary), a widow at the temple in Jerusalem granted a vision of Christ. See *Luke* 2:36–7: 'And there was one Anna, a prophetess, the daughter of Phanuel, of the tribe of Aser; she was far advanced in years, and had lived with her husband seven years from her virginity. And she was a widow until fourscore and four years; who departed not from the temple, by fastings and prayers serving night and day'. On the historical context for this section, see Stafford 1999: 30–1.

respect.[108] And it is right that each church be under the protection of God and of all Christian people; and that church sanctuary is to prevail within the walls and is to be honoured no differently than protection from the king's own hand.[109] Thus, every church-sanctuary is Christ's own sanctuary and every Christian has a great obligation to treat that sanctuary with great respect.[110] Further, it is the responsibility of every Christian to sincerely love and honour God's Church, and he is to seek it out often and willingly for his own benefit.[111] Those in orders also must serve and minister there most often and intercede readily for all Christian people.[112] Accordingly, clergy who serve at the altar must ensure always that they especially set their lives in order in a manner rightly fitting to the Church. The Church is properly the spouse of the priest, and he who heeds God's law is to have nothing thenceforth to do with one who has taken orders, unless he utterly perish in mortal sin; and then must the Church's reeve take notice of that and resolve it and judge it just as the books instruct.[113] And no one must ever damage a church or threaten it with wrongdoing in any way.[114] Yet nonetheless, churches far and wide are now weakly protected and oppressed by evil and entirely deprived of ancient rights and stripped inside of everything proper.[115] Moreover, the Church's servants are everywhere deprived of honour and protection.[116] And woe unto him who causes this, even if he does not intend it, for each of those is assuredly the enemy of God himself who is the enemy of God's churches and who weakens or violates the rights of God's churches;[117] as it is written: *For anyone becomes the enemy of Christ who attempts to wrongly make use of*

108 Cf. *Sanctuary* 30, Bethurum 10b, l. 118, and 10c, ll. 41–5. On Wulfstan's use of the image of the maternal church in this passage and elsewhere, see Atkinson and Burton 2002: 52–3.

109 Cf. *EGu.* 1, *Sanctuary* 2, I Cn. 2.2, VI Atr. 14, *On the Laws of God* n. 15, and *On Justice* n. 6.

110 C.C.C.C. 201 replaces the second clause of this sentence with, 'and Christ justly possesses every ecclesiastical immunity'.

111 Cf. Bethurum 10c, ll. 151–2.

112 Cf. V Atr. 4.1, I Cn. 6a, *Clerical Compensation* 1, *Canons* 1, *On the Duties of the Laity* n. 5, and Napier 37, p. 179, l. 9. See also the version of this passage in *On the Sins of the Clergy*.

113 See above, *Polity* XXII, *Canons* 8 and 68a, and §29 in the A recension of Wulfstan's Canon Law Collection. See Cubitt 2009: 1041.

114 Cf. Bethurum 10b, ll. 33–5.

115 Cf. V Atr. 10.2 and Bethurum 20.3 (*Sermo Lupi ad Anglos*), ll. 40–2.

116 Cf. Bethurum 20.3 (*Sermo Lupi ad Anglos*), ll. 33–4.

117 Cf. *Sanctuary* 26, Bethurum 10c, ll. 45–51, and Napier 30, p. 143, ll. 15–19.

the goods of the Church, etc.[118] And St. Gregory spoke fearsomely about this also, when he said thus: W*hoever plunders the Church of Christ or violates its sanctity is to be anathema. Responding to which, all said: Amen.*[119] Everyone has a great duty to defend himself vigorously against these things; and each friend of God is to always watch over himself, so that he not mistreat the bride of Christ too greatly.[120] We all must love and praise one God and diligently adhere to one Christian faith and reject every heathen practice with all our might.[121] And let us faithfully uphold one royal lord, and let each friend support the other with true devotion.[122]

XXXVI. On All Christian People

It is right that all Christian people properly uphold their Christian faith, and live the life appropriate to them according to the law of God and the customs of the world;[123] and diligently arrange all manner of things according to the guidance of those who can guide them wisely and truly.[124] And this, then, is the most important of precepts: that each person love the one God over all other things and resolutely have one faith in him who first created us all and purchased us again at a dear price. And we also have need to reflect sincerely how we always may keep God's own commandments most rightly and perform all that we – or those who were our sponsors – promised when we received baptism.[125] This, then, is first: that one promises when one

118 Cf. Atto of Vercelli, *De pressuris ecclesiasticis*, 138.14. On this passage, see Bethurum 1957: 323–4 and 326–7.

119 Cf. Bethurum 10c, ll. 45–51 and Napier 30, p. 143, ll. 15–19.

120 Cf. Bethurum 10b, ll. 33–5.

121 Cf. *EGu.* Pr.1; V Atr 1, 34; VI Atr. 1.6; VIII Atr. 44; IX Atr. *explicit*; X Atr. 1; *Northumbrian Priests' Law* 47, 67; *On Justice* n. 50; *Canons* 16; and *On the Proper Support* n. 4.

122 Cf. VIII Atr. 44.1.

123 Cf. VIII Atr. 31.

124 Cf. *Evil Rulers*, n. 5.

125 Cf. Bethurum 10c, 'On Christianity' ('Be Cristendome'), ll. 36–8: 'And accomplish all of that which we or those who were our sponsors at the font promised when we received baptism' ('7 eal þæt gelæstan þæt þæt we behetan þa we fulluht underfengan oððon þa þe æt fontbæþe ure forespecan wæran'). The binding force of baptismal promises is a common theme in Wulfstan's work, and he particularly emphasises the social and political consequences that result from breaking those promises. This interaction of legal and religious influences his word choice here: the word *forespeca*, here used to signify the role of godparent or baptismal patron, also appears in Old English legal texts as a term for courtroom advocate. The extent to which the legal and religious functions of the *forespeca* overlapped is indicated by

seeks baptism to always spurn the devil and zealously avoid his evil teachings and always reject his injustice and eternally resist all of his company; and swiftly thereafter one sincerely proclaims many times with true faith that one thenceforth will always believe in one God forever, always love him over all other things, zealously heed his teachings forever, and keep his own commandments properly. And then that baptism will become like a covenant of all those words and all those promises, fulfil it who will.

And what I say is true: thenceforth, angels oversee every man forever after his baptism, how he fulfils what he earlier promised when he sought baptism. Let us reflect upon that repeatedly and sincerely abide by that which we promised when we received baptism, just as is our obligation. And let us order our words and deeds rightly, fervently cleanse our inmost thoughts, truly keep our oath and pledge, and frequently reflect on the great judgment to which we all must go; and zealously shield ourselves against the swelling flame of hellish torments, and earn for ourselves the glories and happiness which God has prepared for those who work his will in the world.[126] Amen.

---

the so-called 'Fonthill Letter', a record of a property dispute in which the author's godparental relationship to a failed thief leads to him serving as his legal advocate at trial. Rabin 2007: 223–55.

126 The final lines of *Polity* are derived nearly *verbatim* from the final lines of Bethurum 20.3 (*Sermo Lupi ad Anglos*): 'And very diligently accomplish that which we promised when we received baptism or those who were our sponsors at baptism. And let us order our words and works properly and diligently cleanse our consciences, and carefully fulfil oath and pledge, and have some loyalty between us without deception. And let us often reflect on that great judgment to which we all must go; and zealously shield ourselves against the swelling flame of hellish torments, and earn ourselves the glories and the happiness which God has prepared for those who work his will in the world' ('7 gelæstan swyþe georne þæt þæt we behetan þa þe fulluht underfengan, oððon þa þe æt fulluhte ure forespecan wæran, 7 utan word 7 weorc rihtlice fadian, 7 ure in geþanc clænsian georne, 7 að 7 wed wærlice healdan, 7 sume getrywða habban us betweonan butan uncræftan. 7 utan gelome understandan þone miclam Dom þe we ealle to sculon 7 beorgan us georne wið þone weallendan bryne helle wites, 7 geearnian us þa mærþa 7 þa myrhða þe God hæfð gegearwod þam þe his willan on worolde gewyrcað', ll. 169–77). On the connection between these two passages, see Rabin 2006: 393–4.

II
HOMILIES AND
HOMILETIC TRACTS

1. *ON THE LAWS OF GOD AND THE WORLD* (NAPIER 51)

This homily, likely the earliest surviving example of an address by Wulfstan to the royal council, survives only in London, British Library, Cotton Tiberius A.iii. Two possible dates have been proposed for its composition: Jost raises the possibility that it may have served as an address to open legal deliberations at the 1008 Enham meeting, while Wormald suggests that it might better be associated with the meetings in 1014 which promulgated the law-codes IX and X Æthelred.[1] Whichever date is correct, the considerable overlap between this homily and Wulfstan's legislation, especially V–VIII Æthelred, indicates its significance as an early statement of his views on the relationship between secular and ecclesiastical authority. Moreover, the fact that passages from this text recur in the major works of the second half of Wulfstan's career, including II Cnut and the *Institutes of Polity*, suggests that the archbishop himself may have seen this text as an important stage in the development of his thought.[2] Particularly noteworthy in this regard is the homily's discussion of *botleas* crimes, those 'for which no compensation can be made', the earliest extant mention of this category of wrongdoing and a topic he will return to in II Cnut.[3]

1 Jost 1950: 108 and Wormald 1999d: 337n. 344. See also Barlow 1979: 139n. 131 and Lionarons 2010: 170.

2 Lionarons 2010: 170–1 and Richards 2010: 153.

3 Wormald 1999d: 337n. 344 and Lionarons 2010: 171.

TRANSLATION[1]

To all the people:[2]

Beloved people, enact good secular laws and likewise govern so that our
Christian faith will remain steadfast, our lord's kingdom will advance,
and the protection of the people will be greater than it is now.[3] I shall
begin; let him conclude who will, or who knows better. This is a just
law: that one is to govern others in the manner that one desires to
be governed oneself.[4] This is the law which we must follow: first, we
must love and honour one God and reject every other;[5] and we must all
faithfully follow one royal lord[6] and all of us together defend our lives
and our land;[7] and we must diligently promote justice and abolish all
injustice.[8] Additionally, it is our foremost desire that the law of God
take precedence and secular law afterwards; and we desire peace and
friendship to be kept rightly before God and the world.[9] And if anyone
violates it in a way that permits compensation, let him sincerely make
amends for it.[10] Flagrant theft, treachery against one's lord, and evident
murder according to secular law are crimes for which no compensation

---

1 This translation is based on the text in Napier 1883: 274–5.

2 The rubric's indication that this homily was addressed to a general audience seems at
odds with its content, which implies a more specialised reception, most likely by the
royal council. Lionarons suggests that the rubric may be explained by the pairing of
the text in its manuscript with the short tracts forming part of the Pastoral Letter
(Bethurum 13), most of which are also addressed 'To all the people'. Lionarons 2010:
34. On the homily's possible audience, see Jost 1950: 105–6 and Wormald 1999d:
337n. 344.

3 The commission with which Wulfstan opens this homily recalls his reference to the
wise councillors who enacted just laws in *EGu.* Pr.2, *Sanctuary* 24, *Clerical Compensation* 11, and VIII Atr. 36. On this passage, see Davis-Secord 2008: 90–1.

4 *Matthew* 7:12: 'All things therefore whatsoever you would that men should do to
you, do you also to them' ('Omnia ergo quæcumque vultis ut faciant vobis homines,
et vos facite illis'). Cf. VI Atr. 49; I Cn. 18.2; *Sanctuary* 29; Bethurum 7 ll. 169–70;
Bethurum 8b, ll. 78–80; Bethurum 8c ll. 112–3; Bethurum 10c ll. 136–7; Bethurum
13 ll. 55–6; Bethurum 18 ll. 142–3; Napier 30, p. 144, ll. 1–2; Napier 37, p. 179, ll.
27–9; *On the Proper Support* n. 3; and *On the Duties of the Laity* n. 17. An interlinear
note in the manuscript adds the words 'unless that is hateful to the Lord' to the end
of this sentence.

5 Cf. *Exodus* 20:3, *Deuteronomy* 5:7.

6 OE *cynehlaford.* On the significance of Wulfstan's use of this word, see *On Justice*, n. 3.

7 Cf. V Atr. 35.

8 Cf. V Atr. 1.1, VI Atr. 8, X Atr. 2, and II Cn. 1.

9 Cf. V Atr. 1.1, VI Atr. 8, and X Atr. 2.1.

10 Cf. III Eg. 2.2, VIII Atr. 5.1, and I Cn. 3.2.

can be made.[11] Murderers, traitors, those who abandon their lord when he suffers greatest hardship for the needs of the people,[12] perjurers, and oath breakers are all hated by God, unless they repent for it before God and the world.[13] One is to diligently seek out his confessor for holy penance; and, if his confessor is unavailable, one is to seek out a lower-order bishop; and if one must go further, to the archbishop; and afterwards to the Pope, if he must, because of a greater need; we do not at all know where to direct him further after that, except to the highest, which is God himself.[14] And it is our desire that Church sanctuary and the sanctuary received from the hand of a Christian king remain equally inviolable.[15] Now henceforth, read the laws of God more fully. I ask, if it is appropriate of me, Holy Lord, that you have mercy on us all.

11 Cf. II As 4, III Eg. 7.3, VIII Atr. 1.1, I Cn. 2.3, and II Cn. 26 and 64. The connection between this passage and II Cn. 64 has been discussed in Bethurum 1957: 37; O'Brien 1996: 336n. 369; Wormald 1999d: 337n. 344; Lionarons 2010: 171; and Richards 2010: 153.

12 An interlinear note in the manuscript adds the words 'to join with his enemies' to the end of this clause.

13 Cf. Bethurum 10a, ll. 11–3; Bethurum 8c, ll. 161–3, *On Justice*, n. 10, *On the Proper Support*, n. 9, and *On Heathen Practices*, n. 8.

14 The reference to papal authority in this passage is, if not unique in Wulfstan's writings, certainly comparatively rare. Although Wulfstan was not anti-papal, he did demonstrate a marked ambivalence towards papal authority, and on at least one occasion, harshly admonished Pope Benedict VIII against the sin of simony. See Bethurum 1949: 97–104; Bethurum Loomis 1971: 134–5 and Barlow 1979: 270, 299–301.

15 Cf. *EGu.* 1, *Sanctuary* 2, I Cn. 2.2, VI Atr. 14, *On Justice* n. 6, and *Polity* XXXV.

2. ON VARIOUS MISFORTUNES (NAPIER 35)

This homily, a loose adaptation of Æthelred's 'penitential edict' of 1009 (VII Æthelred, translated below at pp. 186–8), survives in two manuscripts, Cambridge, Corpus Christi College 201 and Oxford, Bodleian Library, Hatton 113.[1] The text has long occupied a problematic place in Wulfstan's homiletic canon, largely because it fell prey early on to a reviser of considerably more enthusiasm than skill. The reviser's interpolations, which occur in both manuscripts, have led to questions regarding Wulfstan's authorship and the relationship of this text to Napier 36, also an adaptation of VII Æthelred though by a different author.[2] The translation below follows Napier in bracketing those passages likely inserted by someone other than Wulfstan.[3]

The chief interest of this homily lies in the way in which it revises the specific prescriptions of VII Æthelred for general application.[4] VII Æthelred decreed a series of penitential rituals to be undertaken as a response to the 1009 invasion of England by a Viking army under the leadership of Thurkil the Tall.[5] Here, mentions of the particular circumstances surrounding the 1009 edict have been replaced with a more general reference to any 'great misfortune befall[ing] the realm because of the people's deeds – war or hunger, fire or bloodshed, crop failure or bad weather, the death of men or cattle from a sudden plague'. Together with the Latin and Old English texts of VII Æthelred, it thus provides a useful illustration of the process by which Wulfstan translated law into homily.

---

1 On VII Atr., see Wormald 1999d: 331–2; and Keynes 2007: 179–89. See also Introduction, pp. 32–3 and below, pp. 184–5.

2 Jost 1950: 211–16; Bethurum 1957: 38; and Lionarons 2010: 31–2.

3 See Napier 1883: 169n.

4 Wormald 1999: 331–2; Keynes 2007: 189; and Lionarons 2010: 144–5.

5 On Thurkil, see below, *Cnut 1020*, n. 3.

TRANSLATION[1]

CONCERNING VARIOUS MISFORTUNES[2]

If it comes about that a great misfortune befalls the realm because of the people's deeds – war or hunger, fire or bloodshed, crop failure or bad weather, the death of men or cattle from a sudden plague[3] – then amends always is to be made to God himself. Foremost among all things is that one is to [go to confession,][4] yield to righteousness and renounce sin,[5] and then afterwards do just as David did along with many others: call upon Christ with a remorseful spirit.[6] Also, like the Ninevites, [if counselled to do so,] one is to [cast off for a time gold and adornments, set aside each weapon of war and every legal dispute, and] take up [sackcloth or] wool as clothing for the body and fast very zealously. God is exceedingly merciful: the Ninevites had wholly descended into sin but, as was necessary for themselves, they turned to righteousness, engaged in fasting, and prayed sincerely with a remorseful spirit, and that may serve as an example.[7] Therefore, as often as the need arises, let us immediately proclaim a fast of three days; and everyone is to seek confession most urgently, diligently attend God's church with bare feet [both day and night], and process out with the holy relics and the litany.[8] Furthermore, alms are to be given according to what is deemed necessary: a penny per head, a penny per field, a loaf of the finest ingredients for each usable hearth, or whatever else the royal council considers needful – [sometimes a contribution of wax, sometimes one of malt, sometimes the bathing of the poor or the washing of their feet,[9]

---

1 This translation is based on the text in Napier 1883: 169–72.

2 On the rubric to this homily, see the note to the rubric of VIIa Atr. below.

3 Wulfstan returns to this sequence of misfortunes relatively frequently throughout his writings. See, for instance, Bethurum 5, ll. 102–5; Bethurum 20.1, ll. 50–4 and (in an abbreviated version) Bethurum 20.3, ll. 55–6; Napier 47, p. 243, ll. 1–4, and *On Justice*, n. 17. See also *God's Threat*, n. 7.

4 The bracketed passages are found in the MSS but Napier suggests that they are likely interpolations by someone other than Wulfstan. See Napier 1883: 169. Further discussion on this issue can be found in Jost 1950: 216.

5 Cf. Bethurum 19, ll. 76–8; Bethurum 20.3, ll. 90–2; and Napier 36, p. 172, l. 21.

6 Although a specific reference in unclear here, it seems likely that Wulfstan is alluding to what Cassiodorus designated the seven 'Penitential Psalms': *Psalms* 6, 32, 38, 51, 102, 130, and 143 (6, 31, 37, 50, 101, 129, and 142 according to the Septuagint numbering).

7 Cf. *Jonah* 3:6–10.

8 Cf. VII Atr. 2–2.3 and VIIa Atr. 2–2.1.

9 Cf. *Polity* VII.

sometimes the distribution of alms,] sometimes the assessing of a tithe, either on all men equally or on freemen, sometimes one and sometimes the other; the royal council shall judge according to the needs of the people.[10] And, as is necessary, every priest while celebrating mass is to call upon Christ most urgently without delay[– as masses for every necessity are included in the Church books and one is to diligently attend to them and to holy prayers when the need arises; that is somewhat better than seeking after the efforts of witches and wizards for any necessity –]and all the servants of God [as it is needed] are to inter- cede zealously by reciting the psalms [on behalf of all the people, and at service to sing, prostrate and with outstretched limbs, a certain psalm, the Prayers, and Collect, and fervently pray for favour and mercy for the whole realm,][11] and God's poor[– whom one also is to remember often, so that they also might call to call upon Christ most sincerely –] are to pray wholeheartedly for those who treat them well; and for three days [on which a fast is proclaimed, all of] the poor slaves of every man are to be freed from labour for attendance at church and so that they can keep the fast more willingly and work on their own behalf if they so desire [and also call upon Christ most fervently].[12] Yet if they then do not observe that fast properly, they are to suffer a beating, and if a free man is so greedy as to break the fast or does not hand over his alms properly in the manner proclaimed, he is to compensate for it in the manner that the shire court[13] determines [or in this fashion, if it so happens: a householder with thirty pennies, a thegn with thirty shillings, and wherever that fine comes to be assessed, each penny is to be distributed for God's favour].[14] Moreover, everyone is to willingly distribute their own food, which they would have enjoyed had the fast not been proclaimed, to God's poor in order to obtain God's favour.[15] Yet indeed, the greatest obligation is to turn from sin to righteous- ness, renounce evil, uphold God's law, heed spiritual teachings most diligently, and faithfully fulfil all that was promised in exchange for God's favour. May God preserve us.[16] Amen.

10 Cf. VII Atr. 1–1.3 and VIIa Atr. 2.2, 2.3, and 3.

11 Cf. VII Atr. 2.2a and 3; VIIa Atr. 6–6.3.

12 Cf. VII Atr. 2.3 and VIIa Atr. 5.1.

13 On this stipulation, see Wormald 1999d: 332n. 318; and Keynes 2007: 189.

14 Cf. VII Atr. 2.4–5 and VIIa Atr. 3.

15 Cf. VII Atr. 2.2b and VIIa Atr. 4–4.1

16 Cf. VII Atr. 7.1 and VIIa Atr. 8.

3. ON THE PROPER SUPPORT OF THE CHURCH
(NAPIER 22/BETHURUM 13, ll. 53–106)

This text and the two which follow form part of a series of seven homiletic fragments (Napier 19–25) sometimes referred to as the *Sermones ad Populum*. Variations on the *Sermones* group survive in four manuscripts: C.C.C.C. 201, C.C.C.C. 419, Oxford, Bodleian Library, Hatton 113, and London, British Library, Cotton Tiberius A.iii.[1] The configuration and content of the group differ from manuscript to manuscript, and these differences highlight the complexities involved in attempting to ascertain the relationship between the individual fragments. Three of the four manuscripts treat the fragments as discrete units with individual rubrics, yet Hatton 113 joins them into a single continuous text. C.C.C.C. 201 preserves the distinguishing rubrics, yet adds a preface before Napier 19 which indicates that the texts may have circulated together as some sort of pastoral letter – a further complication, as internal evidence suggests that at least a few of the texts had originally been composed for oral delivery as homilies.[2] Moreover, the facts that the order of texts differs slightly between manuscripts, that not every text appears in every manuscript, and that individual fragments were taken over as components of other texts such as Napier 30 and the E-text of the Old English Sunday Letter indicate that the fragments may at one time have circulated independently of one another.[3] Indeed, it is far from clear that the fragments were even composed at the same time. Both Wormald and Pons-Sanz date Napier 23–6 to the period between 1020 and 1023, while dating Napier 19–22 to either *ca.* 1007 (Wormald) or *ca.* 1015 (Pons-Sanz).[4] The difficulty in ascertaining the relationship between these texts is reflected in the widely varying approaches adopted by their modern editors: Napier follows the majority of the manuscripts in editing the fragments as discrete texts; Bethurum edits Napier's 19–22 as a single continuous text which she calls 'A Pastoral Letter' (though she omits C.C.C.C. 201's preface), but leaves out Napier's 23–6 on generic grounds; and Lionarons edits the entire series together based on the text in Hatton 113 as a single composite homily she calls the *Sermo ad Populum*.[5] Ultimately, it remains

---

1 The texts likely also were included in Cotton Otho B.x; however, this manuscript was mostly consumed in the Ashburnham House fire of 1731 so confirmation is impossible. Ker 1957: 227 and Lionarons 2004b: 165.

2 Cf. Bethurum 1957: 339.

3 Scragg 1977: 197; Scragg 1998: 15–21; Lionarons 2004b: 159–65; and Haines 2010: 92.

4 Wormald 2004: 26–7 and Pons-Sanz 2007: 25.

5 Napier 1883: 108–27; Bethurum 1957: 225–32; and Lionarons 2004b: 176–82.

unclear whether Wulfstan composed a single homily which he then divided into sections for more convenient reuse or if he instead composed a series of individual fragments that he later reedited as a single text. Though less likely, one also cannot dismiss the possibility that a later scribe reworked a series of genuine Wulfstan fragments into a composite homily after the archbishop's death.[6]

The three texts translated here (Napier 22–4) are those of the series which Wormald labelled 'quasi-legislative' and Lionarons categorised as among Wulfstan's 'Political Homilies'.[7] Each reworks legal material on a discrete theme – the prerogatives of the Church, tithing obligations, and baptismal regulations – into homiletic or quasi-homiletic form. Of these texts, *On the Proper Support of the Church* (Napier 22/Bethurum 13, ll. 53–106) is likely the earliest as well as the one with the best claim to stand alone as a complete homily. Beginning and ending in a conventional homiletic fashion, the text reads as a fully developed sermon prepared for oral delivery. Though the circumstances behind its composition remain unclear, the discussion of secular and ecclesiastical dues in the second paragraph indicates that it may have been motivated by the need to combat the misperception that the collection of tithes would replace the taxes decreed by royal legislation for the support of the Church.[8]

6 This last possibility is raised in Scragg 1998: 18.

7 Wormald 2004: 17 and Lionarons 2010: 164, 169–70.

8 On this point, see Lionarons 2010: 169.

TRANSLATION[1]

To the People:[2]

Beloved people, let us do what is necessary for us: be diligent about our obligations, renounce our sins, turn from every wrong, and submit wholeheartedly to righteousness. Moreover, let us recognise that there is no rule better than this: that we are to render unto others that which we desire to be rendered unto ourselves;[3] and let us remember that we have one Heavenly Father and that we all are brothers in the Christian faith. Therefore, no Christian is to act all too wickedly towards others, because all that he does now to bring pain to others wrongfully through words or deeds shall afterwards harm him many times over, unless he first repents of it. Instead, let us work diligently to please the almighty God, to have true peace among ourselves and good will towards all, and always to donate to the Church the portion that we can, and earn for ourselves eternal happiness.

Let us be obedient, so that we may uphold our Christian faith more virtuously, and reject every heathen practice,[4] preserve our true faith, devote ourselves to attending church often and frequently by day and night, live the life that our confessors commend to us, always assiduously keep our oath and pledge, properly observe holy seasons and fast-days, readily distribute alms and, with a willing spirit, pay the dues owed to the Church, namely the tenth portion of all those things which God has granted us in this transitory life as well as the first fruits of our labours and our crops, and we will earn with that little offering much more for our own benefit.[5] Furthermore, this must be understood as well: that we

---

1 This translation is based on the texts in Napier 1883: 112–15 and Bethurum 1957: 228–32.

2 The rubric occurs only in C.C.C.C. 201 and Oxford, Bodleian Library, Hatton 113.

3 *Matthew* 7:12: 'All things therefore whatsoever you would that men should do to you, do you also to them' ('Omnia ergo quæcumque vultis ut faciant vobis homines, et vos facite illis'). Cf. VI Atr. 49; I Cn. 18.2; *Sanctuary* 29; Bethurum 7 ll. 169–70; Bethurum 8b, ll. 78–80; Bethurum 8c ll. 112–13; Bethurum 10c ll. 136–7; Bethurum 13 ll. 55–6; Bethurum 18 ll. 142–3; Napier 30, p. 144, ll. 1–2; Napier 37, p. 179, ll. 27–9; *On the Laws of God* n. 4; and *On the Duties of the Laity* n. 17.

4 Cf. *EGu*. Pr.1; V Atr 1, 34; VI Atr. 1.6; VIII Atr. 44; IX Atr. *explicit*; X Atr. 1; *NPL* 47, 67; *Polity* XXXV; *On Justice* n. 50; and *Canons* 16.

5 Cf. *Canons* 49 and VIII Atr. 6. Bethurum suggests that this passage has its ultimate origin in *Ecclesiastes* 3:3: 'Water quencheth a flaming fire, and alms resisteth sins' ('ignem ardentem extinguit aqua et elemosyna resistit peccatis'). See Bethurum 1957: 341.

must also humbly pay the yearly dues that our predecessors[6] previously promised to God, specifically plough-dues, dues owed to Rome, dues for the upkeep of the church, and dues for the lighting of the church; and he who does as I say acts for his own great benefit.[7] Certainly, it is entirely true, believe it who will, that a time will come for each of us when we will wish, more than anything remaining to us in this world, that, while we could, we had always willingly behaved in the way that God desired; but when that time comes, we will receive only the reward that we earned while alive.[8]

Woe unto that person, then, who has hitherto earned the pains of Hell! In that place, eternal flame is fiercely intermingled and there is eternal terror, there is eternal suffering, and there is sorrow and sadness and perpetual grief for all time, there is loss and lamentation, there is every misery and the gathering of all the devils. Woe unto that person who must abide there in torment! It would have been better for him had he never become a man when he did. There is no one alive who can recount all of the agonies a person must suffer who falls entirely into those torments; and it is all the worse because no relief will ever come to him as long as the world shall last. There shall be the murderers, there shall be the perjurers, there shall be the adulterers and the foul fornicators, there shall be the witches and the child-killers, there shall be the thieves and pillagers, the robbers and the plunderers and, swiftest to relate, all the sinners who anger God, except those who turn aside and repent the more sincerely.[9] For the love of God, we enjoin each person to reflect upon himself. Let us wholeheartedly turn away from sin and, with our inmost hearts, beg God to protect us from that terror. Let us diligently shun wickedness, murder, manslaughter, theft, robbery, and treachery; and let us shield ourselves from fornication and every kind of corruption; and let us fervently love righteousness and renounce every

---

6 The reference to 'our predecessors' ('ure yldran') likely is a specific reference to Kings Æthelstan, Edmund, and Edgar, whose provisions on Church dues provide the immediate sources for Wulfstan's treatment of the topic. See esp. I As. Pr.1, I Em. 2, II Eg. 2–5, and IV Eg. 1.4 and 6. Robertson 1925: 337 and Bethurum 1957: 342.

7 Cf. II Eg. 2.3, 3, Bethurum 13, l. 74, *Canons* 54, *On Tithes*, n. 4, and *On Christian Practices*, n. 6.

8 I Cnut 18, 18a.

9 Cf. Bethurum 3, ll. 66–73 and Bethurum 7, ll. 122–34. See also II Cn. 7; Bethurum 7, l. 131; Bethurum 10a, l. 14; Bethurum 13, l. 95; Bethurum 20.3, l. 165; Napier 42, p. 203, l. 24; Napier 57, pp. 298, ll. 15–6; *On Heathen Practices*, n. 8; *On Justice*, n. 10; and *Polity* II and IX. For an abbreviated version of this list, see *On the Laws of God*, n. 13.

injustice.[10] Let us confess our sins to our confessors while we may and can, and repent and avoid sin hereafter, and give to the Church as much as we are most able; then shall we protect ourselves against eternal punishment and earn for ourselves the heavenly kingdom.

10 Cf. Bethurum 8c, ll. 160–3; Bethurum 20.3, 133–40; and VI Atr. 28.2.

4. *ON THE DUTIES OF THE CLERGY* (NAPIER 52)

This homily and its companion, *On the Sins of the Clergy* (Napier 53) survive in only a single manuscript, London, British Library, Cotton Tiberius A.iii. Together, the two texts are a revised and abbreviated version of *The Institutes of Polity*, chapter XVII, 'Concerning Priests'. Given their closer affinity to the later version of this chapter in II *Polity*, it is likely Wulfstan composed them sometime *ca.* 1019 or 1020. This date is far from certain, however, and Wormald suggests that they may have been composed a few years earlier while Pons-Sanz offers no opinion.[1]

The principal question regarding these two texts is whether they merely represent variant versions of *Polity* XVII or if Wulfstan instead intended them to be circulated independently as homilies. Bethurum, Whitelock, and Jost viewed the texts as *Polity* variants, yet the nature of Wulfstan's revisions suggests that he may have been reworking them for oral delivery.[2] Fewer signs of these revisions occur in *On the Duties* than in *On the Sins*, but there are several worth noting. As Lionarons points out, not only has Wulfstan shortened his original to produce a far more focused text, but he has also replaced the rubric from *Polity* with one more in keeping with his homiletic writings.[3] Equally significant is the texts' presence in Tiberius A.iii, a manuscript of Canterbury origins containing clerical texts, including a number of Wulfstan homilies. That these texts, the only excerpts from *Polity* to circulate independently of the other chapters, should have been included in a compilation of this sort suggests that they were viewed as homilies or, at the very least, homiletic fragments. As such, although they lack many of the stylistic markers found in the archbishop's other sermons (especially an opening address to 'Leofan men'), it seems right to agree with Lionarons' conclusion that 'they should be restored to the Wulfstanian homiletic canon'.[4]

---

1 Wormald 2004: 27 and Pons-Sanz 2007: 25.

2 Bethurum 1957: 38; Jost 1959: 85–102; Whitelock 1965: 220–1; and Whitelock 1966: 22.

3 Lionarons 2010: 165–6.

4 Lionarons 2010: 35.

TRANSLATION[1]

To mass-priests:[2]

A priest in his parish must wisely and sensibly lead and instruct the spiritual flock which he is to protect. He must both preach well and set a good example for others; and at God's judgment, he must render into God's hand an account both of his own deeds and of those people he is to oversee.[3] Thus if he acts rightly,[4] he may not hesitate before either the humble or the mighty[5] to declare that which is most just to men,[6] for he does not do as he ought if he is ashamed to proclaim what is right; and should he conceal it with his silence, he will be repaid bitterly for it in the life to come.[7] Should any of our shepherds overlook even one sheep, we will require that he pay for it. How then will those shepherds fare at God's fearful judgment, who cannot protect the spiritual flocks which they should guide into the hands of Christ,[8] but because of their ignorance they know neither how to lead, how to teach, nor how to tend? Now we think, with what, then, will they pay for them? Woe unto them, then, that they ever received a spiritual flock which they could not protect.[9] How can a blind man lead another? How can an

---

1 This translation is based on the text in Napier 1883: 275–6.

2 Lionarons observes that, 'the change in the rubric from *Polity*'s "Concerning Priests" to the homily's "To Masspriests" is the first indication that the text was rewritten for oral delivery'. Lionarons 2010: 165.

3 *Polity* XVII reads, 'of their own deeds and of those people they are to oversee'. It then follows this sentence with, 'And if they shall have done anything, they may not hesitate, neither out of fear nor love of any person, to proclaim justice and forbid injustice. The shepherd will be of little use to the fold who will not protect the flock, which he must defend with an outcry if he can do nothing else, if the corruptor of the people begins to raid. There is no corruptor as evil as the devil himself. He is concerned with thing always: how he might most defile the souls of men. Therefore must those shepherds who would protect the people against the corruptor be most watchful and vigorous in their warnings. Those are the bishops and the mass-priests who must protect and oversee their spiritual flock with wise teaching'.

4 *Polity* XVII: 'Thus if he would protect himself …'

5 *Polity* XVII: '… either out of love or fear …'

6 *Polity* XVII inserts, 'Nor may he hesitate before either the humble or the mighty …'

7 The final clause of this sentence ('and should … to come') is omitted from *Polity* XVII. It reads instead, 'He will fare miserably if, through his weakness, the flock which he must protect should perish, and he himself with it'.

8 *Polity* XVII: 'who cannot protect the spiritual flocks which Christ purchased with his own life, and which they must protect if they can.'

9 *Polity* XVII: 'Woe unto them, then, that they ever received that which they could not protect'.

ignorant man teach another? Woe unto them who receive a spiritual flock and can tend neither to themselves nor to the flock which they must protect, and worse are those who can and will not.

5. *ON THE SINS OF THE CLERGY* (NAPIER 53)

This text likely was composed at the same time as *On the Duties of the Clergy* (Napier 52) and follows it on fol. 94v. of London, British Library, Cotton Tiberius A.iii, its sole manuscript witness.[1] Like *On the Duties*, *On the Sins* is excerpted from chapter XVII of the *Institutes of Polity*, beginning with the sentence on which its predecessor leaves off. Also like *On the Duties*, *On the Sins* has been extensively shortened and revised, almost certainly by Wulfstan himself.[2] The revisions suggest that Wulfstan intended this text also to be read as an independent homily, rather than just a variant of *Polity* XVII.[3] Not only has a new rubric been added to the text, but Wulfstan also incorporates a traditional homiletic conclusion: 'Holy Lord, have mercy upon us all! Amen'.[4] Taken together with its companion, the preponderance of evidence thus seems to indicate that Wulfstan revised, or perhaps was in the process of revising, these texts to circulate as homilies separate from the remainder of *Polity*.

---

1 For a discussion of this text's date and circumstances of composition, see the introduction to *On the Duties of the Clergy*, p. 138 above.

2 The evidence that Wulfstan himself carried out the revisions to these two texts has been surveyed in Lionarons 2010: 164–6.

3 The suggestion that *On the Duties* and *On the Sins* are only variants of *Polity* XVII occurs in Bethurum 1957: 38; Jost 1959: 85–102; Whitelock 1965: 220–1; Whitelock 1966: 22. On this point, see the introduction to *On the Duties of the Clergy*, p. 138 above.

4 On the concluding prayer, see Lionarons 2010: 166.

TRANSLATION[1]

To mass-priests:

Alas, there are many of those who seek the priesthood wrongfully, to take priestly orders out of a desire for worldly gain, and they do not know that which they should know.[2] About them the prophet spoke most fearsomely[3] and said thus: *Woe unto the priests who eat the sins of the people, etc.* That is, in English: Woe to the priests, he said, who devour the people's sins.[4] Those are the ones who know not to warn the people against sins and punish sins, but take their money in the form of tithes and many other dues; yet they neither teach them well with preaching, nor lead them well with examples, nor intercede for them with prayer.[5] There is great need, then, that he who erred beforehand readily repent for it henceforth;[6] and he who would be protected by God must amend himself thereby, or he will perish entirely in the afterlife. Bitter will be the repayment he receives as a dead man, unless he compensates fully with masses, psalm-singing, and charity. Holy Lord, have mercy upon us all! Amen.

1 This translation is based on the text in Napier 1883: 276–7.

2 *Polity* XVII: 'Alas, alas, there are many of those who, as it may seem, seek the priesthood wrongfully, most for idle glory and worldly wealth, and they do not know that which they should know'.

3 'most fearsomely': omitted from *Polity* XVII.

4 *Hosea* 4:8. *Polity* XVII: 'Woe to the priests, he said, who devour and consume the people's sins'.

5 *Polity* XVII: 'Those are the ones who will not or cannot or dare not warn the people against sins and punish sins, but nonetheless desire their money in the form of tithes and all Church dues; yet they neither lead them well with examples, nor teach them well with preaching, nor heal them well with penances, nor intercede for them with prayer; instead, they scavenge people's possessions for whatever they can grab, just as gluttonous ravens do from a carcass wherever they can. It is all the worse, once they have it all: then they do not treat it at all as they should, but they decorate their women with that which should be on the altars; and they exploit for their own worldly pride and idle vanity that which they should put towards the worship of God in Church affairs or towards assistance to the needy or towards the ransoming of captives or towards some matters which might be of enduring benefit both to themselves and to those who give to them their goods for the love of God'.

6 The text following 'henceforth' is omitted from *Polity* XVII.

6. *ON JUSTICE, VIRTUE AND THE LAW* (NAPIER 50)

Napier 50 is among the most puzzling of Wulfstan's homilies; yet as a late-career summation of his political vision, it also is among his most compelling. The text survives only in C.C.C.C. 421, a manuscript compiled after the archbishop's death, containing only one other authentic Wulfstan homily (Bethurum 3) but two spurious texts (Napier 47 and 49). This fact, along with the text's patchwork structure and obvious debt to the laws of Cnut (which he refused to accept as Wulfstan's compositions) led Jost to ascribe this text to a 'Wulfstan-imitator'.[1] This claim has since been refuted on the basis of both internal and external evidence, and the homily now holds a secure place in Wulfstan's canon.[2] The text undoubtedly dates to the end of Wulfstan's career, yet how close to the end remains subject to debate. Bethurum argues for a date after 1020 and Lionarons goes so far as to suggest that this may be Wulfstan's final sermon.[3] Somewhat more plausible is Wormald's dating of *ca.* 1017–1018: commonalities in structure and source material between *On Justice* and Cnut's legislation of 1018 indicate that the two texts are, at the very least, contemporaneous, and it seems likely that the sermon was preached as part of the deliberations involved in composing the laws.[4]

The homily consists of a series of passages from Wulfstan's other writings woven together into an extended meditation on secular authority, Christian morality, and, in its final movement, the fate of a fallen people in a world hastening towards its end. The structure of the text is somewhat more awkward than many of Wulfstan's earlier works: passages are taken from other texts largely without revision and bound together by only the barest of transitions. Bethurum suggests that this awkwardness may indicate that the surviving text is only an unfinished draft, a set of notes for oral delivery, or simply a late composition produced when the archbishop's powers were in decline.[5] More recently, however, Lionarons has demonstrated that the text is far more skilfully composed than hitherto recognised.[6] Tracing the ways

---

1 Jost 1950: 249–61.

2 Bethurum 1957: 39–40; Whitelock 1966: 21–2; and Kennedy 1983: 64–5.

3 Bethurum 1957: 40 and Lionarons 2010: 175.

4 Wormald 1999d: 335–6. The similarities between this text and Cnut's 1018 law-code were first noticed in Kennedy 1983: 64ff. The 1018 date has also been accepted in Pons-Sanz 2007: 25.

5 Bethurum 1957: 40–1.

6 Lionarons 2004a: 413–28 and Lionarons 2010: 171–5.

in which Wulfstan draws together passages from both his earlier and later works, she claims that this sermon marks his return 'to the writing of his early years to give a last warning to the *witan* about the last days that would inevitably arrive, coming full circle from the beginning of his career a quarter of a century earlier'.[7]

7 Lionarons 2010: 175.

TRANSLATION[1]

A SERMON[2]

We declare to our royal lord[3] and desire to make known to all the people that this is foremost: that we all submit wholeheartedly to God almighty, uphold his commandments, renounce all injustice, accustom and persuade ourselves to the performance of every kind of righteous deed, confess our sins – just as is necessary for us – and fervently repent and henceforth refrain from them as zealously as we can, and always obey our lord loyally and faithfully.[4] Moreover, God's Church is to be held in greater respect and possessed of greater protection than it has hitherto been;[5] in particular, sanctuary within the walls of God's church and sanctuary received from the hand of a Christian king are to be held equally inviolable.[6] Also, it is fitting that the Christian king of a Christian people be, as is proper, a comfort to his people and a just shepherd over a Christian flock.[7] It is likewise fitting for him that he promote Christianity with all his might, everywhere encourage and protect God's Church, always defend the honour of the Church,[8] and reconcile and bring peace to all Christian folk with just law, as readily as he can; and he shall embrace righteousness in every way before God and the world. For in this way, he shall himself thrive first and his people also if he embraces justice before God and the world. And it is fitting for him to zealously aid those who seek justice and always fiercely restrain those who pursue wickedness. He must punish evil men severely with

---

1 This translation is based on the text in Napier 1883: 266–74.

2 Preceding this text in the manuscript is Wulfstan's eschatological homily *Secundam Lucam* (Bethurum 3). It is possible that the scribe intended the two homilies to be read as a single unit, with the eschatological conclusion to this text echoing the apocalyptic themes of *Secundam Lucam*. See Lionarons 2004a: 417–18.

3 The term Wulfstan uses here is *cynehlaford*, a term which may indicate an expansion of traditional notions of lordship and anticipate the notion of the 'liege lord' that will emerge in the next century. See Abels 1988a: 94. Cf. *On the Laws of God* n. 6.

4 Cf. IX Atr. 1. For an earlier version of this injunction, see VI Atr. 1–1.1.

5 Lionarons argues that the repeated references to how things have been 'hitherto' (*ær þysan* and *ær þysum* in the text) provide evidence that the homily was only composed after Cnut had assumed the throne and restored stability to the kingdom. See Lionarons 2004a: 419.

6 Cf. *EGu.* 1, *Sanctuary* 2, I Cn. 2.2, VI Atr. 14, *On the Laws of God* n. 15, and *Polity* ch. XXXV.

7 Cf. VIII Atr. 2.1 and *Polity* II. The remainder of this paragraph is drawn from *Polity* II.

8 This clause can also be translated as an injunction to defend the property of the Church.

secular discipline, and he must detest and destroy murderers, traitors and perjurers,[9] homicides and parricides, enemies of the Church and slayers of priests, those who violate holy orders and those who violate their marriage vows, thieves and vandals, robbers and plunderers, liars and hypocrites, those who break their oaths and those who deny their faith, and he is to harshly repel all of the enemies of God.[10] In the pursuit of justice he must be both merciful and severe: merciful to the good and strict with the evil. Indeed, for how shall relief and comfort come to God's servants and God's poor except through Christ and a Christian king? He must study the learning found in books most attentively, and diligently heed God's commandments, and pursue wisdom with his council, if he wishes to obey God faithfully.

Every just throne stands on three pillars: first, *those who pray*; second, *those who labour*; and third, *those who fight*. *Those who pray* are the clergy, who must serve God and fervently plead for all the people day and night. *Those who labour* are the workers who must toil for that by which the entire community may live. *Those who fight* are the warriors who must protect the land by waging war with weapons. On these three pillars must each throne rightly stand.[11] If any of them weaken, immediately the throne will tremble; and if any of them fracture, then the throne will crumble to pieces, and that will bring that people all to ruin. Therefore, they are to be diligently steadied, strengthened, and reinforced with God's wise teachings and with just worldly law; in that way they will bring lasting guidance to the people. And what I say is true: if Christian faith weakens, the kingdom will soon crumble.[12]

Furthermore, we proclaim to the nobles, generals, judges, and reeves that they have the obligation to zealously renounce injustice and embrace righteousness before God and the world,[13] and never through foolishness, nor out of bribery or friendship, neglect their wisdom so that

9 Richard Abels suggests that Wulfstan's use of the word 'hlafordswican' (lit. 'traitors to their lord') identifies the betrayal of an individual lord with a broader notion of treason to one's king and nation. See Abels 1988a: 94–5.

10 Cf. II Cn. 7; Bethurum 7, l. 131; Bethurum 10a, l. 14; Bethurum 13, l. 95; Bethurum 20.3, l. 165; Napier 42, p. 203, l. 24; Napier 57, pp. 298, ll. 15–16; *On the Proper Support*, n. 9; On *Heathen Practices*, n. 8; and *Polity* IX. For an abbreviated version of this list, see *On the Laws of God*, n. 13.

11 On the homiletic use of this passage, see Davis-Secord 2008: 92–4.

12 This paragraph is taken from Polity IV. For a full discussion of Wulfstan's sources, see the notes for that section.

13 Cf. II Cn. 7.1; *Episc.* 9; *Cn. 1020* 15; Bethurum 11, l. 127; Bethurum 13, l. 103; Bethurum 21, ll. 26–7; and *Polity* II. The similarities between this passage and *Cn. 1020* 15 are discussed in Abels 1988a: 94; Cubitt 2009: 1041.

they twist injustice into justice or pronounce unjust rulings harmful to the poor;[14] rather, they are to aid the clergy in the observance of God's laws better than they have done before this. Too widely and for too long have God's laws been reviled and his doctrines despised, and secular law has been horribly perverted in this realm on every side; and it is evident far and wide that God has been angered by this wickedness for all too long. Let those who now must guide this people repent whole-heartedly, just as God desires, if they wish to appease God rightly and preserve themselves on that great day better than they did previously when they promoted wickedness to their own ruin. For this reason we have endured many wounds and indignities, and if we are to receive any remedy then we must strive to deserve it from God better than we have done hitherto. Indeed, formerly treachery was everywhere greater than wisdom, and at that time he was considered wisest who was most devious and who understood most cunningly how to profess falsely that lies were truth and the unjust how to judge others to their detriment; but woe unto them for their cunning and all of their pride![15] Nor did it prosper before this within or without, but there was hostility and hunger, fire and bloodshed on every side over and over again;[16] and robbery, murder, slander, hatred, and thieves' looting have harmed us most gravely, and likewise bad weather has often brought us crop failure.[17] Therefore, as it may seem, there have been and remains in this realm many injustices and inconstant loyalties among men.[18] Many are forsworn and griev-ously perjured, and pledges have been broken over and over again; and it is evident among this people that the wrath of God has fallen furiously upon us, recognise it who can.[19] So let us, according to our obligation, act to bring about a remedy, renounce wickedness, and yield to righteous-ness; then, if we so desire, we may soon merit God's mercy.[20]

14 Cf. *Polity* IX.

15 Cf. *Evil Rulers*, n. 8.

16 About the pairing 'bryne and blodgite' (translated here as 'fire and bloodshed'), Andy Orchard writes, 'It is apt testament to the troubled times in which he lived that among the many alliterative doublets with which he peppers his prose, the phrase *bryne and blodgite* ("burning and bloodletting"), which is found no fewer than nine times in extant Old English, should appear only in works that for one reason or another have been associated with Wulfstan'. Orchard 2007: 311.

17 Cf. Bethurum 5, ll. 102–5; Bethurum 20.1, ll. 50–4 and (in an abbreviated version) Bethurum 20.3, ll. 55–6; Napier 47, p. 243, ll. 1–4, and *On Various Misfortunes*, n. 3. See also *God's Threat*, n. 7.

18 Cf. Bethurum 20.3 (*Sermo Lupi ad Anglos*), ll. 48–61.

19 Cf. Bethurum 20.3 (*Sermo Lupi ad Anglos*), ll. 93–6 and Napier 27, p. 129, ll. 1–10.

20 Cf. IX Atr. 1; Bethurum 13, ll. 53–5; and Napier 27, p. 129, ll. 10–12.

And it is also right that God's servants, bishops and abbots, monks and monastic women, priests and nuns observe the rule and live according to the canons or forfeit their worldly honour; and that those who live their lives virtuously are to be zealously encouraged and honoured; and that those who will not yield to God's law are to be deemed outlaws unless they return to righteousness.[21] Rather, every man is to submit wholeheartedly to righteousness and every monk to his monastery or depart from this realm altogether.[22] Moreover, it is right that neither anyone bearing weapons nor laymen eat or drink in the monastery refectory among the monks unless accompanied by our lord or anyone else who has a greater fear of God so that it is the better for his presence before God and the world and their rule is not the more dishonoured.[23] Additionally, priests and nuns are to order their lives properly for God's mercy and their own benefit; and we admonish and instruct all of God's servants, especially the mass-priests, to obey God, preserve their purity, and protect themselves against God's wrath and the raging fire that burns in hell.[24] They know full well that they are not to have the companionship of a woman in fornication, but it is even worse that some have two or more, and some abandon the one they had previously and, while the woman is still living, take another, as it does not behoove any Christian to do, especially not those in orders who must set a proper example to others and forbid wrongdoing.[25] Now it seems strange to them to hear this, for they have made their miserable behaviour as routine as if there were no harm in a priest living his life just like a layman.[26] Christ himself ordained celibacy, and his holy apostles who followed him here on earth, so we as servants of God must obey.[27] It came to pass after Christ's passion and after his resurrection from death and his ascension to Heaven, and after the passions of his apostles and martyrs, that the true faith was greatly diminished by devilish heretics: *that is, the priest Arian and the bishop Macedonius and many others.*[28]

21 This admonition presents in condensed form a series of injunctions expressed at greater length elsewhere in Wulfstan's writings. Cf. V Atr. 4.1, 7, and 9.1; VI Atr. 2.2 and 4; and I Cn. 6a.

22 Cf. V Atr. 5 and VI Atr. 3.

23 This 'peculiar' ('eigenartig') provision, to borrow Jost's descriptor, is otherwise unattested and without any known source. See Jost 1950: 251.

24 Cf. I Cn. 6.1.

25 Cf. VI Atr. 5.2.

26 Wulfstan here quotes Ælfric's Pastoral Letter to Bishop Wulfsige, §14.

27 A quotation from Ælfric's Pastoral Letter to Bishop Wulfsige, §2.

28 A condensation of Ælfric's Pastoral Letter to Bishop Wulfsige, §4, and §36 in the

It then came to pass that Constantine, the great emperor and son of the noble Saint Helen, the blessed queen, rose to power in the city of Rome, and he held sway over the entire earth.[29] He then called a very great synod at the city called Nicea in order to establish the proper doctrine concerning the holy trinity and Christ's humanity. The first synod was, just as we said, in Nicea of three hundred and eighteen bishops; afterwards, the next was of one hundred and fifty bishops in Constantinople; the third was of two hundred bishops in Ephesus; and the fourth was of six hundred bishops and thirty priests in Chalcedon, and they all were men who led holy lives. These four synods are to be heeded, just like the four Gospels. They likewise established all of the offices which we perform in God's service: for mass, for matins, and for all of the canonical hours. Afterwards, there were very often other synods of wise bishops widely throughout the world, but these were the first, and they forbade entirely and forever all fornication by those who serve at the altar, namely bishops and priests. Let them now reflect, those who are so arrogant that they neglect God and the judgment of so many holy men such as were gathered at these synods and everywhere afterwards, what reward they can expect for themselves; and indeed, they need not expect but know with certainty that they must receive an evil reward unless they desist and the wrath of God fearsomely because they so enrage God in that they live all of their lives in wickedness. Indeed, there are too many of those who have sinned before this, yet he who is willing to renounce these sins and embrace chastity will have God's mercy and, in his worldly status, he is to be deemed worthy of the privileges accorded to a thegn.[30]

And it is right, if something suddenly befalls the people – it may be invasions, it may be sudden plagues, it may be bad weather or crop failure, it will be what it will be – that amends always is to be made to God himself;[31] and that our lord permit judgment to be passed on all the wicked who refuse to desist in every part of England and, willingly or unwillingly, they are to yield to righteousness or be driven from the realm altogether.[32]

C.C.C.C. 201 version of his first Old English Pastoral Letter to Archbishop Wulfstan.

29 Wulfstan's account of the early Church synods here closely resembles that in *Polity* XXII, especially the version preserved in C.C.C.C. 201. The source for both discussions is Ælfric's Pastoral Letter to Bishop Wulfsige, §5–6, 12–13, and 93–101, and his first Old English Pastoral Letter to Archbishop Wulfstan, §61–3.

30 Cf. VIII Atr. 28, *Canons* 68b, I Cn. 6a.2a, and *Concerning Clerical Compensation* 1.

31 Cf. Napier 35, p. 169, l. 15–p. 170, l. 3.

32 Cf. VIII Atr. 40.

And in the name of God we instruct, enjoin, and decree that no Christian ever is to wed anyone of his own family within six degrees of kinship, nor the widow of a kinsman as closely related as that, nor a close relative of his previous wife or of his godfather, nor an avowed nun.[33] Nor is a Christian man ever to wed any divorced woman or take more than one wife, but he is to keep to that one as long as he lives, if he desires to properly heed God's laws and protect his soul from hellfire.[34] Woe unto that person who pursues injustice all too long, unless he turn aside.[35] And every widow who lives a virtuous life shall be under the protection of God and the king; and each of them is to remain without a husband for twelve months, and afterwards she may choose as she pleases.[36] Likewise, we also command, in the name of almighty God and all of his saints, that no man be so presumptuous as to wed a nun in orders or a woman under monastic vows.[37] If anyone has done so, he is to be an outlaw before God and excommunicated from the Christian faith, and he is to be liable to the king for all that he possesses, unless he swiftly renounces [that union] and greatly repents before God.[38] And he who wishes to cleanse this land properly, to cast out injustice and embrace righteousness, must zealously forbid and resist such wickedness.[39]

Moreover, let the restoration of security and the restoration of the currency be seriously considered in every way:[40] restoration of security in a manner that is best for householders and worst for thieves; and restoration of the currency so that there is a single one throughout the country, without any counterfeit;[41] and false weights and deceptive

33 An identical injunction appears in *On the Duties of the Laity*, n. 12. On this passage, see Lynch 1998: 167.

34 Cf. I Cn. 7, 7.1 and *On the Duties of the Laity*, n. 13.

35 Cf. *Polity* IX.

36 Cf. V Atr. 21–21.1 and VI Atr 26–26.1. Stephanie Hollis points out that the appearance of this injunction in both Æthelred's legislation and this homily marks a shift in the treatment of widows during this period: 'in representing the protection of widows as a particular responsibility of the king, [Wulfstan] replaces the formulaic exhortation to give aid to widows, orphans, and strangers with more socially specific legislation'. Hollis 2004: 449.

37 Cf. VI Atr. 12.1 and 39; I Cn. 7.1; II Cn. 50.1; and *NPL* 63.

38 Cf. *Cn. 1020*, §16–17.

39 Cf. II Cn. 7.1. On the injunction to cleanse the realm, see *Polity* II; VI Atr. 7, VIII Atr. 40, II Cn. 4, *EGu.* 11, and *On Heathen Practices*, n. 6. The demand to cast out injustice ('unriht alecgan') also occurs in *Cn. 1020* 3.

40 Cf. V Atr. 26.1.

41 Cf. VI Atr 32–32.1, II Cn 8.

measures are to be corrected assiduously and every wickedness renounced henceforth.[42]

And tithes are to be rendered properly, according to God's mercy and the king's and that of all Christian people, and according to the rule established by King Edgar.[43] The dues to Rome are to be paid every year by Saint Peter's Day, and he who does not pay it is to give an additional thirty pence to Rome and pay to the king 120 shillings according to English law.[44]

Holy days and fasts are to be observed properly: the Sunday holiday is to be kept diligently from noon on Saturday until dawn on Monday, and we forbid trade and public meetings on that holy day.[45] Likewise, the Ember-fast is to be kept properly, just as Saint Gregory himself decreed to the English people.[46] All obligations to God are to be assiduously fulfilled, every virtue promoted and sin rejected, and then God soon will show mercy to this people.[47] And let us all together, clerical and lay, become resolute before God and the world and have peace and harmony among ourselves according to God's law, and every dispute is to be settled as best we can,[48] nor let us permit the devil to deceive or divide us, just as he often did at our previous assemblies.[49] Instead, let us all submit to God with one heart, praise and worship him, rightly hold

42 Cf. V Atr. 24, VI Atr. 28.2 and 32.2, II Cn. 9, Bethurum 10c l. 88, and *Episc.* 6.

43 Cf. VIII Atr. 7. See also *Cn. 1020* 13, *Polity* X, and *On Christian Practices* n. 6.

44 Cf. II Eg. 4, V Atr. 11.1, VI Atr. 18, I Cn. 9, *EGu.* 6.1, *Canons* 54, *On Christian Practices* n. 6, and *NPL* 57.1. See also n. to *Canons* 54.

45 Cf. VI As. 10; V Atr. 13–13.1; VI Atr. 22.1 and 44; I Cn. 14.2–15; *EGu.* 7; *Canons* 19; *Cn. 1020* 18; *NPL* 55; Napier 43 l. 94; *On Tithes* n. 5; and *On the Duties of the Laity* n. 16.

46 Cf. VI Atr. 23 and *On Tithes*, n. 6. Ember-fasts take place on the Wednesday, Friday, and Saturday of the weeks between the third and fourth Sundays of Advent, between the first and second Sundays of Lent, between Pentecost and Trinity Sunday, and the week beginning on the Sunday after Holy Cross Day. A possible source for this injunction is the (possibly spurious) 'Rule given by S. Gregory to the English on the Ember Fasts' (*ca.* 597x604), ed. in Haddan and Stubbs 1869–71: 52–3. Wulfstan's interest in the place of the Ember-fast in the liturgical calendar is indicated by the inclusion of several texts on the subject in the manuscript compilations dubbed by subsequent scholars his 'commonplace books'. See Cross 1992: 63–4 and Jones 1998c: 237.

47 Cf. *EGu.* 5.1; V Atr. 12.2 and 26; VI Atr. 3, 21.1, and 30; VIII Atr. 14; I Cn. 14; and *On Christian Practices* n. 14.

48 Cf. V Atr. 19; VI Atr. 25.1; I Cn. 17.2; *Polity* X; Bethurum 10a, ll. 21–4; and *On Tithes* n. 9.

49 On the term for assembly used in this passage, *gegaderung*, see Liebermann 1913: 11n. 16.

to our Christian faith and our loyalty to our lord, and entirely renounce all heathen practices.[50]

Furthermore, let us recall that it is near this world's end, believe it who will, and the time of the devil Antichrist;[51] however, the devil deceives men's thoughts, so that they remember it too rarely.[52] And believe it who will, we know truly that it inexorably approaches, for this world is full of sorrow and from day to day it grows ever worse.[53] Indeed, we may see how short and how wretched this life is, how miserable and how sorrowful, how troublesome and how arduous, how precarious and how cruel, how hostile and how deceptive![54] This world is in haste and storm, in disease and bad weather, so that now there cannot be many altogether of whom some are not sick and weak. Yet, though it so happens that people will live in this world for a time, nevertheless they will always be in struggle and sorrow, for this world is not worthy to be loved all too much.[55] There is a great need for us who are appointed as preachers of God to frequently warn God's people against the horror at hand for mankind, namely the archenemy Antichrist, lest they be caught unaware and then too quickly taken in by the devil.[56] Lo, what living man is there that will not be deceived by the devil, unless God almighty preserves him and he is the better prepared beforehand?[57] Truly, is it any wonder, though the incarnate devil may sorely persecute the wicked, when God allows him to perform such a miracle among his own saints, in that through the archenemy, Enoch and Elias shall be martyred, whom God himself previously had preserved in body and soul for many hundreds of years for one reason, that they might uplift the people through their teaching so that they all might not perish together through that devil who strikes fear into all people and torments the

---

50 Cf. *EGu.* Pr.1; V Atr 1, 34; VI Atr. 1.6; VIII Atr. 44; IX Atr. *explicit*; X Atr. 1; *NPL* 47, 67; *Polity* XXXV; *Canons* 16; and *On the Proper Support of the Church* n. 4.

51 Cf. Bethurum 4, ll. 74–7. Wulfstan wrote several sermons dealing with the Antichrist. On the role of the Antichrist in Wulfstan's eschatological thought, see Emmerson 1983: 1–10; Lionarons 2004a: 421–4.

52 Cf. Bethurum 4, ll. 79–81.

53 Given the origin of the previous lines, the immediate source for this sentence is likely Bethurum 4, ll. 77–9. For similar claims, see also Bethurum 1b, ll. 2–5; Bethurum 3, ll. 14–15; Bethurum 20.3 (the *Sermo Lupi ad Anglos*), ll. 7–11; and Napier 40, p. 189, ll. 5–9.

54 Cf. Napier 40, p. 189, ll. 3–4.

55 Cf. Napier 40, p. 189, ll. 8–9. On this passage, see Lionarons 2004a: 424–7.

56 Cf. Bethurum 1b, ll. 25–8.

57 Cf. Bethurum 4, ll. 92–3.

whole world? There is no one living who may or can say how evil it will be in that devilish time.[58]

In God's name, we pray that every Christian will sincerely reflect upon himself, take warning against that terror, submit to God wholeheartedly, turn away from sin as best he can, and strive so that he might have a share in that heavenly kingdom where there is eternal bliss and he will always be with the one who lives and rules always without end. Amen.[59]

---

58 Bethurum 5, ll. 88–98. Enoch and Elias (Elijah), whom the Hebrew Bible lists as having been translated to Heaven prior to their deaths, were often identified by patristic writers as the two witnesses to the apocalypse mentioned in *Revelation* 11:3. Wulfstan's source for this passage is the *Libellus Anticristi* of Adso of Montier-en-Der, ed. Sackur 1898: 99–113. See esp. pp. 111–12. On Wulfstan's use of Adso, see Emmerson 1983: 1–10; Wilcox 1991: 1–19. Lionarons's comments on the analogous passage in Bethurum 5 may be relevant here also: 'It may not be too speculative to imagine that Wulfstan at this point saw his role as equivalent to theirs, becoming in an odd way a precursor to (as well as a descendant of) Enoch and Elias in their preaching against Antichrist at the end of time'. Lionarons 2010: 56.

59 Cf. Bethurum 4, ll. 92–6; Bethurum 6, ll. 214–17; and Bethurum 7, ll. 22–5.

7. ON THE DUTIES OF THE LAITY (NAPIER 59)

The manuscript of the York Gospels (York, Minster Library, Additional 1) was produced at Canterbury sometime around the year 1000 and later brought to York Cathedral, perhaps by Archbishop Wulfstan himself. *Ca.* 1020, a gathering of four leaves was added to the end of the manuscript and the new space used to record a series of texts related to the administration of York Minster and its estates.[1] Among the additions were four texts directly attributable to Wulfstan: Cnut's proclamation of 1020 and three homilies, edited by Napier as numbers 59–61 and translated here as *On the Duties of the Laity, On Heathen Practices*, and *On Christian Practices*. There seems little reason to doubt that the texts were composed at roughly the same time as they were incorporated into the manuscript. The presence of annotations in Wulfstan's handwriting indicates that he oversaw the transcribing of these texts and intended them to be read as a group.[2] As Simon Keynes points out,

> The care taken by Wulfstan to assemble these texts, to have them written on a specially prepared gathering of leaves which was then placed at the end of the gospel book, and finally to make certain corrections, suggests strongly that he attached particular importance to them: indeed, they represent a considered summary of Wulfstan's views on the proper ordering of a Christian society, and by placing them in the gospel book Wulfstan evidently intended not only to enhance the authority behind them but also to ensure that his message would not be forgotten.[3]

Notwithstanding the importance seemingly attached to these pieces by Wulfstan, Bethurum omitted them from her edition, claiming that they smacked too much of the law to be considered true homilies.[4] Yet while the texts are often indistinguishable from law, as Wormald demonstrated by comparing extracts from the York homilies to passages from Wulfstan's legislation, their manuscript context and traditional homiletic structure indicate that they were composed as sermons and meant to be read as such.[5]

Like Napier 52 and 53, *The Duties of the Laity* (Napier 59) is closely related to the *Institutes of Polity*, in this case chapter XVI; however, the homiletic introduc-

---

1 Keynes 1986: 81. See also the catalogue in the Appendix.

2 Ker 1971: 390–1; Keynes 1986: 92; and Treharne 2012: 61–2.

3 Keynes 1986: 92.

4 Bethurum 1957: 38–9.

5 Wormald 1999a: 242–3. On this point, see also Wilcox 1992: 201.

tion and conclusion as well as the use of direct address all leave no question that it was intended to function as an independent sermon.[6] Its emphasis on the importance of obedience to the laws of God and proper behaviour within marriage echo the themes of many of the archbishop's later writings while the command to properly render Church dues and resist 'the devil's blandishments' foreshadow the themes of *On Heathen Practices* (Napier 60) and *On Christian Practices* (Napier 61). As such, though the text can stand on its own, within the manuscript it appears to serve as a sort of general statement of the principles elaborated upon by the two homilies that follow.[7]

6 See below, n. 2.

7 On this point, see also Bethurum 1957: 38; Lionarons 2010: 35; and Treharne 2012: 66–7.

TRANSLATION[1]

SERMON OF THE WOLF[2]

Beloved people, do as I instruct, hear what I will say for your benefit, take heed he who can for his own need. For all Christians, the great obligation is to obey God's laws and zealously heed his divine teachings;[3] and the greatest obligation of all is assigned especially to those in holy orders, for they are to fervently both preach and set an example of God's justice for others.[4]

Now it is our desire carefully to instruct the servants of God, so that they themselves prudently remember, with God's help, to love purity, humbly serve the almighty God, and frequently intercede for all Christian people;[5] and to diligently attend to their studies and prayers, and to fervently preach and set an example of God's justice; and to frequently teach, just as they most diligently can, the clergy to arrange their lives according to the rule and the lay according to the law, just as they should.[6] Moreover, we instruct all Christians always to love God with their innermost heart, to adhere diligently to virtuous Christian practices, to readily heed their spiritual teachers, and to reflect and inquire upon God's teachings and laws again and again for their benefit.[7] And, so that he can understand the true faith aright, we instruct every Christian to learn especially both the paternoster and creed, so that after he dies he will rest in sanctity with Christian fellowship and receive

---

1 This translation is based on the text in Napier 1883: 307–9.

2 Oxford, Bodleian Library, Junius 121 incorporates a shorter version of this text into *Polity* (listed as 'XVI. On God's Servants'); however, this text's use of direct address – which occurs nowhere in *Polity* – suggests that it has been deliberately composed for homiletic purposes. It remains unclear, however, whether the homily predates the version in *Polity* or *vice versa*.

3 Cf. VI Atr. 42.2; II Cn. 84.1; *Sanctuary* 19; *Polity* VI; Napier 37, p. 179, ll. 21–3; Bethurum 5, ll. 113–18; and Bethurum 20.3 (*Sermo Lupi ad Anglos*), ll. 192–4.

4 The demand that clerics both preach and set an example (*bodian 7 bysnian*) occurs frequently in Wulfstan's writings. The closest analogues to this passage appear to be *Canons* 69 and Napier 36, p. 179, l. 5.

5 Cf. V Atr. 4.1, I Cn. 6a, *Clerical Compensation* 1, *Canons* 1, *Polity* XVII and XXXV, and Napier 37, p. 179, l. 9.

6 Cf. Bethurum 20.3 (*Sermo Lupi ad Anglos*) ll. 61–5. The version in Junius 121 follows this sentence with a brief passage drawn from the opening sentences of the homily *On Various Misfortunes* and then concludes with a condensed quotation of VIII Atr. 28.

7 Cf. I. Cn. 21.

prayers or be deserving of the sacrament while still alive.[8] For that reason, he is not a good Christian who does not learn it, nor may he who does not know it lawfully sponsor another at baptism or confirmation until he learns it, so that he knows it well.[9] And we instruct that grave sins and devilish deeds be zealously resisted at all times, and he who falls into sin through the devil's blandishments is to repent fervently in keeping with his confessor's guidance.[10] Likewise, we instruct that foul lustfulness, illicit fornication, and all forms of adultery always be vehemently rejected.[11] And in the name of God we instruct, enjoin, and decree that no Christian ever is to wed anyone of his own family within six degrees of kinship, nor the widow of a kinsman as closely related as that, nor a close relative of his previous wife or of his godfather, nor an avowed nun.[12] Nor is a Christian man ever to wed any divorced woman or take more than one wife, but he is to keep to that one as long as he lives, if he desires to properly heed God's laws and protect his soul from hellfire.[13] And we zealously instruct every person always to bear in mind the fear of God and to keep a horror of sin day and night, dreading the Day of Judgment and trembling in terror of Hell, and always anticipating the End of Days.[14] And we fervently instruct each of our friends to turn from sin and to guide others from iniquity, and above all to love the Lord, and again and again to bear in mind that which is man's greatest obligation to recall most frequently: that is, as we said before, that they are to steadfastly preserve righteous faith in the true God, who is the master and maker of all creation, and to adhere properly to the true Christian faith; and that they are to zealously heed their spiritual teachers and to assiduously follow God's precepts and laws;[15] and that they are to diligently preserve and protect God's churches everywhere and to visit them frequently with candles and offerings, and there again and again themselves pray sincerely to Christ; and that they are to pay their Church dues every year according to the law and properly observe holy days and fasts; and that they are to diligently

---

8 Cf. Theodulf, *Capitula* XXII, *Canons* 22, and Bethurum 8c, ll. 1–6.

9 Cf. *Canons* 22 and I Cn. 22.6.

10 Cf. I Cn.23.

11 Cf. I Cn. 24.

12 An identical injunction appears in *On Justice*, n. 33. On this passage, see Lynch 1998: 167.

13 Cf. I Cn. 7, 7.1 and *On Justice* n. 34.

14 Cf. I Cn. 25; Bethurum 10c, ll. 149–51; Napier 37, p. 179, ll. 13–16; and *Polity* VI.

15 Cf. VI Atr. 42.2, II Cn. 84.1, Bethurum 5 l. 113, and *Sanctuary* 19.

avoid trade on a Sunday as well as assemblies on that holy day;[16] and that they always are to protect and honour the servants of God; and that they are to console and feed God's needy; and that they are not to constantly burden widows and orphans, but to uplift them willingly; and that they are not to trouble or persecute strangers or those who come from afar; and that they are not to offer overmuch injustice to others, but every person is to treat others to the best of his ability with that same justice that he desires for himself.[17] May God's name always be eternally blessed, and may there be glory and honour to him forever in the world.

16 Cf. *EGu.* 7; VI As. 10; VI Atr. 22.1 and 44; I Cn. 15; *Canons* 19; *Cn. 1020* 18; *NPL* 55; Napier 43 l. 94; *On Tithes* n. 5; and *On Justice* n. 45.

17 *Matthew* 7:12: 'All things therefore whatsoever you would that men should do to you, do you also to them' ('Omnia ergo quæcumque vultis ut faciant vobis homines, et vos facite illis'). Cf. VI Atr. 49; I Cn. 18.2; *Sanctuary* 29; Bethurum 7 ll. 169–70; Bethurum 8b, ll. 78–80; Bethurum 8c ll. 112–3; Bethurum 10c ll. 136–7; Bethurum 13 ll. 55–6; Bethurum 18 ll. 142–3; Napier 30, p. 144, ll. 1–2; Napier 37, p. 179, ll. 27–9; *On the Laws of God* n. 4; and *On the Proper Support* n. 3.

8. ON HEATHEN PRACTICES (NAPIER 60)

This piece follows *On the Duties of the Laity* (Napier 59) in the York Gospels (York, Minster Library, Additional 1), and likely was composed at the same time, *ca.* 1020.[1] The homily's rubric and Latin tag link it with its successor, *On Christian Practices*, which is headed in the same way.[2] Although the text reads somewhat awkwardly ('as a heaping up of quotations from Wulfstan's earlier works', to quote the judgment of one recent commentator[3]), its scope and combination of topics add interest to what might otherwise be little more than a rehashing of old themes. While the title – presumably Wulfstan's own – identifies the homily's subject as 'heathen practices', the text itself locates the persistence of heathenism within a sequence of social ills extending progressively from idol worship to the decay of family and community.[4] Treharne asserts the occurrence of these themes in this homily reflects 'a particular rhetorical situation, which is certainly post-1020, and which thus suggests that the attendant horrors of the process of conquest were still very apparent five or more years into Cnut's ascendancy'.[5] Whether the circumstances behind the text's composition are as specific as Treharne proposes, the sense of decline pervading *On Heathen Practices* is very much in keeping with the themes of moral corruption and social decay so characteristic of Wulfstan's later writing.

---

1 See the introduction to *On the Duties of the Laity*, above pp. 154–5.

2 See below, p. 163.

3 Meaney 2004: 483.

4 Cf. Keynes 1986: 94.

5 Treharne 2012: 63.

TRANSLATION[1]

ON HEATHEN PRACTICES

No Christian is to heed pagan superstitions, but he is to despise entirely all of the filth of the heathens.[2] Indeed, great is everyone's obligation always to be wary of the devil's wiles and always to diligently avoid heathen practices insofar as he can do so.[3] Moreover, if it befalls that a Christian ever henceforth anywhere engages in heathen practices or worships idols anywhere in the land, he is to repent for it sincerely before God and the world; and he who commits that transgression too frequently, is to pay his wergild as a penalty if under English law or his *lahslit* if under Danish law, according to the severity of the deed.[4] And if witches or wizards, fornicators or prostitutes, murderers or perjurers[5] come to be found within the realm, they are to be expelled zealously from the country and the realm cleansed, or they must be utterly wiped out unless they desist and repent most deeply.[6] And let evil deeds be punished sternly in every part of the realm.[7] Here in this land are enemies of the sacred and despisers of God's law, murderers and parricides, Church-haters and priest-killers, violators of holy orders and violators of their marriage vows, prostitutes and child-killers, thieves and criminals, robbers and vandals, perjurers and hypocrites and all too many evil tyrants who empty the realm through their butchery, breakers of oaths and violators of trusts, and all too widely there has

---

1 This translation is based on the text in Napier 1883: 309–10.

2 Cf. §152 in the B recension of Wulfstan's Canon Law Collection.

3 Cf. VI Atr. 1.

4 Cf. *EGu.* 2, V Atr. 31, and VI Atr. 51. In the MS. this sentence is surrounded by a jagged line, which Ker suggests may be Wulfstan's attempt to excise this sentence, 'because he did not wish to introduce a specific penalty, more suitable to a law-code, into his general exhortation'. Ker 1971: 318–19. On *lahslit*, see n. to *EGu.* 2.

5 On this phrase, see n. to *EGu.* 11.

6 Cf. *EGu.* 11, VI Atr. 7, VIII Atr. 40, II Cn. 4, and *Cn. 1020* 15. Jonathan Davis-Secord points to the catalogue of sinners in this homily as exemplary of Wulfstan's use of such lists in his work generally: 'The lists are essentially set pieces in that they are relatively independent within their homily as a whole. For example, they have their own internal organisations as lists of doublets, and their content, while not incongruous, does not specifically advance the main argument of their homily. Given these large compound-laden passages, the presence of the compounds registers not just at the level of individual sentences but also at the larger discourse level of the entire homily, differentiating the set pieces from the rest of the text'. Davis-Secord 2008: 68.

7 Cf. II Cn. 4.

been little faith among men.[8] Nor, at times, does the kinsman protect his kin any more than he does a stranger, nor a brother his brother, nor often a child his father or mother.[9] Nor does anybody at all keep his faith as well as he should, before God and the world. But, as is necessary, let repentance fervently be made and the realm be cleansed, if one desires to earn God's mercy.[10]

8 Cf. II Cn. 7; Bethurum 7, l. 131; Bethurum 10a, l. 14; Bethurum 13, l. 95; Bethurum 20.3, l. 165; Napier 42, p. 203, l. 24; Napier 57, pp. 298, ll. 15–16; *On the Proper Support*, n. 9; *On Justice*, n. 10; *Polity* II and IX. For an abbreviated version of this list, see *On the Laws of God*, n. 13.

9 Cf. Bethurum 3, ll. 54–5; Bethurum 5, ll. 98–100; Bethurum 20.3, ll. 61–5; and Napier 27, p. 128, ll. 10–13.

10 Cf. *Polity* II, VI Atr. 7, VIII Atr. 40, II Cn. 4 and 7.1, *EGu.* 11, and *On Justice*, n. 39.

9. *ON CHRISTIAN PRACTICES* (NAPIER 61)

On Christian Practices (Napier 61) is the last in the series of homilies preceding Cnut's 1020 proclamation in York, Minster Library, Additional 1. The rubric and Latin tag indicate that it was meant to be read alongside its predecessor, *On Heathen Practices* (Napier 60), likely composed at the same time.[1] As is the case with the homilies preceding it in the series, *On Christian Practices* is made up of passages borrowed from Wulfstan's other works. Even more so than its companions, however, the text's somewhat awkward construction raises questions as to whether it was ever actually preached. Yet, even if not composed as a homily *per se*, the text's inclusion in the York compilation suggests that it may have been intended as a resource – perhaps for Wulfstan's successor, Ælfric Puttoc[2] – on the moral and practical obligations of an ecclesiastical administrator. Like Napier 23 (*On Tithes and Tithing*) and canon 54 of the *Canons of Edgar*, the text deals principally with the proper times and procedures for the rendering of Church dues based on the practices established in II Edgar 2–5.[3] It might also be noted that, when read alongside the other York Gospel texts, the homily's final injunction concerning the punishment of those who withhold their dues provides a neat transition to *Cnut 1020*, a major concern of which is the state's power to enforce both royal and ecclesiastical decrees.[4]

---

1 Bethurum 1957: 38–9; Keynes 1986: 94–5; and Lionarons 2010: 35. See also the introductions to *On the Duties of the Laity* and *On Heathen Practices* above, pp. 154–5 and 159.

2 Treharne 2012: 66.

3 Cf. Lionarons 2010: 169–70.

4 On this point, see Treharne 2012: 67.

TRANSLATION[1]

ON CHRISTIAN PRACTICES:[2]

For indeed from Christ were Christians named, and Christ is our head and we his members.[3] Christ is the head of all Christians, and all Christians are considered the limbs of Christ if they please their Lord properly.[4] And they should properly adhere to the Christian faith most diligently and seek out Christ's churches often for their own benefit and properly discharge their obligations to Christ. And this is first, that tithes be collected annually on that which God provided for the needs of the people during the year in grain and flax and every kind of produce.[5] And the field-tithe always falls on the tenth acre already tilled by the plough, according to God's mercy and the king's and that of all Christian people, and according to the rule established by King Edgar.[6] The tithe on all young animals is to be paid by Pentecost or face penalty, and that on the earth's produce by the Feast of All Saints;[7] and the dues to Rome are to be paid every year by Saint Peter's Day, and he who does not pay it is to give an additional thirty pence and bring it to Rome[8] and pay to the king 120 shillings according to English law.[9] Church dues are

1 This translation is based on the text in Napier 1883: 310–11.

2 The rubric explicitly connects this text with its predecessor in the manuscript, *On Heathen Practices.*

3 The first part of this sentence is a quotation of Isidore, *Etymologies,* 7.4.1 ('Christians are named from Christ', 'A Christo enim Christiani cognominati') while the second part combines *Ephesians* 5:23 ('Christ is the head of the Church', 'Christus caput est Ecclesiæ') and 5:30 ('Because we are members of his body, of his flesh, and of his bones', 'quia membra sumus corporis eius, de carne eius, et de ossibus eius'). See also *1 Corinthians* 12:12–14.

4 Cf. Bethurum 8b, ll. 69–71; Bethurum 8c, ll. 100–1; Bethurum 10c, ll. 5–8; and Bethurum 18, ll. 125–6. Similar language appears frequently in the works of Ælfric, in particular in his *Sermon on the Lord's Prayer (Feria III De Dominica Oratione* in the Catholic Homilies, first series), ll. 27–8. On this passage, see Orchard 2004: 72.

5 Cf. *Deuteronomy* 14:22.

6 The tithes listed in the remainder of this homily are those set forth in II Eg. 2–5. Similar accounts of tithing practices occur in *EGu.* 6.1, I Cn. 9 and 14, V Atr. 12.2, VI Atr. 21.1, VIII Atr. 9–14, *Canons* 54, *On Justice* nn. 43 and 44, *On Tithes,* n. 4, and *On the Proper Support,* n. 7.

7 Pentecost takes place seven weeks after Easter Sunday. The Feast of All Saints takes place on 1 November.

8 A note in what is most likely Wulfstan's handwriting adds here 'uel sende' ('or send it'), perhaps showing, as Gareth Mann suggests, 'his awareness of the sapping costs involved in travel to Rome for any pilgrim, not just a new archbishop'. See Keynes 1986: 94 and Mann 2004: 265n. 293.

9 The Feast of Saint Peter occurs on 29 June. See also n. to *Canons* 54.

to be paid by Martinmas according to English law, and he who does not
do so is to pay them twelve-fold and pay 120 shillings to the king.[10] It is
fitting that plough-dues be paid every year fifteen nights after Easter[11]
or face punishment, and dues for the lighting of the church are to be
paid on Christmas, Candlemas, and Easter or face punishment; one may
do so more often if he so desires.[12] Dues for the souls of the dead are
always best paid while the grave remains open. Holy days and fasts are
to be properly observed, or face punishment.[13] All obligations to God
are to be rendered assiduously, entirely as is required, and if anyone will
not do so, he is to be punished with secular penalties.[14]

10 Martinmas occurs on 11 November.

11 On the possible pagan origins of this stipulation, see Chaney 1963: 274.

12 Candlemas is celebrated on 2 February. On the significance of Candlemas, see Chaney
    1963: 275.

13 Cf. *On Tithes* n. 10.

14 Cf. *EGu.* 5.1 and *On Justice* n. 47.

10. *ON TITHES AND TITHING* (NAPIER 23)

This text, one of a series of fragments sometimes referred to collectively as the *Sermones ad populum* (Napier 19–25), is preserved in only three of the four manuscripts in which the series occurs: Cambridge, Corpus Christi College 201; Cambridge, Corpus Christi College 419; and British Library, Cotton Tiberius A.iii.[1] Based on II Edgar 2–5, the fragment concerns the proper times and procedures for the rendering of Church dues, a common theme in Wulfstan's writings. Though analogous passages appear in his earlier work, the similarity between the enumeration of dues here and those in the homily *On Christian Practices* (Napier 61), the law-code I Cnut, and the *Canons of Edgar* suggests that this text may have been composed fairly late in archbishop's career, perhaps between 1020 and 1023.[2] We can only speculate, yet it is possible that Wulfstan composed this text as a way of elaborating on the distinction between tithing and Church dues discussed in *On the Proper Support of the Church*.[3] Following Wulfstan's death, a lightly revised version of this fragment was incorporated in its entirety into the E-text of the Old English Sunday Letter.[4]

---

1 On these texts, see the introduction to *On the Proper Support of the Church*, above pp. 133–4.

2 Bethurum 1957: 36–7; Wormald 2004: 27; and Pons-Sanz 2007: 25.

3 Wormald 1999a: 243 and Lionarons 2010: 169–70.

4 Haines 2010: 92.

TRANSLATION[1]

To all the people:[2]

Each year, let us render our plough-dues fifteen nights after Easter,[3] the tithe on the young animals by Pentecost and that on the fruits of the earth by the equinox or, indeed, by the Feast of All Saints; and the hearth-tax is to be paid to the diocese each year by St. Peter's Day, and the Church-dues on Martinmas, and the dues for the lighting of the church three times per year: first, a halfpennyworth of wax on Candlemas, and again on Easter eve, and a third time on the Feast of All Saints.[4] Moreover, the Sunday holiday is to be observed from noon on Saturday until dawn on Monday, and every other holy day as has been decreed for it. We also earnestly forbid trade on Sundays and all forms of assembly, unless there is a great necessity for it.[5] And every ordained fast is to be observed with complete devotion, whether it is an Ember-fast, a Lenten fast, or another type of fast.[6] And a fast shall be proclaimed for all the festivals of St. Mary and for those of each apostle, except we do not decree a fast for that of St. Philip and St. James because of the Easter holiday; and every Friday a fast shall be observed, unless it is a holy day.[7] We also forbid ordeals and oaths on holy days, Ember days, during Lent, on legally-appointed fast days, between Advent and Epiphany, and from the Septuagesima until the fifteenth night after Easter.[8] And as is

---

1 This translation is based on the text in Napier 1883: 116–19.

2 The rubric occurs only in C.C.C.C. 201 and London, British Library, Cotton Tiberius A.iii. A version of this sermon, most likely revised by someone other than Wulfstan, was incorporated into the E-text of the Old English Sunday Letter at lines 56–98. See Haines 2010: 91–3.

3 On the possible pagan origins of this stipulation, see Chaney 1963: 274.

4 The enumeration of Church dues, based on II Eg. 2–5, occurs in several of Wulfstan's works. Cf. Bethurum 13, l. 74ff, *Canons* 54, *On Christian Practices*, n. 6, *On the Proper Support*, n. 7. For notes on the dates on which the dues are to be paid, see *On Christian Practices*. On the significance of Candlemas (traditionally celebrated on 2 February), see Chaney 1963: 275.

5 Cf. VI As. 10; *EGu.* 7; VI Atr. 22.1 and 44; I Cn. 15; *Canons* 19; *Cnut 1020* 18; *NPL* 55; Napier 43 l. 94; *On Justice* n. 45; and *On the Duties of the Laity* n. 16.

6 Cf. *On Justice*, n. 46.

7 Cf. V Atr. 14.1; VI Atr. 22.3; I Cn. 16a; and Napier 43, p. 208, ll. 14–20.

8 Septuagesima refers to the ninth Sunday before Easter and the third before Ash Wednesday. The seventy-day period comprised of the nine weeks before Easter and Easter Week itself was taken to represent the seventy years of the Babylonian Captivity. Cf. *EGu.* 9, V Atr. 18, VI Atr. 25, I Cn. 17, *Canons* 24, and Napier 43 p. 208, ll. 20–4.

proper, during holy seasons there shall be peace and harmony among all Christians, and every dispute is to be settled.[9] Additionally, so that every Christian understands, we instruct that one is not to be buried in the church after death without the payment of dues for his soul; rather, dues for the soul are always to be paid while the grave remains open.[10] For the love of God, we enjoin every Christian to readily understand his own obligations, for we all must reach a time when we will desire more than anything in this world that we had faithfully done God's will for as long as we could; but when that time comes, we will receive only the reward that we earned while alive.[11] Let us act respectfully towards our father and mother,[12] give protection to the wretched widows and orphans, and willingly aid the unfortunate, strangers, and those come from afar. Let us shelter the cold, clothe the naked, give food to the hungry, and drink to the thirsty. Let us comfort the afflicted and give hope to the despairing, free the captive (if it is appropriate for us to do so), visit the sick, generously provide coffins for the needy when they have died, and afterwards bury them. One who does these things acts for his own great benefit.[13]

---

9 Cf. V Atr. 19; VI Atr. 25.1; I Cn. 17.2; Bethurum 10a, ll. 21–4; and *On Justice* n. 48.

10 Cf. VIII Atr. 9–13, *On Christian Practices* n. 13, and *Canons* 29.

11 Cf. I Cnut 18, 18a. See also II Cn. 68.

12 Cf. *Exodus* 20:12, *Deuteronomy* 5:16, and *Ephesians* 6:2.

13 Cf. Napier 43 p. 209, ll. 1–9.

11. *ON BAPTISM AND CONFIRMATION* (NAPIER 24)

This text is preserved as one of the *Sermones ad populum* (Napier 19–26) in Cambridge, Corpus Christi College 201; Cambridge, Corpus Christi College 419; Oxford, Bodleian Library, Hatton 113; and BL Cotton Tiberius A.iii.[1] Although the manuscripts signal the start of the text with a rubricated initial, it lacks a rubric and the obvious transition in the first sentence suggests that it was never intended to stand alone as an independent homily. At the same time, the revisions to the final paragraphs in C.C.C.C. 201 and C.C.C.C. 419 may indicate that it also may not have been originally designed to form part of a cohesive series with the other *Sermones ad populum*.[2] The texts with which this fragment are most closely affiliated are Wulfstan's homily on *The Christian Life* (Bethurum 10c), the *Canons of Edgar*, and I Cnut, though it seems more likely that the fragment represents a restatement of earlier themes than a source on which Wulfstan later drew. Both Wormald and Pons-Sanz date the text to after 1020.[3]

---

1 On these texts, see the introduction to *On the Proper Support of the Church*, above pp. 133–4.

2 On this point, see Scragg 1998: 19–21; and Lionarons 2004b: 163, 172.

3 Wormald 2004: 27 and Pons-Sanz 2007: 25.

TRANSLATION[1]

Let us act, therefore, in the manner that we will now suggest:[2] let us always be loyal and true to our Lord and, with all our might, forever promote his worship and carry out his will;[3] for all that we ever do in the name of our true fidelity to our Lord, we do for our own great benefit, for certainly God will keep faith with him who rightly keeps faith with his lord. Likewise, it is every lord's great duty to govern his people justly.[4] And we entreat and enjoin the servants of God – who must pray on behalf of our royal lord and all Christian people, and who live by the charity of good men – that they fervently labour to deserve this, live their lives as the Bible instructs them and their elders teach them, and diligently perform their service; then will they be able to benefit well both themselves and all Christian people. In addition, we entreat and enjoin that every child is to be baptised within thirty nights; if it then happens to die without being baptised, and if it is because of the priest, then he is to forfeit his order and repent fervently.[5] If it is because of a neglectful relative, then the person responsible is to forfeit all his property and depart from the realm, or deeply repent within the realm as the bishop directs. We also instruct that no one is to remain unconfirmed for too long; and that the child's patrons[6] are to take heed to guide the child in the true faith, in God's service, and in the necessary deeds, and henceforth always to direct the child towards that which will please God and be of benefit to himself; then will they truly be just what they are called, godparents, if they win over their godchild for God.[7]

God is the father of us all, and he made that known when he sent hither

---

1 This translation is based on the text in Napier 1883: 119–22.

2 C.C.C.C. 419 reads instead: 'And once again I mean to instruct you.'

3 Cf. Bethurum 10c, ll. 165–6 and *Canons* 1. Wulfstan's phrasing here also recalls the pledge of loyalty preserved as the first item in the Old English oath compilation, *Swerian*.

4 This passage also occurs in I Cnut 20–20.3. On the reuse of this passage in Cnut's legislation, see Richards 2010: 145. For similar injunctions, see *Canons* 1 and Bethurum 10c, ll. 165–8.

5 C.C.C.C. 419 states that baptism is to take place within seven nights, although the other manuscripts all read 'thirty'. For similar injunctions, see Ine 2 and *Canons* 15. See also *NPL* 10–10.1.

6 Lit. 'those who receive the child'.

7 MSS. Hatton 113 and C.C.C.C. 201 interpose Napier 25 and part of Napier 26 after this paragraph and before the homily's final lines. Lionarons argues that this revision indicates that Wulfstan intended the reworked Napier 24, 25, and 26 to serve as a final section to an expanded version of Bethurum 13. See Lionarons 2004b: 172.

his own son, Christ from heaven: here he was born a man through that pure maiden, Saint Mary, and he endured death for all mankind; and through his death, he released us all from eternal death and won for us eternal life. Through a pure maiden was Christ born and through a pure baptism are we made Christian; which we must also maintain with all purity if we are to achieve anything at all. Though sinless, Christ suffered for us, and so must we suffer and endure through the many consequences of our sins, and deserve from God that he should, through his very great mercy, free us from eternal death and grant us rest in the life to come.[8]

Let us fulfil that which is our great duty: to always keep in our mind the time to come. When the wretched body and the soul part from one another, then will our earthly friends entirely abandon us and, needs must be, they will be unable to do us any good, but whatever we receive shall be at the discretion of the one God.[9] To him always may there be praise and worship throughout the world, world without end, amen.[10]

---

8 This paragraph (which also appears in Napier 30, pp. 150, l. 23–p. 151, l. 8) is a loose adaptation of the Nicene Creed. See also Bethurum 7 and 7a.

9 Cf. Napier 30, p. 151, ll. 8–14. See also the anonymous sermon to be delivered on Tuesday during Rogationtide, ed. in Bazire and Cross 1983: ll. 43–5.

10 An alternative version of this final paragraph survives in C.C.C.C. 201: 'And let us fulfil that which is our great duty: be mindful in every way of our own need and to always keep in our mind the time to come when the wretched body and the soul will part. Then we will understand full well that our earthly friends entirely abandon us and, needs must be, they will be unable to do us any good, except what they will do for our souls. But all that we experience shall be at God's discretion. Let us recall that often, and always praise God over all other things with our inmost hearts, and zealously do his will, and he will reward us as we most desire. To him always may there be praise and worship, world without end, amen.' D.G. Scragg has suggested that the revisions to this passage are the result of a later 'Wulfstan imitator'. Lionarons, on the other hand, argues that the revisions are Wulfstan's own, the result of his reworking this paragraph as the conclusion of the *Sermo ad Populum*. See Scragg 1998: 19–21; Lionarons 2004b: 163.

III
SOURCES AND ANALOGUES

1. GOD'S THREAT TO A SINNING ISRAEL[1] (BETHURUM 19)

This homily survives in three manuscripts: Cambridge, Corpus Christi College 201, Oxford, Bodleian Library, Junius 121, and London, British Library, Cotton Nero A.i. Pons-Sanz, dates the text to Wulfstan's London episcopacy on linguistic grounds, yet both Bethurum and Wormald view it as a more mature composition, possibly produced in the years leading up to the crisis of 1014.[2] The text largely consists of a paraphrase and loose translation of *Leviticus*, chapter 26. The lengthy string of Latin quotations from Jerome's Vulgate that makes up the first half of the text led Bethurum to speculate that this homily 'was probably preached to the clergy as a model, for the first part could hardly have meant anything to a popular audience'.[3] Whether such was the case or not, it does provide a useful illustration of the way in which Wulfstan revised his sources for homiletic use. His 'translation' of the Biblical text is less an accurate rendering than a reworking of his material in order to draw a direct parallel with the England of his own time. The homily thus offers an early instance of the sort of Biblical parallelism that Wulfstan would come to rely on increasingly heavily in 1014 and afterwards.[4]

1 This title was given to the text by Bethurum and I have retained it for ease of reference. The manuscript titles the text, 'On Divine Admonishment'.

2 Bethurum 1957: 104; Wormald 2004: 26; and Pons-Sanz 2007: 19, 25.

3 Bethurum 1957: 355.

4 Cf. Wilcox 2000b: 87–92 and Lionarons 2010: 148–9.

TRANSLATION[1]

ON DIVINE ADMONISHMENT

Beloved people, let us search through the Bible diligently and often
for what they experienced who loved God and upheld God's laws, and
for what they experienced who angered God and broke God's laws,
and take warning for ourselves thereby. God himself invoked a clear
example, and spoke thus in ancient times to Moses the leader: *Thus
speaks the Lord: If you walk in my precepts, and keep my commandments,
and do them, I will give you rain in due seasons. And the ground shall bring
forth its increase, and the trees shall be filled with fruit. The threshing of
your harvest shall reach unto the vintage, and the vintage shall reach unto the
sowing time: and you shall eat your bread to the full, and dwell in your land
without fear. I will give peace in your coasts: you shall sleep, and there shall
be none to make you afraid. I will take away evil beasts: and the sword shall
not pass through your quarters. You shall pursue your enemies, and they shall
fall before you. Five of yours shall pursue a hundred others, and a hundred of
you ten thousand: your enemies shall fall before you by the sword. I will look
on you, and make you increase: you shall be multiplied, and I will establish my
covenant with you. You shall eat the oldest of the old store, and, new coming
on, you shall cast away the old. I will set my tabernacle in the midst of you, and
my soul shall not cast you off. I will walk among you, and will be your God,
and you shall be my people.*[2]

*And the Lord also said: If, however, you do not hearken to me nor fulfil my
commandments, I shall inflict poverty, hunger, and pestilence upon you, and I
shall make your lives a waste, and your enemies will persecute you, and you
shall flee when no man pursueth you; and I will make to you the heaven above as
iron, and the earth as brass, and all your strength shall be in vain. The ground
shall not bring forth her increase, nor the trees of the field yield their fruit.*[3]
*I will bring in upon you the sword and you shall be delivered into the hands
of your enemies, and your land shall be desolate and your cities destroyed.*[4]
*And when the land is made desolate because of the sins of the people and those
who remain are wasting away, they shall confess their sins and the sins of
their fathers whereby they despised me and despised my commandments. Then*

---

1 This translation is based on the text in Bethurum 1957: 251–4.

2 *Leviticus* 26:3–12.

3 A paraphrase of *Leviticus* 26:14–20. Bethurum notes that Wulfstan's language here
is very close to that found in the corresponding passage in *Deuteronomy* 28:20–1.
Bethurum 1957: 355.

4 A paraphrase of *Leviticus* 26:25.

they shall turn from their uncircumcised hearts and cry out to me, and I will remember our former covenant, and the land shall enjoy her sabbaths.[5] *These are the words which the Lord gave to the children of Israel by the hand of Moses.*[6]

Alas, beloved men, by such examples we may take warning for ourselves, if we are willing to reflect upon our duty, as is necessary for us. And whoever cannot understand the Latin, listen now to some part of what that Latin says in English: *Thus speaks the Lord: If you walk in my precepts, etc.* Our Lord commanded Moses the leader to guide the people and zealously admonish them, and he spoke to him thus: he said, if you uphold my laws rightly, then I will send weather which will cause all of your produce and the crops in your fields to flourish greatly. I will provide you with abundant wealth and sustenance, and you will dwell in the land free from care, in peace and security under my protection. I will shield you against every kind of harm, so that you will be neither devoured nor cut down, you will suffer neither war nor hunger, and your enemies' army will not trouble you. I will also give you the strength for victory and such great power that you, for sport, will defeat or disperse as many of your enemies as you can count.[7] I will counsel you and greatly exalt you, and make known my friendship with true faith, grant you happiness and great favour, have you as a thegn, and be unto you a protector, if you obey me in a manner that pleases me.

But if you turn your heart from me and neglect or show disdain for my teachings and my laws, then for you swiftly will there be an increase in suffering from barrenness and misery, strife and sorrow, war and hunger; and your hearts will grow exceedingly timid and the power of your enemies will grow much greater, and often you will flee shamefully, dispersed and greatly terrified by an insignificant force. Crop failure will befall you often because of bad weather, and you will be brought very low by theft and pestilence, and you will be given into the power of your enemies, who will afflict and oppress you terribly.[8] They will lay waste to your land, burn your cities, ransack your property,

---

5 A paraphrase of *Leviticus* 26:39–43.

6 *Leviticus* 26:45.

7 Wulfstan's translation here recalls, in positive form, the sequence of misfortunes he employs elsewhere in his writings to characterise the sufferings of the English. See, for instance, Bethurum 5, ll. 102–5; Bethurum 20.1, ll. 50–4 and (in an abbreviated version) Bethurum 20.3, ll. 55–6; Napier 47, p. 243, ll. 1–4; *On Various Misfortunes*, n. 3; and *On Justice*, n. 17.

8 Cf. *On Justice*, n. 17, and *On Various Misfortunes*, n. 3.

and destroy your country. And when the land has been made desolate because of its sins and the host of people has mostly vanished, then the remnant, anguished and sorrowful, will begin to mourn for their sins with their grief-stricken spirits, and to lament despondently that they and their elders so angered me because they refused to obey my laws but instead despised me in in every way. And then, though it were late, the hardness of their stubborn hearts will be greatly softened by the grim punishment and fierce chastisement which I will inflict upon that people as retribution; and then they will call and plead with me for help, and renounce sin and turn to righteousness. Also, then, will I become mindful of my past promises and of those things I granted to their ancestors in times gone by; and then afterwards I shall counsel and enrich them, if they will obey me properly. I will protect that land and defend that people, and I will grant that people happiness and favour, as long as they love and faithfully obey me. These are the words of God which God himself imparted and Moses set down, and it all may serve as an example to every people, heed it who will. May God preserve us. Amen.

2. EVIL RULERS (BETHURUM 21)

Although one of Wulfstan's shorter homilies, this text is also among his most problematic, not least because of the complications surrounding the different manuscript versions. The text is preserved in three manuscripts: Oxford, Bodleian Library, Hatton 113; London, British Library, Cotton Nero A.i; and two distinct versions in the first and second booklets of Cambridge, Corpus Christi College 201.[1] While obviously copies of the same homily, the differences between the four versions are significant enough to undermine modern editorial attempts to establish a single authoritative text. It thus offers, in Andy Orchard's words, a perfect illustration of 'the issues and pitfalls surrounding the editing of Wulfstan's writing'.[2] Equally problematic is the text's date of composition, which Bethurum places 'late in [Wulfstan's] career', Wormald locates somewhere around 1012, and Pons-Sanz simply lists as unknown.[3] If the circumstances surrounding its composition remain mysterious, however, its manuscript placement does offer some sense of how it was understood by its earliest readers. Three of the four versions directly follow texts of the *Sermo Lupi ad Anglos*, and the implied transition in the Cotton Nero A.i and Hatton 113 rubrics suggests that the two homilies may have been intended to be read together.[4] Likewise, given both its location in the manuscripts and the coda added to the versions in Hatton 113 and Cotton Nero A.i, it may also be the case that, as Lionarons suggests, the text was meant to provide a transition between Wulfstan's homiletic and legal writings.[5]

---

1 See the catalogue of the contents of C.C.C.C. 201 in the appendix.

2 Orchard 2002: 314. I should note that for this translation, I have relied on editions by Bethurum and Orchard (Bethurum 1957: 276–7; Orchard 2002: 328–40.) in attempting to convey some sense of the more significant variations between the different texts.

3 Bethurum 1957: 364; Wormald 2004: 26; and Pons-Sanz 2007: 25.

4 Bethurum 1957: 364 and Anlezark 2006: 67.

5 Lionarons 2010: 162. On the coda, see n. 11 below.

TRANSLATION[1]

Here is another just admonition and true exhortation necessary for the realm.[2] [Let him pay heed who will]:[3]

Beloved people, let us understand exactly what is necessary for us: that henceforth we will always order our ways wisely and prudently before God and the world[4] and turn from sin to righteousness, for it is clear and obvious that this has been put off for all too long;[5] and too little control and secular discipline have been exercised, as ought to have been done, over those who have sinned most often before God and harmed this realm. Yet what I say is true, let him take heed who will: that as a very great punishment, those who abuse and violate divine teachings and secular laws[6] in this realm in any way may be greatly condemned before the world and they are to be dishonoured everywhere in the land, and thereby shall it be made certain that virtue be upheld and wickedness rejected. Accordingly, it is the worse that, widely throughout the land, what should be scorned often has been praised, what ought to be praised has been too greatly scorned, and what should be loved has been too greatly loathed.[7] And formerly, when times were good, a person taken in wickedness and crime on any occasion was wholly disgraced among men unless he turned the more swiftly to his Lord; and the person who made a habit of telling lies was condemned by all those who loved God; and then, when virtue was loved and vice despised, the people were wise and praiseworthy before God and the world. Yet now, the person

1 This translation is based on the text in Bethurum 1957: 276–7 with reference to that in Orchard 2002: 328–40.

2 The rubric up to the phrase 'necessary for the realm' appears only in Hatton 113 and Cotton Nero A.i. Bethurum points out that three of the four versions of this text immediately follow the *Sermo Lupi ad Anglos* in their respective manuscripts, so the rubric might serve as a specific reference to that text. Bethurum 1957: 364. Of the two versions of the text in C.C.C.C. 201, the first is rubricated in Old English 'To all the people' and the second in Latin 'A sermon of the wolf'. A full catalogue of the variations between the different texts can be found in in Orchard 2002: 331–2. Where significant, these differences have been noted below.

3 This addition to the rubric occurs only in Cotton Nero A.i, but it is almost certainly in Wulfstan's own hand. Ker 1971: 322; Orchard 2002: 316.

4 'The formula *for Gode 7 for worolde* presents one of the prominent themes within the homily in its implicit contrast between the divine and the worldly, and more particularly between religious and secular authority'. Lionarons 2010: 162.

5 Cf. *Polity* XXXVI.

6 See note to *Episc.* 1.

7 Cf. Bethurum 20.3 (*Sermo Lupi ad Anglos*), ll. 152–60.

who can survive successfully with deceit and overcome truth with falsehood appears the cleverer and much the wiser, but woe to him for that
cunning and all of his accomplishment unless he desists.[8] Indeed, it is
right that we love those who love God and fervently despise those who
anger God;[9] and we are not to have any interaction with them before
they submit and repent sincerely;[10] and as for those who will not do
so, let us all discipline them with worldly punishment, lest we have
any involvement with their sins now and with their sufferings later.
And let us do what is necessary for us: let us please God, adhere to
God's laws, and grow steadfast for the common benefit; and moreover,
readily consider much that may be wise and necessary for the entire
realm before God and the world. [Amen. Wise were the councillors
who set down secular laws to support divine law for the guidance of
the people, and who assigned compensation to Christ and king, so that
many people must, out of need, submit to justice.][11]

---

8 Cf. Bethurum 9, ll. 133–8 and, more closely, *On Justice*, n. 15. Lionarons argues
  that the closeness of this latter parallel indicates that the two texts may have been
  composed at about the same time. See Lionarons 2010: 163.

9 Wulfstan's language here recalls that of the loyalty oath found at the beginning of
  the Old English oath compilation, *Swerian*: 'By the Lord, before whom this relic is
  holy, I will be faithful and true to N, and love all that he loves and despise all that
  he despises, according to the law of God and the custom of the world' ('On ðone
  Drihten, þe ðes haligdom is fore halig, ic wille beon N hold 7 getriwe 7 eal lufian ðæt
  he lufað 7 eal ascunian ðæt he ascunað, æfter Godes rihte 7 æfter woroldgerysnum').

10 Cf. Napier 57, p. 296, l. 34.

11 MSS. Hatton 113 and Cotton Nero A.i only. Cf. *EGu.* Pr.2, *Sanctuary* 24, *Clerical
   Compensation* 11, and VIII Atr. 36.

3. *AN ADMONITION TO BISHOPS*

This short text survives solely in London, British Library, Cotton Nero A.i, in which it follows *Polity* VI (*'Likewise, on Bishops'*), a brief Latin passage on ecclesiastical garb, and a set of injunctions concerning episcopal behaviour. The title is Jost's, as the text lacks a rubric in the manuscript.[1] It is unclear if Wulfstan composed the text especially for inclusion in the manuscript, or whether it was composed on a separate occasion and then transcribed here. Equally unclear is whether the manuscript preserves the entirety of the text, or if the surviving version is simply a fragment of a longer homily or set of canons.[2] The latter seems unlikely, though: the *Admonition*'s structure as a series of reprimands elaborating on the principle established in the first clause and rounded out by the injunction in the last suggests that the surviving text constitutes a complete unit. Based on its location in the manuscript and lack of rubric, modern readers have speculated that it may have been intended as either a continuation of the injunctions preceding it, a summary of Wulfstan's comments on bishops designed to echo the admonitions at the end of *Polity* VI, or a homiletic fragment inserted to round out a series of related texts.[3] The date of the text is unknown; however, the parallels with the later versions of *Polity* and the *Canons of Edgar* as well as the homilies Bethurum 16, 17, and 20 indicate that it was probably composed later in the archbishop's career, perhaps between 1018 and 1023.

---

1 Jost 1959: 262.

2 Lionarons 2010: 42.

3 Loyn 1971b: 47; Whitelock 1981: 413; Wilcox 2000a: 403; and Lionarons 2010: 42.

TRANSLATION[1]

[1] Bishops must always proclaim God's justice and forbid injustice;[2] and indeed, just as soon as bishops fall silent about what is right and as soon as they grow fearful and come to be ashamed of what is right,[3] and they mumble with their mouths when they should cry out, immediately their integrity greatly diminishes.[4]

[2] Yet nonetheless it is an evil truth which I speak: some of us are inclined to be too accommodating and too eager for praise;[5] and we offer sweet words to men for their friendship and thereby most often flatter needlessly, and we remain silent all too much about the truth.

[3] Moreover, we also have a terrible habit: over and over again we exemplify in ourselves what we should forbid most zealously everywhere, that is worldly pride and idle vanity;[6] and we embrace drunkenness too eagerly, and indeed, we believe that our acclaim grows far and wide when we intoxicate others too greatly.[7]

[4] Yet it would be appropriate for us all, if we desired what is right, that we intoxicate both our own intellect and that of each of those who come to us with wisdom, and not with other drink in great excess, but with proper distinction according to one's capacity.[8]

1 This translation is based on the text in Jost 1959: 262–8 with reference to Whitelock: 1981: 413–17.

2 Cf. Bethurum 17, ll. 14–15 and *Polity* VI. On this passage, see Wilcox 2000a: 403–4; Orchard 2007: 328.

3 Cf. Bethurum 16b, ll. 24–6. The text up until this point is written in Wulfstan's own handwriting. See Ker 1971: 322.

4 A favourite phrase of Wulfstan's, probably influenced by *Isaiah* 58:1. Cf. *Polity* V; Bethurum 16b, ll. 17–22; Bethurum 17, ll. 41–3; and Bethurum 20.3 (the *Sermo Lupi ad Anglos*), ll. 180–4.

5 Wulfstan's criticism of those who are 'too accommodating and too eager for praise' ('to liðie 7 to lofgeorne') recalls the final line of *Beowulf*, in which the hero is described – perhaps ambivalently? – as 'most beloved by men and most eager for glory' ('leodum liðost ond lofgeornost', l. 3182). Wulfstan's use of the first person plural here is in keeping with his practice elsewhere of directing his admonitions at himself as well as his colleagues, as he does at the end of *Polity* V. Cf. Whitelock 1981: 413.

6 Cf. *Polity* XVII.

7 Cf. *Canons* 58 and 66. The most likely source for this injunction is Ælfric's Pastoral Letter to Bishop Wulfsige, §74.

8 Possibly an allusion to the Vulgate translation of *Psalms* 22:5: 'and my cup, which intoxicates me, how brilliant it is' ('et calix meus inebrians quam præclarus est'). If so, Wulfstan's adaptation of the verse would be in line with the interpretation propounded by Augustine: 'We do not mean to say, "nobody must be inebriated", but rather, "Go ahead and get inebriated, but from the right source". If the Lord's

[5] Lo, it has always poorly suited bishops that they, for the purpose of idle boasting, wrongfully curried favour with secular men everywhere too greatly; and it is worse that they willingly flatter unworthy men in search of praise.[9]

[6] We delude ourselves with entertainers, and give them our money, and we willingly offer flattery in exchange for shameful words; we desire praise and to shield ourselves from insult. All of these are vain and displease God.

[7] And it is never appropriate for us to obtain anything unlawfully,[10] nor indeed is it sensible that we squander what has been rightly obtained on foolishness; but it is always most rightly appropriate for us to comfort God's needy willingly with money and food, insofar as we can.

[8] Moreover, it is suitable for us to give our friends loving hospitality, as is appropriate.

[9] And indeed, it is never suitable for bishops to linger too long on the bench at a drinking hall, either at home or on a journey, but they are to be moderate in both.[11]

[10] But we are accustomed, as we never should be, to consider whatever pleases us to be right and to pursue our desires all too greatly.

[11] And we also always reflect the most upon those things which we should the least: we contemplate worldly cares and idle pursuits, and we seek after glory and worldly vanity.[12]

[12] And we also love unlawful gain too greatly: we sell sometimes for a price that which we properly should give for free.[13]

[13] And what I say is true, recognise it who will: ever since bishops have turned wholly away from canonical practices to worldly practices,

---

excellent chalice intoxicates you, your inebriation will be evident in your actions. It will show itself in your holy love for justice, and finally it will be obvious from the way you lose your senses, but lose them only in the estrangement of your mind from earthly things to fly to heaven.' See Boulding 2003: 155.

9 Cf. Bethurum 10c, l. 84 and *Polity* XVII.

10 Cf. I As. 5 and *Polity* X.

11 The source for this admonition is c. X of the *Capitula ecclesiastica* of Haito of Basel: 'Tenth, that [bishops] are not to enter taverns, nor be sitting at home or busy themselves with travel'. See Jost 1959: 265.

12 Cf. *Polity* XI.

13 Cf. the Letter from Brother Ælfric to Archbishop Wulfstan (no. 2a in Fehr 1914), c. XV.

their honour has been diminishing greatly.[14] Therefore, there is much need for repentance immediately.

[**14**] Lo, let us think on that often and frequently, and diligently order our practices with integrity, and understand what is true: that immature behaviour is never appropriate for one of mature age all too greatly;[15] nor is an old man without fault when he makes himself like a child through foolish actions or behaviour.[16]

14 Cf. *Canons* 68b. See also VI Atr. 5.4 and VIII Atr. 29.

15 Cf. the second section ('For bishops, wisdom and discretion …') following *Polity* VI.

16 The final eight words (in the Old English, the last six) are in Wulfstan's handwriting. Ker 1971: 322.

4. TWO VERSIONS OF VII ÆTHELRED (VII AND VIIA ATR.)

The set of laws traditionally referred to as VII Æthelred was composed by Wulfstan and issued in the king's name following a meeting of the royal council at Bath in 1009.[1] Prescribing a set of penitential rituals to be undertaken in response to invasion of the Viking 'great army' under the leadership of Thurkil the Tall, the text survives in four distinct versions:

1. The twelfth-century legal compilation *Quadripartitus* includes a Latin translation of a now-lost Old English original that likely represented the earliest version of the text as well as the one with the greatest claim to have circulated as an officially-sanctioned piece of royal legislation;

2. Cambridge, Corpus Christi College 201 preserves an Old English version referred to as VIIa Æthelred. This version, which differs slightly from that in *Quadripartitus*, might be a draft Wulfstan produced while preparing the 'official' text, but is more commonly thought to be a revision he composed in the process of reworking VII Æthelred as a homily;[2]

3. A homiletic version (Napier 35, *On Various Misfortunes*) survives in C.C.C.C. 201 and Oxford, Bodleian Library, Hatton 113. Although this version suffers from the interpolations of an over-zealous 'Wulfstan-imitator', the majority of the text is unquestionably Wulfstan's own;[3]

4. A second homiletic version (Napier 36) also survives, although this text was almost certainly composed by someone other than Wulfstan. As Lionarons points out, this version 'reads as if it had been written from memory by someone who remembered most of the content and some, albeit not all, of the words of Napier 35'.[4] Although the first two versions of VII Æthelred are translated below and the third elsewhere in this volume, this version, being of lesser interest and (if truth be told) lesser quality, has been omitted.

VII and VIIa Æthelred testify to Wulfstan's belief – indeed, the belief of most of his contemporaries – that religious devotion could effectively defend the

---

1 On the text's date, see Keynes 2007: 179.

2 On the relationship between VII and VIIa Æthelred, see Wormald 1978: 58–9 and Wormald 1999d: 330–2.

3 For more on this text, see the introduction to the translation included in this volume, above pp. 32–3.

4 Lionarons 2010: 31.

nation against external threats, whether natural or man-made.[5] VII Æthelred, a more specific text than its Old English counterpart, draws upon well-established Anglo-Saxon and Carolingian penitential practices in order to unite the realm under a sustained programme of moral self-examination.[6] Rituals of penance here serve as an ideological instrument designed to unify the community in the face of a common threat and to emphasise the moral dimensions of the struggle. In contrast, the somewhat shorter VIIa Æthelred dispenses with many of Latin's specific prescriptions in favour of a more admonitory approach. In part, this revision may have resulted from changing political circumstances: as Wormald points out, the more general tone meant that 'it was no longer the law of a king who was thoroughly discredited by the time the collection in C.C.C.C. 201 was put together'.[7] Perhaps more importantly, though, it translated the specific response to the crisis of 1009 into a statement of principle concerning the proper response of a people to misfortune more generally, a statement Wulfstan would further develop in his homiletic treatment of this text in Napier 35. As such, it is wrong to suggest that VII and VIIa Æthelred, like Wulfstan's other homiletic legislation, offer simply two more examples of legislation that 'was never so loquacious, so vague, or so futile';[8] rather, these texts, along with Napier 35, offer vivid illustrations of Wulfstan's developing vision of a would-be holy society confronting the threats of the outside world.

5 On this point, see Jones 2004: 325 and Keynes 2007: 181–2.

6 The sources of VII Æthelred have been detailed in Keynes 2007: 181–8 and Cubitt 2011: 179–92.

7 Wormald 1999d: 332.

8 This judgment occurs in Richardson and Sayles 1966: 27. On this comment, see Keynes 2007: 181.

TRANSLATION

VII Æthelred[1]

KING ÆTHELRED AND HIS COUNSELLORS DECREED THIS AT BATH:[2]

[1] First, that the one God is to be praised and honoured above all, and that all should obey their king according to the best customs of their ancestors, and together with him defend his kingdom.[3]

[1.1] And they first agreed to call upon God's mercy and help by fasting, almsgiving, confession, and abstaining from sins and injustice.

[1.2] Thus, a penny or the value of a penny is to be given from every ploughland.[4]

[1.3] And everyone who has a household is to ensure that that each of his hired-men[5] gives one penny. If anyone does not have it, the lord is to give it for him; and every thegn is to give one-tenth of all he has.[6]

[2] And we have decreed that every Christian who has reached adulthood is to fast for three days upon bread, water, and raw herbs.[7]

[2.1] And each person is to go to confession and, with bare feet, to church; and by repenting and abstaining, repudiate all his sins.[8]

[2.2] And for three days every priest is to go barefoot in the procession along with his people.

---

1 This translation is based on the text in Liebermann 1903–16: v. I, pp. 260–1 with reference to those in Robertson 1925:108–13 and Whitelock 1981: 375–9.

2 This statement recalls the brief prologues found in much of Æthelred's other legislation, as in I Atr. Pr.: 'This is the decree that King Æthelred and his council devised at Woodstock'. Cf. Wormald 1999d: 331.

3 Cf. V Atr. 34 and 35, VI Atr. 1, VIIa Atr. Pr.

4 Cf. VIIa Atr. 2.2.

5 This word is in Old English although its meaning is problematic. The word used is *hyremannus*, a term encompassing dependants with property of their own, yet the analogous clause in VIIa Atr. 5 refers to *hiredmanna*, 'hired men'. The difference in terminology most likely results from an error on the part of the Quadripartitist, whose Old English was shaky at best. See Robertson 1925: 336.

6 Cf. VIIa Atr. 5.

7 Cf. VIIa Atr. 1.

8 Cf. VIIa Atr. 2 and *On Various Misfortunes*, n. 8. Keynes points out that processions of this sort were particularly associated with Rogation days, referred to as *gangdagas* ('walking days') in Old English. Keynes 2007: 182–3.

[**2.2a**] And moreover, every priest is to sing thirty masses, and every deacon and cleric thirty psalms.[9]

[**2.2b**] And for three days everyone is to be served meals without meat; and food and drink in the amount that would have been eaten is to be shared out among the poor.[10]

[**2.3**] And all slaves are to be freed from work on those three days so that they will be able to fast better and make what they wish for themselves.[11]

[**2.3a**] These are the three days: the Monday, Tuesday, and Wednesday just before the feast of Saint Michael.[12]

[**2.4**] If anyone breaks the fast: a slave is to pay with the lash,[13] a poor freeman is to pay thirty pence and a king's thegn 120 shillings; and this money is to be distributed to the poor.[14]

[**2.5**] And let every priest, town reeve, and tithing-man[15] oversee the almsgiving and fasting, so that they can swear to it on holy relics.[16]

[**3**] And we command that a mass entitled 'Against the Pagans' is to be sung daily at Matins in every religious foundation by the entire community for the king and his people.[17]

[**3.1**] And at each of the canonical hours, all members of the community, lying on the ground with limbs extended, are to chant the psalm, 'Lord, how they are multiplied',[18] and the Collect against the pagans; and this is to be done as long as we have the need.[19]

[**3.2**] And in every monastery or community of monks, every priest

9 This clause has no equivalent in VIIa Atr.

10 Cf. VIIa Atr. 4.1 and *On Various Misfortunes*, n. 15.

11 Cf. Af. 43, VIIa Atr. 5.1, and *On Various Misfortunes*, n. 12. See also Pelteret 1995: 90–3.

12 On 29 September. On this clause, see Cubitt 2011: 191.

13 That is, he is to be whipped. Cf. Wi. 10 and *EGu.* 8.

14 Cf. VIIa Atr. 3 and *On Various Misfortunes*, n. 14. It is likely that the fine of 120 shillings is a scribal error, and both VIIa Atr. and *On Various Misfortunes* list the amount as only 30 shillings. See Wormald 1999d: 331.

15 That is, the head of a tithing, an administrative unit consisting of one-tenth of a hundred. The obligations of the tithing-man are not mentioned in VIIa Æthelred.

16 Cf. VIIa Atr. 2.3 and *On Various Misfortunes*, n. 10.

17 Cf. VIIa Atr. 6, 6.2.

18 *Psalm 3*.

19 Lit. 'as long as the need is in our hands'. Cf. VIIa Atr. 6.3 and *On Various Misfortunes*, n. 11.

is to individually celebrate thirty masses for the king and for all the people, and every monk [chant] his psalter thirty times.[20]

[4] And we command that everyone, for the love of God and all the saints, is to render their Church-dues[21] and proper tithes, just as was done and done better in the days of our ancestors; that is, according to every tenth acre turned up by the plough.[22]

[4.1] And all dues are to be paid, for the love of God, to the appropriate mother church.

[4.2] And no one is to take from God that which belongs to him and which our forebears granted to him.

[5] And we forbid anyone to be sold out of the country. If anyone presumes to do so, he is to be excluded from the blessing of God and all the saints, and from the entire Christian communion, unless he does penance and makes amends as his bishop shall instruct.[23]

[6] And we forbid to all people all forms of theft.

[6.1] And all persons, poor or wealthy, are entitled to legal remedies.

[6.2] And if anyone has committed theft, let him return all that has been stolen and make amends, as was the practice before and will be afterwards.

[6.3] And if a reeve has committed theft, he shall make amends at twice the rate imposed upon anyone else.

[7] And if anyone is behind in his almsgiving, let it be paid between now and the feast of Saint Michael, or the full penalty shall be assessed.

[7.1] And every year henceforth God's dues are to be paid in every case as decreed above, for the friendship of God and all the saints, so that the omnipotent God will grant us mercy, and victory over our enemies, and peace. Let us earnestly beseech him to grant us mercy and grace here and rest without end in the future. Amen.[24]

---

20 Cf. VIIa Atr. 6–6.2.

21 This word is in Old English.

22 Cf. *EGu.* 6.3, VIII Atr. 12, and I Cn. 8.2.

23 The sale of people into foreign slavery was one of Wulfstan's principal concerns and recurs frequently in his work. Wormald points out that its mention here is one of the chief indicators of the archbishop's involvement in the text's composition. Wormald 1978: 63.

24 Cf. VIIa Atr. 8 and *On Various Misfortunes*, n. 16.

VIIa Æthelred[25]

THIS WAS DECREED WHEN THE GREAT ARMY CAME TO THIS LAND:[26]

We all must strive diligently so that we may receive God's mercy and compassion and, with his help, withstand our enemies.[27]

[1] Now we ordain that the whole realm consume only bread, herbs, and water in shared penance for three days, that is, the Monday, Tuesday, and Wednesday before Michaelmas.[28]

[2] And everyone is to come to church barefoot, without gold or ornaments, and they are to go to confession.[29]

[2.1] And all shall process out with the holy relics and fervently call

---

25 This translation is based on the text in Liebermann 1903–16: v. I, p. 262 with reference to those in Robertson 1925: 114–15 and Whitelock 1981: 379–82.

26 The rubric likely refers to the Danish invasion of 1009, the year in which the Latin version of VII Atr. was promulgated. Pons-Sanz suggests that this text was composed at the same time as VII Atr.; however the retrospective rubric indicates that Wulfstan only may have undertaken an Old English translation of VII Atr. sometime after the production of the original Latin text. Alternately, it is also possible that the rubric simply refers to the transcription of the text rather than its composition. Liebermann judges the rubric to be inauthentic, though his conclusion stems from his assumption that the text was an official piece of royal legislation rather than an adaptation of the laws composed by the archbishop for purposes of his own. Wormald observes that the progress of VII Atr. from Latin text through Old English translation and into homily (*On Various Misfortunes*, Napier 35) results in changes to the rubric that imply an increasingly general application of the text. While the Latin opens with 'This was established by King Æthelred and his councillors at Bath' ('Hoc instituerunt Æþelredus rex et sapientes eius apud Badam') and the Old English begins with the rubric translated above; the homily's rubric reads only, 'Concerning Various Misfortunes' ('On mistlican gelimpan'). See Liebermann 1903–1916: v. 3, p. 180; Wormald 1999d: 331–2; Keynes 2007: 179–80; Pons-Sanz 2007: 22; and Lionarons 2010: 144–5.

27 Cf. VII Atr. 1–1.1 and 7.1.

28 Cf. VII Atr. 2 and 2.3a. This clause provides the basis for the 1009 dating of the text. As Keynes summarises, 'Internal evidence indicates that the code was issued in a year in which Monday, Tuesday and Wednesday fell "before" Michaelmas (29 September), which thus must itself have fallen between Thursday and Sunday; and the version of the code in *Quadripartitus* specifies that the three days were *proximi* before Michaelmas, perhaps implying that Michaelmas itself fell on a Thursday. The options for the date of *VII Æthelred* can be narrowed in this way to 1009 and 1015. In 1015, the Danes arrived in September, not August, which would leave little time for necessary arrangements; on which basis it seems reasonable to settle for 1009'. Keynes 2007: 179.

29 Cf. VII Atr. 2.1 and *On Various Misfortunes*, n. 8. The possible origins of the Anglo-Saxon practice of penitential processions are discussed in Keynes 2007: 181–3.

upon Christ with their innermost hearts.[30]

[**2.2**] And a penny or the equivalent of a penny is to be paid by every hide.[31]

[**2.3**] And it is to be brought to church and subsequently divided in three with the confessor and town reeve acting as witnesses.[32]

[**3**] And if anyone does not pay this, then he shall compensate for it in the manner that the law decrees: a householder with thirty pence, a slave with a beating, and a thegn with thirty shillings.[33]

[**4**] And wherever that levy comes to be assessed, every penny is to be distributed for God's favour.

[**4.1**] Furthermore, all the food that would have been enjoyed had the fast not been decreed is to be diligently distributed for God's favour after the fast to the poor, the bedridden, and those so afflicted that they are not able to fast.[34]

[**5**] And every retainer is to give a penny as alms, or his lord is to give it for him if he does not have it himself, and those of high status shall pay tithes.[35]

[**5.1**] And slaves are to be released from work on these three days to attend church and keep the fast more readily.[36]

[**6**] And in every monastery, the whole community is to chant from their psalters on these three days.[37]

---

30 Cf. *On Various Misfortunes*, n. 8. See also Ælfric's *Sermon on the Greater Litany* (*Letania maiore* in the Catholic Homilies, first series): 'On these days, we should carry out our prayers, follow our relics out and in, and praise the almighty God with zealousness'. ('We sceolon eac on ðysum dagum began ure gebedu & fylian urum haligdomum ut 7 in 7 þone ælmihtigan god mid geornfulnysse herian', ll. 40–1). On this clause, see Keynes 2007: 187.

31 Cf. VII Atr. 1.2.

32 Cf. VII Atr. 2.5 and *On Various Misfortunes*, n. 10. On the division of church income, see also VIII Atr. 6.

33 Cf. VII Atr. 2.4 and *On Various Misfortunes*, n. 14. VII Atr. assesses a penalty of 120 shillings for a thegn's non-compliance rather than the 30 specified here. Wormald notes that while either number could be the result of scribal error, a penalty of 30 shillings is supported by the corresponding passage in *On Various Misfortunes*. See Wormald 1999d: 331.

34 Cf. VII Atr. 2.2b and *On Various Misfortunes*, n. 15.

35 Cf. VII Atr. 1.3.

36 Cf. VII Atr. 2.3 and *On Various Misfortunes*, n. 12. See Pelteret 1995: 90–3.

37 Cf. VII Atr. 3 and 3.2.

[6.1] And each priest is to celebrate mass for our lord and all of his people.[38]

[6.2] Additionally, a special mass is to be celebrated each day in every church because of the peril that confronts us until it is resolved.[39]

[6.3] And at each service, the whole community, prostrate with outstretched arms before God's altar, is to sing the psalm, '*Lord, how are they multiplied*'[40] and the Prayers and Collect.[41]

[7] And all collectively, clerical and lay, are to submit to God whole-heartedly and deserve his mercy.

[8] And every year henceforth, ecclesiastical dues are to be paid with special conscientiousness, so that the almighty God will have mercy on us and enable us to overcome our enemies. May God preserve us. Amen.[42]

---

38 Cf. VII Atr. 3.2.

39 Cf. VII Atr. 3 and 3.2.

40 *Psalm 3*.

41 Cf. VII Atr. 3.1 and *On Various Misfortunes*, n. 11.

42 Cf. VII Atr. 7.1 and *On Various Misfortunes*, n. 16.

5. CNUT'S PROCLAMATION OF 1020

Cnut 1020 follows Napier 59–61 (*On the Duties of the Laity, On Heathen Practice,* and *On Christian Practice*) in the York Gospels (York, Minster Library, Additional 1). The text was initially composed during Cnut's return to Denmark in 1019–1020; however, internal evidence indicates that Wulfstan subsequently revised it for further circulation, oral delivery, or inclusion with the homilies in the manuscript.[1] The greatest density of Wulfstanian language occurs in clauses 14–20, and it seems likely that these clauses along with the concluding 'amen' were added to the original royal writ in order to prepare the text to be read from the pulpit as well as to situate it in the same ideological framework governing Cnut's other legislation.[2]

Cnut had come to power only four years before the release of this letter, so it must be viewed through the lens of the still-recent 1014–1016 conquest of England by the Danes. Although Cnut affirms his closeness with Archbishop Lyfing of Canterbury and endorses the legislation of his English predecessor Edgar, he nonetheless remains a foreign king addressing a defeated people, and clauses such as 4–5 and 9–12 seem designed to underscore his audience's subject status. At the same time, Cnut also promises to rule justly in exchange for obedience, and it is upon this promise that Wulfstan builds in the second half of the letter.[3] Wulfstan's additions to the letter subordinate Cnut's demand for obedience to secular law to a larger call for adherence to the law of God. Although Cnut had been a Christian prior to coming to power, little evidence survives to suggest that he felt any particular devotion before assuming the throne of a Christian kingdom. Thus, even as Wulfstan's revisions offer the conqueror a politically useful Christian context for his rule, they also reinforce a specifically Christian vision of just governance under which the king's authority remains only one component of the greater authority of God.[4]

---

1 Keynes 1986: 95–6; Stafford 1989: 74; Lawson 1992: 584–5; Lawson 1993: 63–4; Bolton 2009: 83–4; and Treharne 2012: 21–7.

2 Keynes 1986: 96 and Bolton 2009: 84.

3 On the place of this text within the history of Cnut's royal promises, see Stafford 1971: 188–9 and Wormald 1999d: 348.

4 Cf. Treharne 2012: 26.

TRANSLATION[1]

[1] King Cnut offers friendly greetings to his archbishops, his subordinate bishops,[2] Earl Thurkil,[3] all his earls, and all his people in England, the twelve-hundred men and the two-hundred men, clergy and laymen.[4] [2] And I proclaim to you that I will be a gracious lord, devoted to the rights of the Church and to just secular law.[5] [3] I have taken to heart the letters and messages from the Pope which Archbishop Lyfing[6] brought to me from Rome: that I should everywhere promote God's worship and cast out injustice and establish a perfect peace through the power which God has chosen to give to me.[7]

[4][8] Now then, I did not withhold my money when a threat to you

---

1 This translation is based on the text in Liebermann 1903–16: v. I, pp. 273–5 with reference to those in Robertson 1925: 140–5 and Whitelock 1981: 435–41.

2 The word used here is *leodbiscopas*, a blanket term for all the categories of episcopal rank (metropolitan, diocesan, suffragan) lower than an archbishop.

3 Thurkil the Tall (b. unknown, d. after 1023) was among Cnut's leading supporters. Leader of a band of Jómsvíkings, Thurkil had alternated allegiances between Sweyn Forkbeard (father of Cnut) and Æthelred for much of the first two decades of the eleventh century. Following his men's murder of Archbishop Alphege of Canterbury in 1012, Thurkil defected once more to the English side, only to rejoin the Danes for Cnut's invasion of England in 1015. Following Cnut's ascension to the English throne, Thurkil became earl of East Anglia, a position he still held when this letter was released. Thurkil was banished from England following a quarrel with Cnut in 1021, although by 1023 the two had reconciled and he was appointed by the king to govern Denmark. Thurkil disappears from the historical record at this point, suggesting that he likely died shortly thereafter. See Lawson 1993 and Bolton 2009: 206–20. Although Wulfstan's attitude towards Thurkil remains unknown, the possible influence of his career on Wulfstan's work has been discussed in Keynes 1991: 75–6.

4 The complicated ethnic makeup of Cnut's realm is indicated by his use of both Scandinavian and English status designators. Significantly, this is the first time 'earl' is used in the Scandinavian sense in the Old English laws. Cnut employs a similar mode of address in a contemporary writ for Christ Church, Canterbury (ed. as no. 26 in Harmer 1952: 181–2). On twelve-hundred men and two-hundred men, see *On Ranks.*

5 Cf. IV Eg. 16, as well as Æthelred's similar promise, recorded in the entry for 1014 in the *Anglo-Saxon Chronicle*, to be a 'gracious lord' ('hold hlaford') following his return from exile.

6 Archbishop of Canterbury from 1018 until his death on 12 June 1020. The letters referred to, addressed to Cnut by Pope Benedict VIII and carried back from Rome by Archbishop Lyfing in 1018, have not survived.

7 The letters may have been from the pope, but the language here is Wulfstan's. Cf. *On Justice*, n. 13; II Cn. 7.1; and *Episc.* 8 and 9.

8 Keynes suggests that articles 4–7 show signs of having been revised or corrected by Wulfstan. Keynes 1986: 83.

was at hand, and with God's help I have dispersed it with my wealth.[9]
[5] At that time, it was made known to me that a danger approached
us greater than we would have preferred; then I myself went, alongside those who travelled with me, to Demark, from which the greatest
danger threatened you;[10] and with God's help I have forestalled it,
so that from now on hostility from there will never threaten you as
long as you obey me faithfully and my life continues. **[6]** Now I thank
almighty God for his help and benevolence, in that I have resolved
the great threat which loomed over us so that we need not anticipate
danger from there, but rather aid and relief if the need should arise.
[7] Now it is my will that we all humbly thank almighty God for his
favour, which through his assistance he has granted to us.

[8] I now charge my archbishops and all my subordinate bishops to be
conscientious concerning the rights of the Church, each in the region
assigned to him; and I also command my ealdormen to support the
bishops in advancing the rights of the Church and my royal authority
and the welfare of the whole people.

[9] If anyone – either cleric or lay, Danish or English – is so bold as
to act in opposition to the law of God and in opposition to my royal
authority or in opposition to secular law, and he refuses to repent and
refrain in keeping with the teachings of my bishops, then I ask, and
indeed command, Earl Thurkil to bring the offender to justice, if he
can.[11] **[10]** If he cannot, then I desire him to wipe him from the earth
or drive him from the land with our combined strength, whether he is
of higher or lower status.[12]

[11] And further, I command my reeves, for the sake of my friendship and all that they possess and their very lives, to govern my people
with righteousness everywhere and to hand down just rulings with

---

9 The precise nature of the threat mentioned here remains unclear. Robertson argues
   that Cnut here refers to his paying off of the army used to invade England before it
   could commit any further depredations, though Liebermann and Whitelock suggest
   that he may instead be alluding to his purchase of support for his claim to the
   Danish throne. See Liebermann 1903–1916: v. III, p. 188; Robertson 1925: 344; and
   Whitelock 1981: 436.

10 Cnut's trip to Denmark is recorded in the 1019 and 1020 entries in the *Anglo-Saxon
    Chronicle*. The trip may have been a response to the death in 1018 of Cnut's brother,
    King Harald of Denmark, and the raids on England that resulted from the ensuing
    lawlessness. See Lawson 1993: 89–91.

11 Cf. II Cn. 83–83.2. On the parallels between clauses 8–10 and *On Christian Practices*,
    see Baxter 2004: 188.

12 Cf. II Cn. 4–4.2.

the oversight of the bishops of their shires, and to act with such mercy thereby that the bishop deems it just and the subject can abide by it.[13] [12] Moreover, if anyone shelters a thief or commits perjury on his behalf, he will be as deserving of punishment before me as the thief, unless he can be cleared by fully vindicating himself before me.[14]

[13] And I decree that the entire populace, clergy and lay, shall faithfully obey the law of Edgar which all people have accepted and to which they swore allegiance at Oxford,[15] [14] for all the bishops proclaim that very great penance must be performed before God for the violation of oaths or pledges.[16] [15] In addition, they further instruct us that we should sincerely seek, love, and honour the eternal merciful God with all our power and all our might, and reject all forms of wrongdoing,[17] especially those of parricides, murderers and perjurers,[18] witches, enchantresses, adulterers, and the incestuous.[19] [16][20] And we also command, in the name of almighty God and all of his saints, that no man be so bold as to wed a nun in orders or a woman under monastic vows.[21] [17] And if anyone has done so, he is to be an outlaw before God and excommunicated from the Christian faith, and he is to be liable to the king for all that he possesses, unless he swiftly renounces [that union] and greatly repents before God. [18] And we yet further emphasise that the holy day of Sunday is to be kept and honoured with all effort from Saturday noon until dawn on Monday,[22] and no one is to be so bold as to either transact business or attend any meeting on that holy

---

13 Cf. I Ew. Pr.; III Eg. 1.1–1.2 and 5.2; VI Atr. 10.2; and II Cn. 1.1 and 18.1.

14 Cf. IV As. 6.3, I Atr. 4.2, And II Cn. 33.1a.

15 This ceremony is recorded in the entry for 1018 in the *Anglo-Saxon Chronicle*. Edgar's laws loom large in Wulfstan's thought. Cf. I Cn. 1 in C.C.C.C. 201; *Polity* X; *On Justice*, n. 43; and *On Christian Practices*, n. 6. It is unclear how assiduous this adherence to Edgar's laws was meant to be, however. According to Wormald, it is likely that, 'the "law of Edgar" had the same sort of significance in this contexts as had the "law of Edward the Confessor" after the Conquest; with the difference that a written law of Edgar did exist. Each offered a symbol of promised continuity at a time when it seemed gravely threatened'. Wormald 1999d: 132.

16 Cf. V Atr. 22.2 and VI Atr. 28.

17 Cf. II Cn. 7.1; *Episc*. 9; *Polity* II; Bethurum 11, l. 127; Bethurum 13, l. 103; Bethurum 21, ll. 26–7; and *On Justice*, n. 13.

18 On this phrase, see n. to *EGu*. 11.

19 Cf. *EGu*. 11, VI Atr. 7, II Cn. 4, and *On Heathen Practices* n. 6. See also n. to *EGu*. 4.

20 §16–17 appear verbatim in *On Justice*. See n. 38.

21 Cf. VI Atr. 12.1 and 39; I Cn. 7.1; II Cn. 50.1; and *NPL* 63.

22 Cf. II Eg. 5.

day.²³ **[19]** And all people, the poor and the wealthy, are to attend their churches²⁴ and pray for their sins and readily observe every mandated fast,²⁵ and sincerely honour the saints-days²⁶ which the priests have set for us.²⁷ **[20]** Thus we all may and can reach the joy of the heavenly kingdom through the mercy of the eternal God and the intercession of his saints, and dwell with him who lives and rules forever without end. Amen.

23 Cf. *EGu.* 7; VI As. 10; VI Atr. 22.1 and 44; I Cn. 15; *Canons* 19; *NPL* 55; Napier 43 l. 94; *On Tithes* n. 5; *On Justice* n. 45; and *On the Duties of the Laity* n. 16. See Haines 2010: 27.

24 Cf. I Cn. 2.

25 The source for this injunction is II Eg. 5.1. See also V Atr. 12–14 and 17; VI Atr. 22–4; VIII Atr. 16; I Cn. 14.1; *Canons* 49; *On Tithes,* n. 6; and *On the Proper Support,* n. 5.

26 Cf. V Atr. 16, VI Atr. 23, I Cn. 17.1.

27 Cf. *EGu.* 3.1, I Cn. 14.2, and *NPL* 11.

6. THE NORTHUMBRIAN PRIESTS' LAW

Although transcribed in Cambridge, Corpus Christi College 201, among the most important of the mid-eleventh century manuscript compilations of Wulfstan's works, it is doubtful that the *Northumbrian Priests' Law* was actually written by the archbishop. The text appears to have been composed in two parts: the first (clauses 1–45) contains a series of injunctions directed at the clergy, while the second (clauses 46–67) consists of decrees directed at Christian Northumbrians more generally.[1] This dual focus on the moral obligations of the priesthood and the proper exercise of Christian duty, alongside the many borrowings from the *Canons of Edgar* and *Edward-Guthrum*, led Dorothy Whitelock to identify Wulfstan as the text's most likely author.[2] Though tentative, Whitelock's attribution nonetheless came to be widely accepted until it was challenged by Patrick Wormald. Noting the irregularity of the text's Wulfstanian diction, Wormald observed that, '[Wulfstan's] influence is as sparse when he was not quoted as it is intense when he was'.[3] Not only does much of the prose lack the distinctive features of Wulfstan's style, but the text's pronouncements on topics such as clerical marriage radically differ from the sorts of policies endorsed by the archbishop.[4] Wormald argued that the text might more plausibly be attributed to one of Wulfstan's two successors at York, Ælfric Puttoc and Cynesige, both of whom spent parts of their careers as followers of the archbishop yet would have felt little necessity to agree with him on every particular.[5] Wormald's attribution has now largely replaced Whitelock's; yet their disagreement illustrates the still-evolving state of Wulfstan scholarship. This evolution can be recursive, though: one consequence of Wormald's argument is that Felix Liebermann's proposed dating of the text to 1028x1060, rejected by Whitelock because she believed that the text must have been composed during Wulfstan's lifetime, must once again be considered possible.[6] More importantly, the possibility that the *Northumbrian Priests' Law* was actually composed by one of Wulfstan's successors provides vivid evidence for the archbishop's extensive influence on ecclesiastical administration in York even after his death in 1023.

1 Liebermann 1903–1916: v. III, pp. 220–1.

2 Whitelock 1965: 221; Whitelock 1966: 10; and Whitelock 1981: 451.

3 Wormald 1999d: 396.

4 Wormald 1999d: 396–7 and Wormald 1999a: 251.

5 Wormald 1999d: 397.

6 Liebermann 1903–1916: v. III, p. 220 and Whitelock 1981: 450.

TRANSLATION[1]

THE NORTHUMBRIAN PRIESTS' LAW[2]

[1] If anyone inflicts harm on any priest, all of his fellows – with the bishop's help – are to be persistent about the compensation, and in every legal matter they are to be, just as it is written, *as one heart and one soul*.[3]

[2] And because of God's prohibition, we forbid that any priest either buy or accept another's church,[4] unless the other ruins himself with a capital crime so that afterwards he is unworthy to serve at the altar.[5]

[2.1] Yet if any priest does so for any other reason, he is to forfeit his status and the fellowship of his colleagues, and he is not to hold mass anywhere until he who properly holds that church possesses it.[6]

[2.2] And he who committed that offence is to pay twenty ores to the bishop, twelve ores to the priest whom he displaced from his church, twelve ores to all of his colleagues, and he is also to forfeit the payment, if he paid anything wrongfully for another priest's church.

[2.3] And every priest is to find for himself twelve bondmen, that he will properly abide by the priests' law.[7]

---

1 This translation is based on the text in Liebermann 1903–16: v. I, pp. 380–5 with reference to those in Tenhaken 1979: 37–48 and Whitelock 1981: 449–68.

2 Title appears in MS. Whitelock suggests that initially it may have referred only to clauses 1–45, and clauses 46–67.1 were added to the text at a later date. See Whitelock 1981: 450.

3 *Acts* 4:32. Cf. *Canons* 5 and §4 in 'Injunctions on the Behaviour of Bishops.' See Whitelock 1981: 409.

4 Cf. Theodulf, *Capitula* c. XIV, *Canons* 9.

5 Cf. *The Old English Penitential* III.2: 'If a mass-priest was polluted by capital sins before he was ordained and previously confessed that and did penance as his confessor instructed him, and if, after he is ordained, he commits the same sins that he previously renounced, he is not worthy to perform any service at God's altar' ('Gif se mæssepreost geleahtrod wæs mid heafodlicum leahtrum ær he gehadod wære 7 þæt ær andette 7 bette swa him his scrift tæhte. gif he eft syððan he gehadod bið þa ylcan leahtras begæð þe he ær bette. ne bið he na wyrðe þæt he ænige þenunga æt godes weofode do').

6 Cf. *Canons* 9 and VIII Atr. 27.

7 The term used here is *festermen*, a word of Old Norse origin which does not appear elsewhere in Old English legislation. This practice is attested by a record of the *festermen* who testified on behalf of someone named Ælfric which survives as the last item in the York Gospels. See Keynes 1986: 98–9. On the use of bondsmen and warrantors, see II Cn. 23–4. On the need for twelve witnesses, see II Cn. 48 and below, *NPL* 51. The reference to twelve bondmen here and similar require-ments in other Old English legislation led early historians of English law to date the origins of the twelve-member jury to the Anglo-Saxon period. Although there are resonances between the twelve bondmen mentioned here and later jury practices, to

[3] And if any priest sins and he holds mass in spite of the bishop's command, he is to pay twenty ores for neglecting that command, and also do penance for the wrong which he committed previously.

[4] If a priest disregards a bishop's own decree, he is to pay twenty ores.

[5] If a priest turns judgment in a dispute over to a layman which he should refer to an ecclesiastic, he is to pay twenty ores.[8]

[6] If a priest disregards an archdeacon's decree, he is to pay twelve ores.

[7] If a priest is guilty of wrongdoing and he holds mass in spite of the archdeacon's command, he is to pay twelve ores.

[8] If a priest refuses to perform baptism or confession, he is to compensate for that with twelve ores and most especially plead fervently with God.[9]

[9] If a priest does not fetch the chrism at the right time, he is to pay twelve ores.[10]

[10] We instruct that every child is to be baptised within nine nights, or there will be a fine of six ores.[11]

[10.1] And if a child dies a heathen[12] within nine nights out of neglect, penance is to be done before God without a secular penalty; and if it occurs after nine nights, penance is to be done before God and twelve ores are to be paid for that neglect, because he remained a heathen for so long.[13]

---

identify such committees of witnesses as the 'original' juries is a bit of an overstatement. The origins and development of the jury-origin myth has been discussed in Stanley 2000: 111–48.

8 Cf. VI Atr. 1, *Canons* 7, and §10 in 'Injunctions on the Behaviour of Bishops' (ed. Whitelock 1981: 408–13). The principal source for this canon is c. 9 of the Council of Chalcedon.

9 Cf. *EGu.* 3.2 and *Canons* 15.

10 Cf. *EGu.* 3.2.

11 Cf. Ine 2, Ælfric's first Old English pastoral letter for Bishop Wulfsige, §71, and *Canons* 15.

12 Lit. 'If a heathen child dies ...'. Meaney points out that the word *hæþen* is never used to refer to an unbaptised child or adult in any of Wulfstan's surviving writings, thus providing one more indication that the *NPL* was composed by someone else. Meaney 2004: 472.

13 Different penances are prescribed elsewhere for lapses of this sort. Cf. *On Baptism*, n. 5. See also Tenhaken 1979: 53 and Whitelock 1981: 455. Notably, Ine 2.1 assigns the penance to the child's guardian rather than to the priest.

[11] If a priest misleads the people concerning a holy day or a fast, he is to do penance before God and pay twelve ores.[14]

[12] If a priest wrongfully receives ordination outside of his diocese, he is to pay twelve ores and a deacon six ores; and he is to forfeit his ordination unless the bishop of the diocese allows the ordination.

[13] If a priest holds mass in an unconsecrated building, he is to pay twelve ores.[15]

[14] If a priest holds mass without a consecrated altar, he is to pay twelve ores.[16]

[15] If a priest consecrates the host in a wooden chalice, twelve ores.[17]

[16] If a priest holds mass without wine, he is to pay twelve ores.[18]

[17] If a priest neglects the host, he is to pay twelve ores.[19]

[18] If a priest holds mass more often than three times in one day, he is to pay twelve ores.[20]

[19] If anyone violates church-sanctuary, compensation is to be paid according to the status of the church and according to its degree of protection.[21]

[20] If anyone engages in trade with a church,[22] he is to compensate for that with *lahslit*.[23]

[21] If anyone compels service from a church, he is to compensate for that with *lahslit*.

14 Cf. *Canons* 48, *EGu.* 3.1. On this clause, see Magennis 1999: 91n. 24.

15 See n. to *Canons* 30.

16 Cf. Ælfric's first Latin Pastoral Letter to Archbishop Wulfstan, §142 and *Canons* 31.

17 Cf. *Canons* 41, Ælfric's first Old English Pastoral Letter to Archbishop Wulfstan, §162, and his Pastoral Letter to Bishop Wulfsige, §58.

18 Cf. Ælfric's first Old English Pastoral Letter to Archbishop Wulfstan, §164a. The importance of wine to the celebration of the mass was a topic Wulfstan emphasised elsewhere. Its mention here was one of the features that led Whitelock to assert Wulfstan's authorship of the text. See Whitelock 1981: 451.

19 Cf. *Canons* 38.

20 Cf. *Canons* 37 and n.

21 Cf. VIII Atr. 4–4.1, I Cn. 3–3a, and *Northumbrian Church-Sanctuary* 4. Based on the more general applicability of clauses 19–24 (beginning with 'If anyone ...' rather than 'If a priest ...'), Whitelock suggests that they may be a later insertion. See Whitelock 1981: 450.

22 That is, if anyone attempts to use a church as currency in a business transaction.

23 Clauses 20–2 are an expansion of V Atr. 10.2 and VI Atr. 15. On *lahslit*, see n. to *EGu.* 2.

[22] If anyone wrongfully expels a priest from his church, he is to compensate for that with *lahslit*.

[23] If anyone injures a priest, compensation is to be made for the injuries and, because of his order, twelve ores is to be given to the bishop as compensation to the church;[24] for a deacon, six ores as compensation to the church.[25]

[24] If anyone kills a priest, he is to compensate for him with his full wergild, and twenty-four ores to the bishop as compensation to the church; for a deacon, twelve ores as compensation to the church.[26]

[25] If a priest dishonours the church, from which all his honour must come, he is to atone for that.[27]

[26] If a priest puts inappropriate things in a church, he is to atone for that.[28]

[27] If a priest removes the possessions of the church, he is to atone for that.[29]

[28] If a priest abandons the church to which he was consecrated of his own volition, he is to atone for that.[30]

[29] If a priest disrespects or shames another with words or deeds, he is to atone for that.[31]

[30] If a priest fights with another, he is to make amends to him and to the bishop.

[31] If a priest abets another in wrongdoing, he is to atone for that.

[32] If a priest denies rightful assistance to another, he is to atone for that.

[33] If a priest allows another to be unwarned of what he knows will do him harm, he is to atone for that.[32]

24 Literally, 'altar-compensation'.

25 Cf. II Cn. 42.

26 The penalties prescribed here are considerably less than those found in texts more closely associated with Wulfstan. Cf. II Cn. 39 and *Clerical Compensation* 2–9.

27 Cf. *Canons* 26.

28 Cf. *Canons* 27.

29 Cf. §42 in the A recension of Wulfstan's Canon Law Collection (§80 in the B recension).

30 Cf. *Canons* 8. See also Ælfric's first Latin pastoral letter to Wulfstan, §194–5, and §14 in the B Recension of Wulfstan's Canon Law Collection.

31 Cf. *Canons* 13.

32 Cf. §5 in 'Injunctions on the Behaviour of Bishops': 'It is appropriate for bishops that

[34] If a priest neglects to cut his beard or hair, he is to atone for that.[33]

[35] If a priest abandons one woman and takes another, *let him be accursed!*[34]

[36] If a priest does not ring or sing the canonical hours at the set time, he is to atone for that.[35]

[37] If a priest enters the church with weapons, he is to atone for that.[36]

[38] If a priest performs the annual services of the church in the wrong sequence, by day or night, he is to atone for that.[37]

[39] If a priest errs while carrying out an ordeal, he is to atone for that.[38]

[40] If a priest commits fraud while conducting an ordeal,[39] he is to atone for that.

[41] If a priest embraces drunkenness, or becomes an entertainer or a singer among drunkards, he is to atone for that.[40]

[42] If a priest conceals what injustice reigns among the men of his parish, he is to atone for that.[41]

---

each warn another if he hears or learns anything himself about another' ('Bisceopum gebyreð þæt ælc oþerne warnige, gyf he hwæt be oðrum gehyre oððe sylf agyte').

33 Cf. §158 in the B Recension of Wulfstan's Canon Law Collection, §115 in Ælfric's first Old English Pastoral Letter, §206 in Ælfric's second Old English Pastoral Letter, and *Canons* 20.

34 This injunction, which limits its condemnation only to a priest *changing* wives, is one of the places where *NPL* differs markedly from Wulfstan's thought. Nowhere in his writing does Wulfstan come even this close to approving of clerical marriage. Cf. *Canons* 50 and VI Atr. 5.1–2. On this point, see Wormald 1999d: 397 and Hollis 2004: 457.

35 Cf. Ælfric's first Latin Pastoral Letter to Archbishop Wulfstan, §62 and his Pastoral Letter to Bishop Wulfsige, §49. See also §29 in the B recension of Wulfstan's Canon Law Collection, *Polity* VII, and *Canons* 45.

36 Cf. §75 in the A recension of Wulfstan's Canon Law Collection and §159 in the B recension, Ælfric's first Old English Pastoral Letter to Archbishop Wulfstan, §189, Ælfric's first Latin Pastoral Letter to Archbishop Wulfstan, §178, and Ælfric's Pastoral Letter to Bishop Wulfsige, §80. See also *Northumbrian Church-Sanctuary* 3 and *Canons* 46.

37 Cf. *Canons* 50.

38 For this and the next injunction, see also *Canons* 63.

39 Lit. 'If a priest deceives while binding', presumably a reference to the binding of an individual's burn or wound (so that the healing process may be inspected several days later) in the course of an ordeal.

40 Cf. *Canons* 58 and 59 and n. On this clause, see Magennis 1999: 109n. 191.

41 Cf. Theodulf, *Capitula* c. XXVIII and *Canons* 6.

[43] If a priest permits the yearly dues to go uncollected, he is to atone for that.[42]

[44] If a priest fails to attend a synod, he is to atone for that.[43]

[45] If a priest refuses to submit to what is right, but rebels against the bishop's decree, he is to atone for it or he is to be cut off from those in orders and lose both companionship and every dignity unless he submits and atones for it very deeply.[44]

[46] If anyone violates the law of God or the law of the people, he is to atone sincerely for that.[45]

[47] We must all revere and love one God and fervently adhere to one Christian faith and wholly reject every heathen practice.[46]

[48] Accordingly, if anyone comes to be discovered who henceforth practices any heathen rituals, either through sacrifice or through divination or through any form of witchcraft or the worship of idols, if he is the king's thegn, he is to pay ten half-marks: half to Christ, half to the king.[47]

[49] If he is a landholder of another kind, he is to pay six half-marks: half to Christ, half to the local lord.

[50] If he is a peasant,[48] he is to pay twelve ores.

42 Cf. *Canons* 54 and n.

43 Cf. *Canons* 3–6 and n.

44 Cf. VIII Atr. 27 and I Cn. 5.3. See also above, *NPL* 2.1.

45 Noting the change in clausal openings here from 'If a priest ...' to 'If anyone ...'. Whitelock argues that this clause marks the beginning of a later addition to the text, perhaps by a different author more concerned with the behaviour of the laity than with that of the cleric. She also points out that clauses 46–7 are nearly identical to clauses 66–7, suggesting the possibility that the clauses serve as a framing device for the added material. See Whitelock 1981: 450. The source for this clause is VI Atr. 50.

46 Cf. *EGu.* Pr.1; V Atr 1, 34; VI Atr. 1.6; VIII Atr. 44; IX Atr. *explicit*; X Atr. 1; *Northumbrian Priests' Law* 67; *Polity* XXXV; *On Justice* n. 50; *Canons* 16; and *On the Proper Support* n. 4.

47 Cf. *Canons* 16 and II Cn. 5.1. Wulfstan's influence on this clause and c. 54 has been discussed in Jurovics 1978: 204–5; Meaney 2004: 478–9.

48 The term used here is *færbena*, a word of uncertain meaning. The similar penalty for wrongdoing indicates that the *færbena* is equal in status to the *ceorl* and *cyrlisc man* (both here also translated 'peasant') of clauses 53 and 60 and the *tunesman* ('townsman') of clause 59; however, the precise nature of his obligations to his lord remain unclear. Liebermann suggests that the *færbena* may be a freeman without property who may travel without the permission of a lord. Whitelock, on the other hand, pointing out that *bena* means 'suppliant', follows the *Bosworth-Toller Supplement* in interpreting *færbena* as one who must ask permission from his lord to travel. See Liebermann 1903–1916: v. III, p. 224; Liebermann 1908: 337–40; and Whitelock 1981: 462.

[51] If a king's thegn denies the charge, then twelve are to be chosen for him, and he is to select twelve kinsmen and twelve neutral witnesses, and if his oath fails then he is to pay *lahslit*: ten half-marks.[49]

[52] If a landholder denies the charge, then just as many witnesses of his same status are to be chosen for him as for a king's thegn; if that fails, he is to pay *lahslit*: six half-marks.

[53] If a peasant denies the charge, then just as many witnesses of his same status are to be chosen for him as for the others: if that fails, then he is to pay *lahslit*: twelve ores.

[54] If there is a hallowed space on anyone's property near a stone or a tree or a well or any silliness of this sort, then the one who made it is to pay *lahslit*: half to Christ, half to the local lord.[50]

[54.1] And if the local lord will not aid in the enforcement, then Christ and the king are to receive the compensation.

[55] We everywhere forbid trade on a Sunday and every public meeting and every type of labour and every type of transport, either by wagon or by horse or by carried load.[51]

[56] One who does any of these is to pay a penalty: a freeman twelve ores, a slave with a beating; except for travellers, who may carry food out of necessity; and in times of conflict one may, out of necessity, journey a distance of up to six miles from York on the eve of a holy day.[52]

[57] One who violates a holy day or a legally mandated fast is to pay a penalty of twelve ores.[53]

[57.1] And we ordain that all dues to Rome are to be paid to the episcopal see by St. Peter's day.[54]

---

49 See above, *NPL* 2.3. The implied equivalence between a priest's and thegn's status is found frequently in Wulfstan's writings. See VIII Atr. 28, *Canons* 68b, I Cn. 6a.2a, *Concerning Clerical Compensation* 1, and *On Justice*, n. 30.

50 Cf *Canons* 16. On this clause, see Meaney 2004: 487–8.

51 Cf. *EGu.* 7; VI As. 10; VI Atr. 22.1 and 44; I Cn. 15; *Canons* 19; *Cn. 1020* 18; Napier 43 l. 94; *On Tithes* n. 5; *On Justice* n. 45; and *On the Duties of the Laity* n. 16. See Haines 2010: 27–8.

52 Cf. Theodulf, *Capitula* c. XXIV: 'And if it becomes necessary to sail or travel, permission is granted' ('Nam et si necessitas fuerit navigandi sive itinerandi licentia datur').

53 Cf. Wi. 11, Ine 3.2, II Cn. 45.1–2 and 46, and *EGu.* 7.1 and 8.

54 Cf. II Eg. 4, V Atr. 11.1, VI Atr. 18, I Cn. 9, *Canons* 54, *On Justice* n. 44, and *On Christian Practices* n. 6. See also n. to *Canons* 54.

[**57.2**] And we ordain that two trustworthy thegns and one mass-priest in each wapentake[55] be chosen to collect it and deliver it again, as they dare to swear to it.

[**58**] If a king's thegn or any local lord holds back, he is to pay ten half-marks: half to Christ, half to the king.[56]

[**59**] If any townsman hides or holds back any penny, the local lord is to pay the penny and seize one ox from that man; and if the landlord fails in this, then Christ and the king are to confiscate the full penalty: twelve ores.

[**60**] If anyone holds back his tithes and he is a king's thegn, he is to pay ten half-marks, a landholder six half-marks, a peasant twelve ores.[57]

[**61**] And on account of God's prohibition, we forbid any man to have more than one wife, and she is to be properly promised and wedded;[58]

[**61.1**] and that any man shall marry anyone more closely related than the fourth degree; nor is any man to marry one spiritually related to him.[59]

[**61.2**] And if anyone does so, let him not have God's mercy, unless he desists and repents as the bishop instructs.[60]

[**62**] Yet if he dies in that sin, he is to be deprived of Christian burial and God's mercy.[61]

[**63**] If anyone fornicates with a nun, they both – he and she – are liable for their wergild.[62]

[**63.1**] And if they die without putting an end to that, let them be deprived of Christian burial and God's mercy.[63]

[**64**] If anyone deserts his living lawful wife and wrongfully weds

---

55 A wapentake is a division of land used in northern England that roughly equates to the hundreds of southern England.

56 Cf. *EGu.* 6.1.

57 Cf. II Eg. 3.1 and *EGu.* 6.

58 Cf. I Cn. 7.3.

59 OE *godsibbe*, that is, his god-parent or god-child. Cf. VI Atr. 12–12.2 and I Cn. 7. See Lynch 1998: 166–7.

60 The penance for incest prescribed here conforms to that prescribed in the *Old English Penitential*, II. 18–19.

61 Cf. I Em. 4.

62 Cf. VI Atr. 12.1 and 39; I Cn. 7.1; II Cn. 50.1; and *Cn. 1020* 16–17.

63 Cf. *Canons* 29 and I Em. 4.

another woman, let him not receive God's mercy unless he does penance for it.[64]

[**65**] But everyone is to keep his lawful wife as is right while she lives, unless it so happens with the bishop's guidance that they both decide to separate and remain chaste henceforth.[65]

[**66**] Henceforth, if anyone violates just laws, he is to atone for it sincerely.[66]

[**67**] We must all love and revere one God and fervently adhere to one Christian faith and wholly reject every heathen practice.[67]

[**67.1**] And we ordain that land transactions, legal fines,[68] sworn statements, honest testimony, just judgments, final settlements, and initial claims are to endure valid and legitimate, and the lord's lawful gift and most of all one Christian faith and one kingdom in the realm forever.[69]

Blessed be the name of the Lord, from henceforth now and forever.[70]

---

64 Cf. *Canons* 21 and II Cn. 54.1.

65 Cf. §129 in the B recension of Wulfstan's Canon Law Collection.

66 Cf. above *NPL* 46.

67 Cf. *EGu.* Pr.1; V Atr 1, 34; VI Atr. 1.6; VIII Atr. 44; IX Atr. *explicit*; X Atr. 1; *NPL* 47; *Polity* XXXV; *On Justice* n. 50; *Canons* 16; and *On the Proper Support* n. 4.

68 *Lahceap* – literally, 'law-business' – a compound referring to the payment of a fine by an outlaw to regain his legal status.

69 Although the the injunction itself is different, this clause shares much of its vocabulary with III Atr. 3.

70 *Psalms* 112:2.

APPENDIX:
MANUSCRIPTS CONTAINING ARCHBISHOP WULFSTAN'S POLITICAL WRITINGS

The following charts catalogue the contents of the manuscripts containing the texts translated in this volume. The manuscripts are organised according to the categories set out in the Introduction (see above, pp. 20–5). The charts are based on the manuscript catalogues found in Ker 1957, Sawyer 1957, Loyn 1971b, Wilcox 2000c, and Gneuss 2001. Texts translated in this volume are identified in **bold**.

a. Manuscripts used or copied from those used by Wulfstan

Cambridge, University Library, Additional 3206
s. XI², probably Worcester
Ker 11, Gneuss 30

A damaged fragment containing text corresponding to ff. 22^v–26^r of Junius 121: fragment of **II *Polity*, cap. XVII**, two short texts entitled *On Priests*, and the opening of the later version of the *Canons of Edgar*.

Cambridge, Corpus Christi College 190
s. XI¹ (vol. I), s. XI^{med} (Vol. II), S. XI² (Vol. III), Worcester
Ker 45, Gneuss 59, 59.5

Volume I		
p. ii	Hymn for the Consecration of Oils on Maundy Thursday	
pp. iii–xii	Table of Contents	
p. xii	Extract from Pope Gregory the Great	
pp. 1–12	*De initio creature*	
pp. 12–94	*Penitential of Pseudo-Theodore*	
pp. 94–110	Excerpts of texts concerning ecclesiastics	
pp. 111–30	Wulfstan's Canon Law Collection, B-recension	Continued on pp. 134–8.
p. 130	Decrees of Pope Gelasius, extracts	
p. 130	Old English charm against theft	Related to that found in *Textus Roffensis* and C.C.C.C. 383.

p. 364	Excommunication ritual	

Volume III

p. 365	Old English formulae for confession and absolution	
pp. 366–84	*Scriftboc*	Also called the *Confessional of pseudo-Egbert*
pp. 384–414	*Old English Penitential*	Old English version of the penitential of Halitgar of Cambrai.
pp. 414–16	Formulae for the use of confessors	
pp. 416–18	*Penitential of Theodore*, extracts	
pp. 418–20	**Mircna laga (Concerning the Mercian Law), Að (Concerning the Mercian Oath)** and **Hadbot (Concerning Clerical Compensation)**	In this MS. *Að* 2 serves as the first clause of *Hadbot.*

London, British Library, Cotton Nero A.i
s. XI[ex] (vol. I), s. XI[in] (vol. II), Worcester or York
Ker 163–4, Gneuss 340–1

Volume I

ff. 3ʳ–16ʳ	I Cnut	
ff. 16ʳ–41ʳ	II Cnut	
ff. 42ʳ–44ᵛ	II–III Edgar	
ff. 45ʳ–48ʳ	*Capitula* to the laws of Alfred and Ine	
f. 48ʳ	*Romscot*	
ff. 48ʳ–50ᵛ	*Judex*	
ff. 51ʳ–57ᵛ	Mosaic preface to Alfred-Ine, fragment	MS. breaks off here, damage occurred prior to being bound with Vol. II. Text followed by twelve leaves added in the sixteenth century by John Joscelyn with a transcription of Alfred-Ine up to Ine 54.2.

Volume II

ff. 70ʳ–76ᵛ	Fourteen sections from I *Polity* corresponding to caps. II–IV, IX, XVII, XXII, XI–XIV, XXI, XV, XXXV, and XXXVI	Annotated in the 'Wulfstan hand'.
ff. 76ᵛ–83ᵛ	Bethurum 10c	Annotated in the 'Wulfstan hand'.
ff. 84ʳ–86ᵛ	**Bethurum 19 (*God's Threat to a Sinning Israel*)**	
ff. 86ᵛ–87ᵛ	I Æthelstan	
f. 87ᵛ	I Edmund	
ff. 88ʳ–89ʳ	III Edgar	
ff. 89ʳ–92ᵛ	V Æthelred	Also at ff. 116ᵛ–119ᵛ below.
92ᵛ–95ᵛ	**Grið (*On Sanctuary*)**	
ff. 95ᵛ–96ᵛ	VIII Æthelred	
f. 96ᵛ	**Norðhymbra cyricgrið (*Northumbrian Church Sanctuary*)**	Ker suggests that leaves may be missing after f. 96ᵛ.
f. 97ʳᵛ	I *Polity: Item de episcopis*	
ff. 97ᵛ–98ᵛ	I *Polity: Item* (beginning 'Biscopas scylan bocum …')	
ff. 99ʳ–100ʳ	*Incipit de sinodo*	Annotated in the 'Wulfstan hand'.
ff. 100ᵛ–102ʳ	**An Admonition to Bishops**	Annotated in the 'Wulfstan hand'.
ff. 102ʳ–109ᵛ	**Five chapters from II *Polity*: XVII, XI, XII, X, and V**	Annotated in the 'Wulfstan hand'.
ff. 110ʳ–115ʳ	Bethurum 20.3	Annotated in the 'Wulfstan hand'.
ff. 115ᵛ–116	**Bethurum 21 (*Evil Rulers*)**	
ff. 116ᵛ–119ᵛ	V Æthelred	Annotated in the 'Wulfstan hand'.
f. 120ʳ	**II *Polity*, caps. I–II**	Annotated in the 'Wulfstan hand'.
ff. 120ᵛ–121ᵛ	leaves left blank	
f. 122ʳ	illegible	
ff. 122ᵛ–127ʳ	Extracts from the Vulgate and Church Fathers on the nature of the bishop as *pastor animarum*	Annotated in the 'Wulfstan hand'.

f. 127ʳ   *De clericis siue ecclesiasticis gradis*

ff. 127ᵛ–174ᵛ   Wulfstan's Canon Law Collection,   Annotated in the
                 B-recension   'Wulfstan hand'.

Oxford, Bodleian Library, Junius 121
s. XI³/⁴, Worcester
Ker 338, Gneuss 644

---

f. 19ᵛ	**II *Polity*, cap. XV: On the Widow**	
f. 20ʳᵛ	*On the Servants of God*	Numbered by the scribe as cap. XVI, though not considered by Jost to be a part of *Polity*.
ff. 20ᵛ–23ᵛ	**II *Polity*, cap. XVII: On Priests**	
ff. 23ᵛ–24ʳ	*To Priests*	Numbered by the scribe as cap. XVIII, though not considered by Jost to be a part of *Polity*.
ff. 24ʳ–25ʳ	*To Priests*	Numbered by the scribe as cap. XIX, though not considered by Jost to be a part of *Polity*.
ff. 25ᵛ–31ᵛ	*Synodal Decrees* (*Canons of Edgar*, later version)	Numbered by the scribe as cap. XX, though not considered by Jost to be a part of *Polity*.
ff. 31ᵛ–32ʳ	**II *Polity*, cap. XXI: On Laymen**	
ff. 32ʳ–34ʳ	**II *Polity*, cap. XXII: On Men in Orders**	
ff. 34ʳ–35ᵛ	*On Men in Orders*	Numbered by the scribe as cap. XXIII, though not considered by Jost to be a part of *Polity*.
ff. 35ᵛ–40ʳ	*De ecclesiasticis gradibus*	See also C.C.C.C. 190, pp. 314–19 and C.C.C.C. 201, pp. 108–12. Numbered by the scribe as cap. XXIV, though not considered by Jost to be a part of *Polity*.
ff. 40ʳ–42ʳ	Napier 46, extract	
ff. 42ʳ–55ᵛ	Old English *Benedictine Office*	Numbered by the scribe as caps. XXV–XXXIII, though not considered by Jost to be a part of *Polity*.
ff. 55ᵛ–57ᵛ	Old English translation of Amalarius of Metz, *De regula canonicorum*, ch. 145	Numbered by the scribe as cap. XXXIV, though not considered by Jost to be a part of *Polity*.
ff. 57ᵛ–59ʳ	**II *Polity*, cap. XXXV: On the Church**	

ff. 59ʳ–59ʳ*	**II *Polity*, cap. XXXVI: On All Christian People**	*Due to a scribal error, two consecutive leaves are numbered 59.
ff. 59ʳ–61ᵛ	Napier 28	Numbered by the scribe as cap. XXXVII, though not considered by Jost to be a part of *Polity*.
ff. 61ᵛ–67ᵛ	*Old English Handbook of Penance*	Numbered by the scribe as caps. XXXVIII–XLI, though not considered by Jost to be a part of *Polity*.
ff. 67ʳ–87ᵛ	*Old English Penitential*	Numbered by the scribe as caps. XLII–XLIII, though not considered by Jost to be a part of *Polity*. This is the final set of texts in the numbered series that includes the *Institutes of Polity*.
ff. 87ᵛ–101ʳ	*Scriftboc*	
ff. 101ʳ–110ᵛ	Ælfric's letter to Wulfsige	
ff. 111ʳ–124ʳ	Ælfric's second Old English letter to Wulfstan	
ff. 124ʳ–130ᵛ	Homily based on Ælfric's letter to Wulfgeat	
ff. 130ᵛ–136ᵛ	Homily for the Sunday after Ascension	
ff. 136ᵛ–137ᵛ	Bethurum 1b	
ff. 138ʳ–42ʳ	Homily for the first Sunday in Advent	
ff. 142ʳ–148ᵛ	Homily for the second Sunday in Advent	
ff. 148ᵛ–154ᵛ	An Easter homily on the Harrowing of Hell	
ff. 154ᵛ–157ʳ	Homiletic adaptation of Ælfric's preface to the Catholic Homilies, first series	
ff. 157ʳ–160ʳ	Homily on the Assumption	

York Minster, Additional I
s. XI$^{1-2}$, York
Ker 402, Gneuss 774

ff. 156^v–157^r	Survey of York Minster estates at Sherburn-in-Elmet, Otley, and Ripon	The Old English texts are written on a series of blank leaves at the end of the MS. The MS. itself is a gospel book.
f. 158^{rv}	**Napier 59 (*On the Duties of the Laity*)**	Annotated in the 'Wulfstan hand'.
f. 159^r	**Napier 60 (*On Heathen Practices*)**	Annotated in the 'Wulfstan hand'.
f. 159^v	**Napier 61 (*On Christian Practices*)**	
f. 160^{rv}	***Cnut 1020***	
f. 161^r	A catalogue of service books, plate, vestments, and bells at Sherburn-in-Elment	
f. 161^v	Bidding prayers	
f. 161^v	List of men who acted as sureties (*festermen*) on behalf of one Ælfric (not to be confused with the Abbot of Eynsham)	

b. Posthumous compilations and miscellanies

Cambridge, Corpus Christi College 201
s. XI^{in} (vol. I), s. XI^{med} (vol. II), s. XI^{med} (vol. III), possibly New Minster, Winchester
Ker 49, Gneuss 65, 65.5, and 66

Volume I		
pp. 1–7	Old English translation of the *Regularis Concordia*	Fragment.
pp. 8–9	Napier 1	
pp. 9–10	Napier 62	
pp. 10–15	Bethurum 6 (Napier 2)	
pp. 15–19	Bethurum 7 (Napier 3)	
pp. 19–22	Bethurum 13 (including ***On the Proper Support of the Church***, **Napier 22**)	

p. 22	**Napier 24 (*On Baptism and Confirmation*)**	Only first paragraph.
pp. 22–4	Napier 25 and 26	Second and third paragraphs of 26 only.
pp. 24–5	**Napier 23 (*On Tithes and Tithing*)**	
p. 25	Bethurum 7a (Napier 26)	
p. 25	Napier 27	
pp. 25–8	**Bethurum 21 (*Evil Rulers*)**	First of two versions in this MS.
pp. 28–9	**Napier 35 (*On Various Misfortunes*)**	
pp. 29–30	Napier 38	
p. 30	**VIIa Æthelred**	
pp. 31–40	Ælfric's first Old English letter for Wulfstan	
pp. 40–3	**II *Polity*, 22, 21, and 35 (fragment)**	
pp. 43–6	***Northumbrian Priests' Law***	
pp. 46–7	II Edgar	
pp. 47–8	III Edgar	
pp. 48–52	V Æthelred	
p. 52	**II *Polity*, cap. 36 (fragment)**	
p. 52	Bethurum 10c (fragment)	
p. 52	Napier 40 (fragment)	
p. 53	I Æthelstan	
pp. 53–6	Bethurum 10b	
pp. 56–7	Bethurum 10c (fragment)	
pp. 57–61	**II *Polity* cap. 25 (fragment)**	
pp. 57–64	Bethurum 11	
pp. 65–6	Bethurum 9	
pp. 66–8	Bethurum 1a and 1b	
pp. 68–71	Bethurum 5	
pp. 71–2	Bethurum 2	
pp. 72–4	Bethurum 3	
pp. 74–8	Bethurum 4	
pp. 78–80	Napier 40	
pp. 80–1	Bethurum 16b	
pp. 82–6	Bethurum 20.2	

Cambridge, Corpus Christi College 419
s. XI[1], Possibly Christ Church, Canterbury
Ker 68 (along with C.C.C.C. 421), Gneuss 108

Cambridge, Corpus Christi College 421
s. XI¹, Possibly Christ Church, Canterbury
Ker 68 (along with C.C.C. 421), Gneuss 109

p. 2	Conclusion to a homily on the Feast of an apostle	Written in a hand different from the rest of the manuscript.
pp. 3–25	Ælfric, *Homily on Pentecost*, Catholic Homilies, First Series	
pp. 25–36	Ælfric, *Homily on the Nativity of One Apostle*, Catholic Homilies, Second Series	
pp. 36–54	Ælfric, *Homily on the Nativity of Holy Martyrs*, Catholic Homilies, Second Series	
pp. 54–76	Ælfric, *Homily on the Nativity of One Confessor*, Catholic Homilies, Second Series	
pp. 76–98	Ælfric, *Homily on the Nativity of Holy Virgins*, Catholic Homilies, Second Series	
pp. 99–150	Ælfric, *Homily on Pentecost*	
pp. 150–70	Napier 47	
pp. 170–208	Napier 49	
pp. 209–21	**Napier 50 (*On Justice, Virtue, and the Law*)**	
pp. 221–6	Ælfric, *In Letania maiore*, Catholic Homilies, First Series	
pp. 254–87	Ælfric, *Feria III de Dominica oratione*, Catholic Homilies, First Series	
pp. 287–324	Ælfric, *Feria IIII de fide catholica*, Catholic Homilies, First Series	
pp. 324–54	Ælfric, *Homily on the Lord's Ascension*, Catholic Homilies, First Series	

London, British Library, Cotton Tiberius A.iii
s. XI^{med}, probably Christ Church, Canterbury
Ker 186, Gneuss 363

ff. 118^r–163^v	*Rule of St. Benedict*, Latin with an Old English gloss	Wormholes, wear to the manuscript, and anomalous location of the table of contents indicate that ff. 118^r–173^v were originally bound before ff. 2^r–116^v.
ff. 164^r–168^v	Epitome of the *Rule of St. Benedict*, with Old English gloss.	
ff. 168^v–169^r	*De festiuitatibus anni*	
ff. 169^r–173^r	*Capitula* drawn up at Aachen in 818	
ff. 3^r–27^v	*Regularis concordia*, with Old English gloss	
ff. 27^v–43^r	A collection of Latin and Old English prognostic texts	
ff. 43^r–44^r	Miscellaneous short extracts in Latin and Old English	
ff. 44^r–56^v	*Old English Handbook of Penance*, extracts	
ff. 57^r–60^r	Selected short prayers and devotions, Latin and Old English	
ff. 60^v–64^v	Ælfric's *Colloquy*, Latin and Old English	
f. 65^{rv}	Four prognostics	
ff. 65^v–73^r	Ælfric's *De temporibus*	
f. 73^{rv}	Miscellaneous short extracts in Latin and Old English	
ff. 73^v–77^v	Old English life of St. Margaret	
ff. 77^v–83^r	Ælfric's homily of Palm Sunday, very corrupt	
ff. 83^r–87^r	Old English *Sunday Letter*, version F (Napier 44)	
ff. 87^r–88^v	Homily, *The Devil's Account of the Next World*	
ff. 88^v–90^v	Bethurum 13/Napier 19–**22 (*On the Proper Support of the Church*)**, **Napier 24 (*On Baptism and Confirmation*)**	On the arrangement of texts in this MS. with particular reference to the treatment of Napier 22, 23, and 24, see above, pp. 133–4.

ff. 90ᵛ–91ʳ	Napier 36
ff. 91ʳᵛ	**Napier 23 (*On Tithes and Tithing*)**
ff. 91ᵛ–92ʳ	Napier 27
f. 92ʳᵛ	**Napier 51 (*On the Laws of God and the World*)**
f. 92ᵛ	Napier 25
ff. 92ᵛ–93ʳ	Bethurum 7a
f. 93ʳᵛ	**Napier 52 (*On the Duties of the Clergy*)**
f. 93ᵛ	**Napier 53 (*On the Sins of the Clergy*)**
ff. 93ᵛ–94ᵛ	*Ordo confessionis*
ff. 94ᵛ–97ʳ	Directions for a confessor
ff. 97–101ᵛ	*Monasteriales indicia*
ff. 101ᵛ–102ʳ	Old English lapidary
ff. 102ʳ–103ʳ	Homily against worldly arrogance
ff. 103ʳ–105ʳ	*Rule of St. Benedict*, ch. 4, Latin and Old English
f. 105ʳᵛ	Old English translation of Alcuin, *De virtutibus et vitiis*, ch. 14
ff. 105ᵛ–106ʳ	Old English translation of Alcuin, *De virtutibus et vitiis*, ch. 26
f. 106ʳ	Old English charm against theft
ff. 106ʳ–7ᵛ	Ælfric's second Old English letter to Wulfstan, fragment
ff. 107ᵛ–115ᵛ	Prayers for the Virgin Mary

Oxford, Bodleian Library, Hatton 113
s. XI³ᐟ⁴, Worcester
Ker 331a, Gneuss 637

ff. 1ʳ–3ʳ	Napier 1	Variant version from that found in C.C.C.C. 201 and Cotton Tiberius A.xviii.
ff. 3ʳ–4ʳ	Napier 62	
ff. 4–10ᵛ	Bethurum 6	
ff. 10ᵛ–11ʳ	Bethurum 7 (first para.)	MS. divides this homily into two parts w/separate rubrics.
ff. 11ʳ–16ʳ	Bethurum 7 (second para.)	

ff. 16^r–21^r	Bethurum 8c	MS. divides this homily into five sections, each with the rubric, 'Item'.
ff. 21^r–27^r	Bethurum 11	
ff. 27^r–31^v	Bethurum 9	
ff. 31^v–34^r	Bethurum 1a and 1b	Both texts copied under a single rubric.
ff. 34^r–38^r	Bethurum 10b	
ff. 38^r–44^r	Bethurum 10c, abbreviated	
ff. 44^r–47^v	Bethurum 5	
ff. 47^v–49^v	Bethurum 2	
ff. 49^v–52^v	Bethurum 3	
ff. 52^r–56^v	Bethurum 4	
ff. 56^v–58^v	Bethurum 14	
ff. 58^v–61^r	Bethurum 12	
ff. 61^r–66^r	*Sermo ad populum* (Bethurum 13/ Napier 19–**22** [*On the Proper Support of the Church*], **24** [*On Baptism and Confirmation*]–26)	On the arrangement of texts in this MS. with particular reference to the treatment of Napier 22 and 24, see above, pp. 133–4.
ff. 66^r–73^r	Napier 29	
ff. 73^r–80^v	Napier 30	
ff. 80^v–81^r	Napier 31	
ff. 81^r–83^r	Napier 32	
ff. 83^r–84^v	Napier 37, extracts	
ff. 84^v–90^v	Bethurum 20.3	
ff. 90^v–91^v	**Bethurum 21 (*Evil Rulers*)**	
ff. 91^v–93^v	**Napier 35 (*On Various Misfortunes*)**	
ff. 93^v–94^v	Napier 37, extracts	
ff. 94^v–102^v	Homily, 'Se hælend crist'	
ff. 102^v–115^v	Homily, *Sermo ad populum in octauis pentecosten dicendus*	
ff. 115^v–124^r	Homily, *Sermo in die natalis domini*	
ff. 124^r–130^v	Homily for the feast of St. Stephen Protomartyr	
ff. 130^v–139^v	Homily for the Feast of St. John the Baptist	

ff. 139ᵛ–144ᵛ Homily for the feast of the Holy   The text of this homily
               Innocents   continues in Hatton 114,
                                                      which was originally
                                                      bound with this MS.

c. Twelfth-century legal anthologies

Cambridge, Corpus Christi College 383
s. XI/XII, probably London, St. Paul's
Ker 65, Gneuss 102

Quire 'a'	II–III Edgar	Copied from London, British Library, Harley 55 in the sixteenth century.
pp. 13–42	Alfred-Ine	Leaves bound out of order.
p. 42	Blaseras, pt. 2	Leaves bound out of order.
p. 1	Blaseras, pt. 1	
p. 1	Forfang	
pp. 1–3	Hundred	
pp. 3–5	I Æthelred	
p. 6	*Treaty of Alfred and Guthrum*	
pp. 7–10	**Laws of Edward and Guthrum**	
pp. 10–12	II Æthelstan	
pp. 43–7	I Cnut	
pp. 47–72	II Cnut	
pp. 72–4	I Edward	
pp. 74–8	II Edward	
pp. 78–9	I Edmund	
pp. 79–81	II Edmund	
pp. 81–3	*Swerian*	
pp. 83–4	*Treaty of Alfred and Guthrum*	Text repeated.
pp. 84–6	Wifmannes beweddung	
pp. 86–7	*Wergild*	
p. 87	Old English Charm Against Theft	Related to that found in *Textus Roffensis* and C.C.C.C. 190. Text crossed out in red ink, probably by scribe.

pp. 87–8	Hit becwæð	
pp. 88–93	II Æthelred	
pp. 93–5	Dunsæte	
pp. 96–102	Rectitudines Personarum Singularum	
pp. 102–7	Gerefa	
pp. 107–8	St. Paul's 'Shipmen' List	Copied onto a blank leaf in the twelfth century.
p. 108	West Saxon Regnal List	Copied onto a blank leaf in the twelfth century.

Strood, Medway Archive and Local Studies Centre, MS. DRc/R1
(Textus Roffensis)
1123 or 1124, Rochester Cathedral
Ker 373

ff. 1ʳ–3ᵛ	Laws of Æthelberht	
ff. 3ᵛ–5ʳ	Laws of Hlothhere and Eadric	
ff. 5ʳ–6ᵛ	Laws of Wihtred	
f. 7ʳᵛ	*Hadbot (On Clerical Compensation)*	
ff. 7ᵛ–8ᵛ	West Saxon Royal Genealogy	
ff. 9ʳ–32ʳ	Laws of Alfred and Ine	
f. 32ʳ	Blaseras	
f. 32ʳ	Forfang	
f. 32ʳᵛ	Ordal	
f. 32ᵛ	Walreaf	
ff. 32ᵛ–37ʳ	II Æthelstan	
ff. 37ʳ–38ʳ	V Æthelstan	
f. 38ʳ	IV Æthelstan	Fragment: IV As. 6 only.
f. 38ʳ	Pax	
ff. 38ᵛ–39ᵛ	*Swerian, Að (Concerning the Mercian Oath)*	*Að* has been appended to *Swerian* and its clauses inverted.
f. 39ᵛ	*Mircna laga (Concerning the Law of the Mercians)*	
ff. 40ʳ–41ᵛ	*Laws of Edward and Guthrum*	
ff. 41ᵛ–42ʳ	Wergild	
ff. 42ʳ–43ʳ	I Edward	
ff. 43ʳ–44ʳ	II Edward	
ff. 44ʳ–45ʳ	I Edmund	

ff. 45ʳ–46ʳ	II Edmund	
ff. 46ʳ–47ʳ	I Æthelred	
f. 47ʳᵛ	William I, 'On Exculpation' (Wl lad)	
ff. 48ʳ–49ᵛ	III Æthelred	
ff. 49ᵛ–57ʳ	Iudicia Dei I–III	
f. 57ᵛ	Cnut's Grant of Sandwich to Christ Church, Canterbury	Fragment.
ff. 58ʳ–80ʳ	Instituta Cnuti	
ff. 80ʳ–81ᵛ	William I, 'Articles' (Wl art)	
ff. 81ᵛ–87ʳ	Canon law excerpts	
ff. 88ʳ–93ʳ	VI Æthelstan	
f. 93ʳᵛ	*Geþyncðu (On Ranks)*	
ff. 93ᵛ–94ʳ	*Be wergylde (Concerning Wergild)*	Titled in other MS. 'Norðleoda laga' ('Law of the North-people').
ff. 94ᵛ–95ʳ	Wifmannes beweddung	
f. 95ʳ	Old English Charm Against Theft	Related to that found in C.C.C.C. 190 and 383.
f. 95ʳᵛ	Hit becwæð	
ff. 96–97ᵛ	Coronation Charter of Henry I	
ff. 98–99ᵛ	Excommunicationes VIII–IX	
ff. 101ʳ–104ʳ	Anglo-Saxon Royal Genealogies	
ff. 105ʳ–16ʳ	Lists of Popes, Emperors, Patriarchs, and English Bishops and Archbishops	
f. 116ᵛ	Supplementary lists (e.g. Papal liturgical innovations)	
ff. 117ʳ–118ʳ	Blank leaves	
ff. 119ʳ–222ʳ	Cartulary of Rochester Cathedral Priory	

BIBLIOGRAPHY

Primary sources

Assmann, Bruno. 1889. *Angelsächsiche Homilien und Heiligenleben, Bibliothek der angelsächsischen prosa*. Kassel: G.H. Wigand.

Attenborough, F.L. 1922. *The Laws of the Earliest English Kings*. Cambridge: Cambridge University Press.

Bazire, Joyce, and J.E. Cross. 1983. *Eleven Rogationtide Homilies*. Toronto: University of Toronto Press.

Bertram, Jerome. 2005. *The Chrodegang Rules: The Rules for the Common Life of the Secular Clergy from the Eighth and Ninth Centuries*. Farnham: Ashgate.

Bethurum, Dorothy. 1957. *The Homilies of Wulfstan*. Oxford: Clarendon Press.

Blake, E.O. 1962. *Liber Eliensis, Camden Third Series*. London: The Royal Historical Society.

Boretius, A. 1883. *Capitularia Regum Francorum I, Monumenta Germaniae Historica*. Hanover: Impensis Bibliopolii.

Boulding, Maria. 2003. *Augustine: Expositions of the Psalms 1–32. Works of Saint Augustine*, Vol. 3. Hyde Park: New City Press.

Clemoes, Peter. 1997. *Ælfric's Catholic Homilies, First Series, Early English Text Society*. Oxford: Oxford University Press.

Colgrave, Bertram, and R.A.B. Mynors. 1991. *Bede's Ecclesiastical History of the English People*. Oxford: Clarendon Press.

Cross, J.E. and Andrew Hamer. 1999. *Wulfstan's Canon Law Collection, Anglo-Saxon Texts*. Woodbridge: Boydell & Brewer.

Darlington, R.R. 1968. *The Cartulary of Worcester Cathdreal Priory (Register 1), The Publications of the Pipe Role Society, New Series*. London: J.W. Ruddock & Sons, Ltd.

Darlington, R.R., P. McGurk, and Jennifer Bray. 1995. *The Chronicle of John of Worcester, Volume II: The Annals from 450 to 1066*. Oxford: Clarendon Press.

Downer, L.J. 1972. *Leges Henrici Primi*. Oxford, England: Clarendon Press.

Dyson, R.W. 2010. *Sedulius Scottus: De Rectoribus Christianis (On Christian Rulers): An Edition and English Translation*. Woodbridge: Boydell Press.

Fehr, Bernard. 1914. *Die Hirtenbriefe Ælfrics, Bibliothek der Angelsachsischen Prosa*. Hamburg: H. Grand.

Fowler, Roger. 1972. *Wulfstan's Canons of Edgar*. Vol. 266, *Early English Text Society*. Oxford: Oxford University Press.

Fulk, R.D., Robert E. Bjork and John D. Niles. 2008. *Klaeber's Beowulf and the Fight at Finnsburg.* 4th edn. Toronto: University of Toronto Press.

Fulk, R.D., and Stefan Jurasinski. 2012. *The Old English Canons of Theodore, Early English Text Society, Supplementary Series,* Vol. 25. Oxford: Oxford University Press.

Godden, M.R. 1979. *Ælfric's Catholic Homilies, Second Series.* Vol. 5, *Early English Text Society, Second Series.* Oxford: Oxford University Press.

Godden, M.R., and Susan Irvine. 2009. *The Old English Boethius: An Edition of the Old English Versions of Boethius's De Consolatione Philosophiae.* 2 vols. Oxford: Oxford University Press.

Haddan, Arthur West, and William Stubbs. 1869–71. *Councils and Ecclesiastical Documents Relating to Great Britain and Ireland.* 3 vols. Oxford: Oxford University Press.

Harmer, Florence E. 1914. *Select English Historical Documents of the Ninth and Tenth Centuries.* Cambridge: Cambridge University Press.

Harmer, Florence E. 1952. *Anglo-Saxon Writs.* Manchester: Manchester University Press.

Irvine, Susan. 2004. *The Anglo-Saxon Chronicle, Manuscript E, The Anglo-Saxon Chronicle: A Collaborative Edition,* Vol. 7. Cambridge: D.S. Brewer.

Jost, Karl. 1959. *Die 'Institutes of Polity, Civil and Ecclesiastical'. Swiss Studies in English.* Bern: Francke Verlag.

Keynes, Simon, and Michael Lapidge. 1983. *Alfred the Great: Asser's Life of King Alfred and Other Contemporary Sources.* New York: Penguin.

Lambarde, William. 1568. *Archaionomia: siue de priscis anglorum legibus libri sermone Anglico, vetustate antiquissimo, aliquot abhinc seculis conscripti, atq[ue] nunc demum, magno iurisperitorum, & amantium antiquitatis omnium commodo, è tenebris in lucem vocati. Gulielmo Lambardo interprete. Regum qui has leges scripserunt nomenclationem, & quid praeterea accesserit, altera monstrabit pagina.* London: Ex officina Ioannis Daij.

Langefeld, Brigitte. 2003. *The Old English Version of the Enlarged Rule of Chrodegang.* Frankfurt am Main: Peter Lang.

Liebermann, Felix. 1903–1916. *Die Gesetze der Angelsachsen.* 3 vols. Halle: Scientia Aalen.

Marsden, Richard. 2008. *The Old English Heptateuch and Ælfric's Libellus de Veteri Testamento et Novo.* Vol. 1, *Early English Text Society.* Oxford: Oxford University Press.

Migne, Jacques-Paul, ed. 1844–62. *Patrologia Latina.* Paris: Garnier.

Morris, Richard. 1868. *Old English Homilies and Homiletic Treatises, E.E.T.S. First Series.* London: N. Trubner & Co.

Napier, Arthur. 1883. *Wulfstan: Sammlung der ihm zugeschrieben homilien nebst Untersuchungen über ihre Echtheit.* Berlin: Weidmannsche Buchhandlung.

Napier, Arthur. 1916. *The Old English version of the Enlarged Rule of Chrodegang together with the Latin original; An Old English version of the Capitula of Theodulf together with the Latin original; An interlinear Old English rendering of the Epitome of Benedict of Aniane, Early English Text Society.* London: Kegan, Paul, Trench, Trübner & Co.

Oliver, Lisi. 2002. *The Beginnings of English Law.* Toronto: University of Toronto Press.

Pope, John C. 1968. *Homilies of Ælfric: A Supplementary Collection.* 2 vols, Oxford: Early English Text Society.

Raith, Josef. 1933. *Die altenglische Version des Halitgar'schen Bussbuches.* Hamburg: Bibliothek der Angelsächsischen Prosa.

Robertson, A.J. 1925. *The Laws of the Kings of England from Edmund to Henry I.* Cambridge: Cambridge University Press.

Robertson, A.J. 1956. *Anglo-Saxon Charters.* 2nd edn. Cambridge: Cambridge University Press.

Sackur, Ernst. 1898. *Sibyllinische Texte und Forschungen.* Halle: Max Niemeyer.

Sauer, Hans. 1978. *Theodulfi Capitula in England. Die altenglischen Übersetzungen, zusammen mit dem lateinischen Text.* Munich: Wilhelm Fink.

Schmid, Reinhold. 1858. *Die Gesetze der Angelsachsen.* 2nd edn. Leipzig: F.A. Brockhaus.

Swanton, Michael. 1993. *Anglo-Saxon Prose.* London: J.M. Dent.

Symons, Dom Thomas. 1953. *Regularis Concordia Anglicae Nationis Monachorum Sanctimonialiumque (The Monastic Agreement of the Monks and Nuns of the English Nation).* London: Thomas Nelson and Sons, Ltd.

Tanner, Norman P. 1990. *Decrees of the Ecumenical Councils.* 2 vols. Washington D.C.: Georgetown University Press.

Tenhaken, Hans P. 1979. *Das Nordhumbrische Priestergesetze.* Dusseldorf: Stern-Verlag Janssen & Co.

Thorpe, Benjamin. 1840. *Ancient Laws and Institutes of England.* London: G.E. Eyre and A. Spottiswoode.

Ure, James M. 1957. *The Benedictine Office: An Old English Text.* Edinburgh: Edinbugh Univesity Press.

Wasserschleben, Friedrich Wilhelm. 1851. *Die Bussordnungen der abendländischen Kirche.* Halle: Verlag von Ch. Graeger.

Wasserschleben, Hermann. 1885. *Die Irische Kanonensammlung.* Leipzig: Bernhard Tauchnitz.

Whitelock, Dorothy. 1930. *Anglo-Saxon Wills, Cambridge Studies in English Legal History.* Cambridge: Cambridge University Press.

Whitelock, Dorothy. 1966. *Sermo Lupi ad Anglos, Methuen's Old English Library.* New York: Appleton-Century-Crofts.

Whitelock, Dorothy. 1979. *English Historical Documents, Volume I: c. 500–1042.* London: Eyre Methuen.

Whitelock, Dorothy. 1981. *Councils and Synods with Other Documents Relating to the English Church: 871–1066.* Vol. I, Part 1. Oxford: Clarendon Press.

Wilkins, David, ed. 1721. *Leges Anglo-Saxonicae Ecclesiasticae et Civiles.* London: William Bowyer.

Winterbottom, Michael. 2007. *William of Malmesbury: Gesta Pontificum Anglorum, Vol. 1: Text and Translation, Oxford Medieval Texts.* Oxford: Oxford University Press.

Woodman, D.A., ed. 2012. *Charters of Northern Houses, Anglo-Saxon Charters.* Oxford: Oxford University Press.

Secondary sources

Abels, Richard. 1988a. *Lordship and Military Obligation in Anglo-Saxon England.* London: British Museum Publications.

Abels, Richard. 1988b. 'Review of James Campbell, *Essays in Anglo-Saxon History*'. *Albion: A Quarterly Journal Concerned with British Studies* no. 20 (2): 293–5.

Abels, Richard. 1998. *Alfred the Great: War, Kingship, and Culture in Anglo-Saxon England.* London: Longman.

Adams, Henry, ed. 1876. *Essays in Anglo-Saxon Law.* Boston, MA: Little Brown and Company.

Anlezark, Daniel. 2006. 'Reading "The Story of Joseph" in MS Cambridge, Corpus Christi College 201'. In *The Power of Words: Anglo-Saxon Studies Presented to Donald G. Scragg on his Seventieth Birthday*, edited by Hugh Magennis and Jonathan Wilcox, 61–94. Morgantown, WV: West Viginia University Press.

Arnold, C.J. 1988. *An Archaeology of the Early Anglo-Saxon Kingdoms.* London: Routledge.

Atkinson, Nancy E., and Dan E. Burton. 2002. 'Harrowing the Houses of the Holy: Images of Violation in Wulfstan's Homilies'. In *The Year 1000: Religious and Social Response to the Turn of the Millenium*, edited by Michael Frassetto, 49–62. New York: Palgrave Macmillan.

Baker, J.H. 1990. *An Introduction to English Legal History.* London: Butterworths.

Barker, Nicholas, ed. 1986. *The York Gospels.* London: The Roxburghe Club.

Barlow, Frank. 1979. *The English Church 1000–1066: A Constitutional History.* New York: Longmans.

Barrow, Julia. 1992. 'How the Twelfth-Century Monks of Worcester Perceived their Past'. In *The Perception of the Past in Twelfth-Century Europe*, edited by Paul Magdalino, 53–74. London: Continuum.

Barrow, Julia. 2004. 'Wulfstan and Worcester: Bishop and Clergy in the Early Eleventh Century'. In *Wulfstan, Archbishop of York: The Proceedings of the Second Alcuin Conference*, edited by Matthew Townend, 141–60. Turnhout: Brepols.

Bateson, Mary. 1895. 'A Worcester Cathedral Book of Ecclesiastical Collections Made About 1000 A.D.' *English Historical Review* no. 10: 712–31.

Baxter, Stephen. 2004. 'Archbishop Wulfstan and the Administration of God's Property'. In *Wulfstan, Archbishop of York: The Proceedings of the Second Alcuin Conference*, edited by Matthew Townend, 161–206. Turnhout: Brepols.

Baxter, Stephen. 2007. *The Earls of Mercia: Lordship and Power in Late Anglo-Saxon England*. Oxford: Oxford University Press.

Bethurum, Dorothy. 1942. 'Archbishop Wulfstan's Commonplace Book'. *PMLA* no. 57 (4): 916–29.

Bethurum, Dorothy. 1949. 'A Letter of Protest from the English Bishops to the Pope'. In *Philologica: The Malone Anniversary Studies*, edited by T.A. Kirby and H.B. Woolf, 97–104. Baltimore, MD: Johns Hopkins University Press.

Bethurum, Dorothy. 1950. 'Six Anonymous Old English Codes'. *Journal of English and Germanic Philology* no. 69: 449–63.

Bethurum, Dorothy. 1963. 'Episcopal Magnificence in the Eleventh Century'. In *Studies in Old English Literature in Honor of Arthur G. Brodeur*, edited by Stanley B. Greenfield, 162–70. Eugene, OR: University of Oregon Press.

Bethurum, Dorothy. 1966. 'Wulfstan'. In *Continuations and Beginnings: Studies in Old English Literature*, edited by E.G. Stanley, 210–46. London: Thomas Nelson and Sons, Ltd.

Bethurum Loomis, Dorothy. 1971. '*Regnum* and *Sacerdotium* in the Early Eleventh Century'. In *England Before the Conquest: Studies in Primary Sources Presented to Dorothy Whitelock*, edited by Peter Clemoes and Kathleen Hughes, 129–47. Cambridge: Cambridge University Press.

Blair, John. 2005. *The Church in Anglo-Saxon Society*. Oxford: Oxford University Press.

Blair, Peter Hunter. 1963. *Roman Britain and Early England, 55 B.C.-A.D. 871*. New York: W.W. Norton and Co.

Blair, Peter Hunter. 1977. *An Introduction to Anglo-Saxon England*. Cambridge: Cambridge University Press.

Bolton, Timothy. 2009. *The Empire of Cnut the Great: Conquest and the Consolidation of Power in Northern Europe in the Early Eleventh Century*. Leiden: Brill.

Brackmann, Rebecca. 2012. *The Elizabethan Invention of Anglo-Saxon England: Lawrence Nowell, William Lambarde and the Study of Old English*. Woodbridge: D.S. Brewer.

Brooke, C.N.L. 1977. 'York Minster from the Ninth to the Early Thirteenth Centuries'. In *History of York Minster*, edited by G.E. Aylmer and Reginald Cant, 12–43. Oxford: Oxford University Press.

Brown, R. Allen. 1969. 'An Historian's Approach to the Origins of the Castle in England'. *Archaeological Journal* no. 126: 131–48.

Budny, Mildred. 1997. *Insular, Anglo-Saxon, and Early Anglo-Norman Art at Corpus Christi College, Cambridge*. 2 vols. Kalamazoo, MI: Medieval Institute Publications.

Burns, J.H., ed. 1988. *The Cambridge History of Medieval Political Thought, c. 350–1450*. Cambridge: Cambridge University Press.

Campbell, James, ed. 1982. *The Anglo-Saxons*. London: Phaidon.

Campbell, James. 2009. 'Aspects of Nobility and Mobility in Anglo-Saxon Society'. In *Soldiers, Nobles and Gentlemen: Essays in Honour of Maurice Keen* edited by Peter Coss and Christopher Tyerman, 17–31. Woodbridge: Boydell.

Carella, Bryan. 2011. 'Evidence for Hiberno-Latin Thought in the Prologue to the Laws of Alfred'. *Studies in Philology* no. 108: 1–26.

Carella, Bryan. 2012. 'Asser's Bible and the Prologue to the Laws of Alfred'. *Anglia* no. 130: 195–206.

Chadwick, H.M. 1905. *Studies on Anglo-Saxon Institutions*. New York: Russell and Russell, Inc.

Chaney, William A. 1963. 'Anglo-Saxon Church Dues: A Study in Historical Continuity'. *Church History* no. 32 (3): 268–77.

Chapman, Don W. 2002. 'Germanic Tradition and Latin Learning in Wulfstan's Echoic Compounds'. *Journal of English and Germanic Philology* no. 101 (1): 1–18.

Clayton, Mary. 1994. 'Ælfric's *Judith*: Manipulative or Manipulated?' *Anglo-Saxon England* no. 23: 215–27.

Clayton, Mary. 2008. 'The Old English *Promissio Regis*'. *Anglo-Saxon England* no. 37: 91–150.

Clemoes, Peter. 1960. 'The Old English Benedictine Office, Corpus Christi College, Cambridge, Manuscript 190, and the Relations Between Ælfric and Wulfstan: A Reconsideration'. *Anglia* no. 78: 265–83.

Clemoes, Peter. 1970. *Rhythm and Cosmic Order in Old English Christian Literature*. Cambridge: Cambridge University Press.

Clemoes, Peter. 1995. *Interactions of Thought and Language in Old English Poetry, Cambridge Studies in Anglo-Saxon England*. Cambridge: Cambridge University Press.

Cooper, Janet M. 1970. *The Last Four Anglo-Saxon Archbishops of York*. Vol. 38, *Borthwick Papers*. York: Borthwick Institute of Historical Research, University of York.

Crook, John. 2004. '"Vir optimus Wlfstanus": The Post-Conquest Commemoration of Archbishop Wulfstan at Ely Cathedral'. In *Wulfstan, Archbishop of York: The Proceedings of the Second Alcuin Conference*, edited by Matthew Townend, 501–24. Turnhout: Brepols.

Cross, J.E. 1991. 'Wulfstan's *De Antecristo* in a Twelfth-Century Worcester Manuscript'. *Anglo-Saxon England* no. 20: 203–20.

Cross, J.E. 1992. 'A Newly-Identified Manuscript of Wulfstan's "Commonplace Book", Rouen, Bibliothèque Municipale, MS. 1382 [U.109], fols 173r–198v'. *Journal of Medieval Latin* no. 2: 63–83.

Cross, J.E. 1993. 'Atto of Vercelli, "De Pressuris Ecclesiasticis", Archbishop Wulfstan, and Wulfstan's Commonplace Book'. *Traditio* no. 48: 237–46.

Cross, J.E., and Alan Brown. 1989. 'Literary Impetus for Wulfstan's Sermo Lupi'. *Leeds Studies in English* no. 20: 270–91.

Cross, J.E., and Alan Brown. 1993 for 1989. 'Wulfstan and Abbo of Saint-Germain-de-Prés'. *Medievalia* no. 15: 71–91.

Cubitt, Catherine. 1997. 'The Tenth-Century Benedictine Reform in England'. *Early Medieval Europe* no. 6 (1):77–94.

Cubitt, Catherine. 2000. 'Virginity and Misogyny in Tenth- and Eleventh-Century England'. *Gender & History* no. 12 (1): 1–32.

Cubitt, Catherine. 2006. 'Bishops, Priests and Penance in Late Saxon England'. *Early Medieval Europe* no. 14 (1): 41–63.

Cubitt, Catherine. 2007. 'Bishops and Councils in Late Saxon England: The Intersection of Secular and Ecclesiastical Law'. In *Recht und Gericht in Kirche und Welt*, edited by Wilfried Hartman and Annette Grabowsky, 151–68. Munich: R. Oldenbourg Verlag.

Cubitt, Catherine. 2009. '"As the Lawbook Teaches": Reeves, Lawbooks and Urban Life in the Anonymous Old English Legend of the Seven Sleepers'. *English Historical Review* no. 124 (510): 1021–49.

Cubitt, Catherine. 2011. 'The Politics of Remorse: Penance and Royal Piety in the Reign of Æthelred the Unready'. *Historical Research* no. 85 (228): 179–92.

Dammery, Richard. 1994. 'Editing the Anglo-Saxon Laws: Felix Liebermann and Beyond'. In *The Editing of Old English: Papers from the 1990 Manchester Conference*, edited by Donald Scragg and Paul Szarmach, 251–61. Woodbridge, Suffolk: D.S. Brewer.

Dance, Richard. 2004. 'Sound, Fury, and Signifiers; or Wulfstan's Language'. In *Wulfstan, Archbishop of York: The Proceedings of the Second Alcuin Conference*, edited by Matthew Townend, 29–62. Turnhout: Brepols.

Davis-Secord, Jonathan. 2008. 'Rhetoric and Politics in Archbishop Wulfstan's Old English Homilies'. *Anglia* no. 126: 65–96.

Davison, B.K. 1967. 'The Origins of the Castle in England'. *Archaeological Journal* no. 124: 202–11.

Duby, Georges. 1982. *The Three Orders: Feudal Society Imagined*. Translated by Arthur Goldhammer. Chicago: University of Chicago Press.

Dumville, David. 1992. *Liturgy and the Ecclesiastical History of Late Anglo-Saxon England*. Woodbridge: Boydell & Brewer.

Dunkel, Wilbur. 1965. *William Lambarde, Elizabethan Jurist: 1536–1601*. New Brunswick, NJ: Rutgers University Press.

Dunning, William Archibald. 1930. *A History of Political Theories: Ancient and Medieval*. New York: The Macmillan Company.

Einenkel, E. 1884. 'Der *Sermo ad Anglos*: ein Gedicht'. *Anglia* no. 7: 200–3.

Elliott, Michael. 2010. 'Ghaerbald's First Capitulary, the Excerptiones Pseudo-Ecgberhti, and the Sources of Wulfstan's Canons of Edgar'. *Notes and Queries* no. 57 (2): 161–5.

Emmerson, Richard Kenneth. 1983. '"Epistola" to "Sermo": The Old English Version of Adso's *Libellus de Antichristo*'. *Journal of English and Germanic Philology* no. 82 (1): 1–10.

Faith, Rosamond. 1997. *The English Peasantry and the Growth of Lordship*. London: Leicester University Press.

Fisher, D.J.V. 1952. 'The Anti-Monastic Reaction in the Reign of Edward the Martyr'. *Cambridge Historical Journal* no. 10 (3): 254–70.

Fleming, Robin. 2011. *Britain After Rome: The Fall and Rise, 400 to 1070*. New York: Penguin.

Fletcher, R.A. 2003. *Bloodfeud: Murder and Revenge in Anglo-Saxon England*. Oxford: Oxford University Press.

Foot, Sarah. 1996. 'The Making of Angelcynn: English Identity Before the Norman Conquest'. *Transactions of the Royal Historical Society* 6th ser. 6: 25–49.

Foot, Sarah. 2000. *Veiled Women*. 2 vols. Aldershot: Ashgate.

Fowler, Roger. 1963. '"Archbishop Wulfstan's Commonplace Book" and the *Canons of Edgar*'. *Medium Aevum* no. 32: 1–10.

Fowler, Roger. 1965. 'A Late Old English Handbook for the Use of a Confessor'. *Anglia* no. 83 (1): 1–34.

Frantzen, Allen J. 1983. *The Literature of Penance in Anglo-Saxon England*. New Brunswick, NJ: Rutgers University Press.

Fulk, R.D. 2010. 'Localizing and Dating Old English Anonymous Prose'. In *English Law Before Magna Carta: Felix Liebermann and Die Gesetze der Angelsachsen*, edited by Stefan Jurasinski, Lisi Oliver and Andrew Rabin, 59–80. Leiden: Brill.

Funke, O. 1962. 'Some Remarks on Wulfstan's Prose Rhythm'. *English Studies* no. 43 (1–6): 311–18.

Gatch, Milton McC. 1977. *Preaching and Theology in Anglo-Saxon England: Aelfric and Wulfstan*. Toronto: University of Toronto Press.

Gatch, Milton McC. 2012. 'Review of Joyce Tally Lionarons, *The Homiletic Writings of Archbishop Wulfstan: A Critical Study*'. *Speculum* no. 87 (1): 252–4.

Gates, Jay Paul. 2010. '*Ealles Englalandes Cyningc*: Cnut's Territorial Kingship and Wulfstan's Paronomastic Play'. *The Heroic Age: A Journal of Early Medieval Northwestern Europe* no. 14: n.p.

Gneuss, Helmut. 2001. *Handlist of Anglo-Saxon Manuscripts: A List of Manuscripts and Manuscript Fragments Written or Owned in England up to 1100*. Tempe, AZ: Arizona Center for Medieval and Renaissance Studies.

Gneuss, Helmut. 2009. *Ælfric of Eynsham: His Life, Times, and Writings*. Translated by Michael Lapidge, *Old English Newsletter Subsidia*. Kalamazoo, MI: Medieval Institute Publications.

Godden, M.R. 1994. 'Apocalypse and Invasion in Late Anglo-Saxon England'. In *From Anglo-Saxon to Early Middle English: Studies Presented to E.G. Stanley*, edited by M.R. Godden, Douglas Gray and Terry Hoad, 130–62. Oxford: Clarendon Press.

Godden, M.R. 2004. 'The Relations of Wulfstan and Ælfric: A Reassessment'. In *Wulfstan, Archbishop of York: The Proceedings of the Second Alcuin Conference*, edited by Matthew Townend, 353–74. Turnhout: Brepols.

Graham, Timothy. 2000. 'John Joscelyn, Pioneer of Old English Lexicography'. In *The Recovery of Old English: Anglo-Saxon Studies in the Sixteenth and Seventeenth Centuries*, edited by Timothy Graham, 83–140. Kalamazoo, MI: Medieval Institute Publications.

Grant, Raymond J.S. 1996. *Lawrence Nowell, William Lambarde, and the Laws of the Anglo-Saxons*. Amsterdam: Costerus.

Greenberg, Janelle. 2010. '"St. Edward's Ghost": The Cult of St. Edward and His Laws in English History'. In *English Law Before Magna Carta: Felix Liebermann and Die Gesetze der Angelsachsen*, edited by Stefan Jurasinski, Lisi Oliver and Andrew Rabin, 273–300. Leiden: Brill.

Grendon, Felix. 1909. 'The Anglo-Saxon Charms'. *The Journal of American Folklore* no. 22 (84): 105–237.

Gretsch, Mechthild. 1999. *The Intellectual Foundations of the English Benedictine Reform, Cambridge Studies in Anglo-Saxon England*. Cambridge: Cambridge University Press.

Grierson, Phillip, and Mark Blackburn. 1986. *Medieval European Coinage, Together with a Catalogue of the Coins in the Fitzwilliam Museum, Cambridge*. Vol. 1. Cambridge: Cambridge University Press.

Hadley, D.M. 2000. *The Northern Danelaw: Its Social Structure, c. 800–1100*. London: Leicester University Press.

Hadley, D.M. 2006. *The Vikings in England: Settlement, Society, and Culture*. Manchester: Manchester University Press.

Hagen, Ann. 1995. *A Second Handbook of Anglo-Saxon Food and Drink: Production and Distribution*. Hockwold cum Wilton: Anglo-Saxon Books.

Haines, Dorothy. 2010. *Sunday Observance and the Sunday Letter in Anglo-Saxon England*. Woodbridge: D.S. Brewer.

Hall, Thomas N. 2004. 'Wulfstan's Latin Sermons'. In *Wulfstan, Archbishop of York: The Proceedings of the Second Alcuin Conference*, edited by Matthew Townend, 93–140. Turnhout: Brepols.

Hamilton, Sarah. 2005. 'Remedies for "Great Transgressions": Penance and Excommunication in Late Anglo-Saxon England'. In *Pastoral Care in late Anglo-Saxon England*, edited by Francesca Tinti, 83–105. Woodbridge: Boydell Press.

Harris, Stephen J. 2003. *Race and Ethnicity in Anglo-Saxon Literature*. London: Routledge.

Harvey, P.D.A. 1993. '*Rectitudines Singularum Personarum* and *Gerefa*'. The *English Historical Review* no. 108 (426): 1–22.

Hattori, Yoshiki. 1990. 'Anticipation of *þæt* Clauses in Wulfstan's *Homilies*'. In *Studies in English Philology in Honour of Shigeru Ono*, edited by Koichi Jin et al., 195–207. Tokyo: Nan'un-do.

Heslop, T.A. 2004. 'Art and the Man: Archbishop Wulfstan and the York Gospelbook'. In *Wulfstan, Archbishop of York: The Proceedings of the Second Alcuin Conference*, edited by Matthew Townend, 279–308. Turnhout: Brepols.

Higham, N.J. 1997. *The Convert Kings: Power and Religious Affiliation in Early Anglo-Saxon England*. Manchester: Manchester University Press.

Higham, N.J., and M.J. Ryan. 2013. *The Anglo-Saxon World*. New Haven, CT: Yale University Press.

Hill, David. 1978. 'Trends in the Development of Towns During the Reign of Ethelred II'. In *Ethelred the Unready: Papers from the Millenary Conference*, edited by David Hill. Oxford: Archaeopress.

Hill, Joyce. 1992. 'Monastic Reform and the Secular Church: Ælfric's Pastoral Letters in Context'. In *England in the Eleventh Century: Proceedings of the 1990 Harlaxton Symposium*, edited by Carola Hicks, 103–17. Stamford: Paul Watkins Publishing.

Hill, Joyce. 1993. 'Reform and Resistance: Preaching Styles in Late Anglo-Saxon England'. In *De l'homélie au sermon: histoire de la prédication médiévale*, edited by Jacqueline Hamesse and Xavier Hermand. Louvain-La-Neuve: Institut d'Etudes Médiévales de l'Université Catholique de Louvain.

Hill, Joyce. 2004. 'Archbishop Wulfstan: Reformer?' In *Wulfstan, Archbishop of York: The Proceedings of the Second Alcuin Conference*, edited by Matthew Townend, 309–24. Turnhout: Brepols.

Hohler, C.E. 1975. 'Some Service Books of the Later Saxon Church'. In *Tenth Century Studies: Essays in Commemoration of the Millenium of the Council of Winchester and the 'Regularis Concordia'*, edited by David Parsons, 60–83, 217–227. London: Phillimore.

Hollis, Stephanie. 2004. '"The Protection of God and the King": Wulfstan's Legislation on Widows'. In *Wulfstan, Archbishop of York: The Proceedings of the Second Alcuin Conference*, edited by Matthew Townend, 443–60. Turnhout: Brepols.

Horner, Shari. 2001. *The Discourse of Enclosure*. Albany, NY: State University of New York Press.

Hough, Carole A. 2000. 'Penitential Literature and Secular Law in Anglo-Saxon England'. *Anglo-Saxon Studies in Archaeology and History* no. 11: 133–41.

Hough, Carole A. 2001. 'Legal and Documentary Writings'. In *A Companion to Anglo-Saxon Literature*, edited by Philip Pulsiano and Elaine Treharne, 170–87. Oxford: Blackwell.

Hough, Carole A. 2006. 'Numbers in Manuscripts of Anglo-Saxon Law'. In *Writing and Texts in Anglo-Saxon England*, edited by Alexander Rumble, 114–31. Woodbridge: D.S. Brewer.

Howe, Nicholas. 2001. *Migration and Mythmaking in Anglo-Saxon England*. Notre Dame, IN: University of Notre Dame Press.

Hudson, John. 2010. 'From the *Leges* to *Glanvill*: Legal Expertise and Legal Reasoning'. In *English Law Before Magna Carta: Felix Liebermann and Die Gesetze der Angelsachsen*, edited by Stefan Jurasinski, Lisi Oliver and Andrew Rabin, 221–50. Leiden: Brill.

Hudson, John. 2012. *The Oxford History of the Laws of England, Volume II: 871–1216*. Oxford: Oxford University Press.

Jayakumar, Shashi. 2009. 'Reform and Retribution: the "Anti-Monastic Reaction" in the Reign of Edward the Martyr'. In *Early Medieval Studies in Memory of Patrick Wormald*, edited by Stephen Baxter, Catherine E. Karkov, Janet Nelson and David Pelteret, 337–52. Burlington: Ashgate.

Jayatilaka, Rohini. 2003. 'The Old English Benedictine Rule: Writing for Women and Men'. *Anglo-Saxon England* no. 32: 147–87.

John, Eric. 1966. 'The King and the Monks in the Tenth-Century Reformation'. In *Orbis Britanniae and Other Studies*, 154–80. Leicester, UK: Leicester University Press.

Jones, Christopher A. 1998a. *Ælfric's Letter to the Monks of Eynsham, Cambridge Studies in Anglo Saxon England*. Cambridge: Cambridge University Press.

Jones, Christopher A. 1998b. 'The Book of the Liturgy in Anglo-Saxon England'. *Speculum* no. 73 (3): 659–702.

Jones, Christopher A. 1998c. 'Two Composite Texts From Archbishop Wulfstan's "Commonplace Book": The *De ecclesiastica consuetudine* and the *Institutio beati Amalarii de ecclesiasticis officiis*'. *Anglo-Saxon England* no. 27: 233–71.

Jones, Christopher A. 2004. 'Wulfstan's Liturgical Interests'. In *Wulfstan, Archbishop of York: The Proceedings of the Second Alcuin Conference*, edited by Matthew Townend, 325–52. Turnhout: Brepols.

Jost, Karl. 1918. 'Review of Bernhard Fehr, *Die Hirtenbriefe Ælfrics*'. *English Studies* no. 52: 105–12.

Jost, Karl. 1932. 'Einige Wulfstantexte und ihre Quellen'. *Anglia* no. 56: 265–315.

Jost, Karl. 1950. *Wulfstanstudien*. Bern: A. Francke.

Jurasinski, Stefan. 2011. 'Violence, Penance, and Secular Law in Alfred's Mosaic Prologue'. *Haskins Society Journal* no. 22: 25–42.

Jurasinski, Stefan. 2012. 'Slavery, Learning and the Law of Marriage in Alfred's Mosaic Prologue'. In *Secular Learning in Anglo-Saxon England*, edited by László Sándor Chardonnens and Bryan Carella, 45–64. Amsterdam: Rodopi.

Jurovics, Rachel. 1978. 'The *Sermo Lupi* and the Moral Purpose of Rhetoric'. In *The Old English Homily and Its Backgrounds*, edited by Paul Szarmach and Bernard F. Huppe, 203–20. Albany, NY: State University of New York Press.

Kantorowicz, Ernst H. 1957. *The King's Two Bodies: A Study in Medieval Political Theology*. Princeton, NJ: Princeton University Press.

Keefer, Sarah Larratt. 1998. 'Ut in omnibus honorificetur Deus: The *corsnæd* Ordeal in Anglo-Saxon England'. In *The Community, the Family and the Saint: Patterns of Power in Early Medieval Europe*, edited by John M. Hill and Mary Swan, 237–64. Turnhout: Brepols.

Kennedy, A.G. 1983. 'Cnut's Law Code of 1018'. *Anglo-Saxon England* no. 11: 57–81.

Ker, N.R. 1948. 'Hemming's Cartulary'. In *Studies in Medieval History Presented to F.M. Powicke*, edited by R.W. Hunt, W.A. Pantin and R.W. Southern, 49–75. Oxford: Oxford University Press.

Ker, N.R. 1957. *A Catalogue of Manuscripts Containing Anglo-Saxon*. Oxford: Oxford University Press.

Ker, N.R. 1971. 'The Handwriting of Archbishop Wulfstan'. In *England Before the Conquest: Studies in Primary Sources Presented to Dorothy Whitelock*, edited by Peter Clemoes and Kathleen Hughes, 315–31. Cambridge: Cambridge University Press.

Keynes, Simon. 1978. 'The Declining Reputation of King Æthelred the Unready'. In *Ethelred the Unready: Papers from the Millenary Conference*, edited by David Hill, 227–53. Oxford: Archaeopress.

Keynes, Simon. 1980. *The Diplomas of King Æthelred 'the Unready', 978–1016*. Cambridge: Cambridge University Press.

Keynes, Simon. 1986. 'The Additions in Old English'. In *The York Gospels: A Facsimile with Introductory Essays*, edited by Nicholas Barker, 81–99. London: The Roxburghe Club.

Keynes, Simon. 1991. 'Crime and Punishment in the Reign of King Aethelred the Unready'. In *People and Places in Northern Europe*, edited by Ian Wood and Niels Lund, 67–81. Woodbridge: Boydell.

Keynes, Simon. 2005. 'A Note on Anglo-Saxon Personal Names'. In *St. Wulfsige and Sherborne: Essays to Celebrate the Millennium of the Benedictine Abbey, 998–1998*, edited by Katherine Barker, David A. Hinton and Alan Hunt, 20–3. Oxford: Oxbow Books.

Keynes, Simon. 2007. 'An Abbot, an Archbishop, and the Viking Raids of 1006–7 and 1009–12'. *Anglo-Saxon England* no. 36: 151–220.

Keynes, Simon. 2008. 'Edgar, *rex admirabilis*'. In *Edgar, King of the English 959–975: New Interpretations*, edited by Donald Scragg, 3–59. Woodbridge: Boydell.

Kinard, James Pinckney. 1897. *A Study of Wulfstan's Homilies: Their Style and Sources*. Baltimore, MD: John Murphy and Company.

Kirby, D.P. 1991. *The Earliest English Kings*. London: Unwin Hyman Ltd.

Klosko, George, ed. 2011. *The Oxford Handbook of the History of Political Philosophy*. Oxford: Oxford University Press.

Knowles, David. 1963. *The Monastic Order in England*. Cambridge: Cambridge University Press.

Kubouchi, Tadao. 1999. 'Texts of "Be Cynestole" in Wulfstan's *Institutes of Polity*'. In *From Wulfstan to Richard Rolle: Papers Exploring the Continuity of English Prose*, 211–17. Woodbridge: D.S. Brewer.

Lambert, Malcolm. 2010. *Christians and Pagans: The Conversion of Britain from Alban to Bede*. New Haven, CT: Yale University Press.

Lapidge, Michael. 2006. *The Anglo-Saxon Library*. Oxford: Oxford University Press.

Lavelle, Ryan. 2002. *Æthelred II: King of the English, 978–1016*. Stroud: Tempus.

Lawson, M.K. 1992. 'Archbishop Wulfstan and the Homiletic Element in the Laws of Æthelred II and Cnut'. *The English Historical Review* no. 107 (424): 565–86.

Lawson, M.K. 1993. *Cnut: The Danes in England in the Early Eleventh Century*. New York: Longman.

Lees, Clare. 1999. *Tradition and Belief: Religious Writing in Late Anglo-Saxon England*. Minneapolis, MN: University of Minnesota Press.

Liebermann, Felix. 1908. 'King Alfred and Mosaic Law'. *Transactions of the Jewish Historical Society of England* no. 6: 21–31.

Liebermann, Felix. 1913. *The National Assembly in the Anglo-Saxon Period*. New York: Burt Franklin.

Lionarons, Joyce Tally. 2004a. 'Napier Homily L: Wulfstan's Eschatology at the Close of his Career'. In *Wulfstan, Archbishop of York: The Proceedings of the Second Alcuin Conference*, edited by Matthew Townend, 413–28. Turnhout: Brepols.

Lionarons, Joyce Tally. 2004b. 'Textual Identity, Homiletic Reception, and Wulfstan's *Sermo ad Populum*'. *Review of English Studies* no. 55 (219): 157–82.

Lionarons, Joyce Tally. 2010. *The Homiletic Writings of Archbishop Wulfstan: A Critical Study*. Woodbridge: D. S. Brewer.

Loyn, H.R. 1971a. 'Towns in Late Anglo-Saxon England'. In *England Before the Conquest: A Festschrift to Professor Dorothy Whitelock*, edited by Peter Clemoes, 115–28. Cambridge: Cambridge University Press.

Loyn, H.R., ed. 1971b. *A Wulfstan Manuscript Containing Institutes, Laws and*

Homilies. British Museum Cotton Nero A.i.x. Early English Manuscripts in Facsimile, Vol. 17. Copenhagen: Rosenkilde and Bagger.

Loyn, H R. 1975. 'Church and State in England in the Tenth and Eleventh Centuries'. In *Tenth Century Studies: Essays in Commemoration of the Millenium of the Council of Winchester and Regularis Concordia*, edited by David Parsons, 94–102, 229–30. London: Phillimore.

Loyn, H.R. 1992. '*De iure domini regis*: A Comment on Royal Authority in Eleventh-Century England'. In *England in the Eleventh Century. Proceedings of the 1990 Harlaxton Symposium*, edited by Carola Hicks, 17–24. Stamford: Paul Watkins Publishing.

Loyn, H.R. 1994. *The Vikings in Britain*. Oxford: Blackwell.

Lynch, Joseph H. 1998. *Christianizing Kinship: Ritual Sponsorship in Anglo-Saxon England*. Ithaca, NY: Cornell University Press.

Maddicott, J.R. 2010. *The Origins of the English Parliament, 924–1327*. Oxford: Oxford University Press.

Magennis, Hugh. 1999. *Anglo-Saxon Appetites: Food and Drink and Their Consumption in Old English and Related Literature*. Dublin: Four Courts Press.

Magennis, Hugh, and Mary Swan, eds. 2009. *A Companion to Ælfric*. Leiden: Brill.

Maitland, Frederic William. 1898. *Township and Borough, The Ford Lectures*. Cambridge: Cambridge University Press.

Mann, Gareth. 2004. 'The Development of Wulfstan's Alcuin Manuscript'. In *Wulfstan, Archbishop of York: Proceedings of the Second Alcuin Conference*, edited by Matthew Townend, 235–78. Turnhout: Brepols.

Marafioti, Nicole. 2008. 'Punishing Bodies and Saving Souls: Capital and Corporal Punishment in Anglo-Saxon England'. *The Haskins Society Journal* no. 20: 39–57.

McClelland, J.S. 1996. *A History of Western Political Thought*. New York: Routledge.

McIntosh, Angus. 1949. 'Wulfstan's Prose'. *Proceedings of the British Academy* no. 35: 109–42.

Meaney, Audrey L. 2004. '"And we forbeodað eornostlice ælcne hæðenscipe": Wulfstan and Late Anglo-Saxon and Norse "Heathenism"'. In *Wulfstan, Archbishop of York: The Proceedings of the Second Alcuin Conference*, edited by Matthew Townend, 461–500. Turnhout: Brepols.

Morrison, Stephen. 1996. 'A Reminiscence of Wulfstan in the Twelfth Century'. *Neuphilologische Mitteilungen* no. 96: 229–34.

Musson, Anthony. 2001. *Medieval Law in Context: The Growth of Legal Consciousness from Magna Carta to the Peasants' Revolt*. New York: Manchester University Press.

Niles, John D. 2009. 'Trial By Ordeal in Anglo-Saxon England: What's the Problem with Barley?' In *Early Medieval Studies in Memory of Patrick*

Wormald, edited by Stephen Baxter, Catherine E. Karkov, Janet Nelson and David Pelteret, 369–82. Farnham: Ashgate.

North, Richard. 2006. 'End Time and the Date of "Völuspá": Two Models of Conversion'. In *Conversion and Colonization in Anglo-Saxon England*, edited by Nicholas Howe and Catherine E. Karkov, 213–36. Tempe, AZ: Arizona Center for Medieval and Renaissance Studies.

Norton, Christopher. 2004. 'York Minster in the Time of Wulfstan'. In *Wulfstan, Archbishop of York: The Proceedings of the Second Alcuin Conference*, edited by Matthew Townend, 207–34. Turnhout: Brepols.

Oakley, Thomas Pollock. 1923. *English Penitential Discipline and Anglo-Saxon Law in their Joint Influence*. New York: Columbia University Press.

O'Brien, Bruce. 1996. 'From *Morðor* to *Murdrum*: The Preconquest Origin and Norman Revival of the Murder Fine'. *Speculum* no. 71 (2): 321–57.

O'Brien, Bruce. 1999. *God's Peace & King's Peace: the Laws of Edward the Confessor*. Philadelphia, PA: University of Pennsylvania Press.

Ogawa, Hiroshi. 2002. 'Aspects of "Wulfstan Imitators" in Late Old English Sermon Writing'. In *Studies in English Historical Linguistics and Philology: A Festschrift for Akio Oizumi*, edited by Jacek Fisiak, 389–403. Frankfurt am Main: Peter Lang.

O'Keeffe, Katherine O'Brien. 1998. 'Body and Law in Late Anglo-Saxon England'. *Anglo-Saxon England* no. 27: 209–32.

Oliver, Lisi. 2013. 'Legal Documentation and the Practice of English Law'. In *The Cambridge History of Early Medieval English Literature*, edited by Clare Lees, 499–529. Cambridge: Cambridge University Press.

Orchard, Andy. 1992. 'Crying Wolf: Oral Style and the *Sermones Lupi*'. *Anglo-Saxon England* no. 21: 239–64.

Orchard, Andy. 2002. 'On Editing Wulfstan'. In *Early Medieval English Texts and Interpretations: Studies Presented to Donald G. Scragg*, edited by Elaine Treharne and Susan Rosser, 311–40. Tempe, AZ: Arizona Center for Medieval and Renaissance Studies.

Orchard, Andy. 2004. 'Re-editing Wulfstan: Where's the Point?' In *Wulfstan, Archbishop of York: The Proceedings of the Second Alcuin Conference*, edited by Matthew Townend, 63–91. Turnhout: Brepols.

Orchard, Andy. 2007. 'Wulfstan as Reader, Writer, and Rewriter'. In *The Old English Homily: Precedent, Practice, and Appropriation*, edited by Aaron Kleist, 311–41. Turnhout: Brepols.

Orchard, Andy. 2012. 'The Library of Wulfstan of York'. In *The Cambridge History of the Book in Britain, Volume I: c. 400–1100*, edited by Richard Gameson, 694–700. Cambridge: Cambridge University Press.

Parsons, David, ed. 1975. *Tenth Century Studies: Essays in Commemoration of the Millennium of the Council of Winchester and the Regularis Concordia*. London: Phillimore.

Pelteret, David. 1995. *Slavery in Early Mediaeval England.* Woodbridge: Boydell.

Pollock, Sir Frederick. 1893. 'Anglo-Saxon Law'. *English Historical Review* no. 8 (30): 239–71.

Pollock, Sir Frederick, and Frederic William Maitland. 1968. *The History of English Law Before the Time of Edward I.* 2nd edn. Cambridge: Cambridge University Press.

Pons-Sanz, Sara M. 2004. '*For Gode and for worolde*: Wulfstan's Differentiation of the Divine and Worldly Realms through Word-Formation Processes'. *English Studies* no. 85 (4): 281–96.

Pons-Sanz, Sara M. 2007. *Norse-Derived Vocabulary in Late Old English Texts: Wulfstan's Works, A Case Study.* Odense: University Press of Southern Denmark.

Powell, Timothy E. 1994. 'The "Three Orders" of Society in Anglo-Saxon England'. *Anglo-Saxon England* no. 23: 103–32.

Pratt, David. 2007. *The Political Thought of King Alfred the Great, Cambridge Studies in Medieval Life and Thought.* Cambridge: Cambridge University Press.

Prideaux-Collins, William. 2003. '"Satan's Bonds are Extremely Loose": Apocalyptic Expectation in Anglo-Saxon England during the Millennial Era'. In *The Apocalyptic Year 1000: Religious Expectation and Social Change, 950–1050,* edited by Richard Landes, Andrew Gow and David C. van Meter, 289–310. Oxford: Oxford University Press.

Rabin, Andrew. 2006. 'The Wolf's Testimony to the English: Law and the Witness in the *Sermo Lupi ad Anglos*'. *Journal of English and Germanic Philology* no. 105 (3): 388–414.

Rabin, Andrew. 2007. 'Old English *forespeca* and the Role of the Advocate in Anglo-Saxon Law'. *Mediaeval Studies* no. 69: 223–55.

Rabin, Andrew. 2010a. 'Evidence for Wulfstan's Authorship of the Old English *Að*'. *Neuphilologische Mitteilungen* no. 111 (1): 43–52.

Rabin, Andrew. 2010b. 'Felix Liebermann and *Die Gesetze der Angelsachsen*'. In *English Law Before Magna Carta: Felix Liebermann and Die Gesetze der Angelsachsen,* edited by Stefan Jurasinski, Lisi Oliver and Andrew Rabin, 1–8. Leiden: Brill.

Rabin, Andrew. 2012. 'Law and Justice'. In *The Blackwell Handbook of Anglo-Saxon Studies,* edited by Jacqueline Stodnick and Renee Trilling. Oxford: Blackwell.

Rabin, Andrew. 2013. 'Holy Bodies, Legal Matters: Reaction and Reform in Ælfric's *Eugenia* and the Ely Privilege'. *Studies in Philology* no. 110 (2): 220–65.

Rabin, Andrew. forthcoming. 'Archbishop Wulfstan's 'Compilation on Status' in the Textus Roffensis'. In *Textus Roffensis: Law, Language, and Libraries in Medieval England,* edited by Barbara Bombi and Bruce O'Brien. Turnhout: Brepols.

Reynolds, Roger E. 1978. *The Ordinals of Christ from their Origins to the Twelfth Century*. Berlin: Walter de Gruyter.

Reynolds, Roger E. 1979. '"At Sixes and Sevens" – and Eights and Nines: The Sacred Mathematics of Sacred Orders in the Early Middle Ages'. *Speculum* no. 54 (4): 669–84.

Reynolds, Susan. 1985. 'What Do We Mean by "Anglo-Saxon" and "Anglo-Saxons"?' *Journal of British Studies* no. 24: 395–414.

Richards, Mary P. 1986. 'The Manuscript Contexts of the Old English Laws: Tradition and Innovation'. In *Studies in Earlier Old English Prose*, edited by Paul Szarmach, 171–192. Albany, NY: State University Press of New York.

Richards, Mary P. 1988. *Texts and Their Traditions in the Medieval Library of Rochester Cathedral Priory, Transactions of the American Philosophical Society*. Philadelphia, PA: The American Philosophical Society.

Richards, Mary P. 1997. 'Anglo-Saxonism in the Old English Laws'. In *Anglo-Saxonism and the Construction of Social Identity*, edited by Allen J. Frantzen and John D. Niles, 40–59. Gainesville, FL: University Press of Florida.

Richards, Mary P. 2002. 'Wulfstan and the Millennium'. In *The Year 1000: Religious and Social Response to the Turning of the First Millennium*, edited by Michael Frassetto, 41–8. New York: Palgrave Macmillan.

Richards, Mary P. 2010. 'I-II Cnut: Wulfstan's Summa?' In *English Law Before Magna Carta: Felix Liebermann and Die Gesetze der Angelsachsen*, edited by Stefan Jurasinski, Lisi Oliver and Andrew Rabin, 137–56. Leiden: Brill.

Richardson, H.G., and G.O. Sayles. 1966. *Law and Legislation from Æthelberht to Magna Carta*. Edinburgh: Edinburgh University Press.

Ryan, Alan. 2012. *On Politics: A History of Political Thought from Herodotus to the Present*. 2 vols. New York: W.W. Norton and Co.

Salvador-Bello, Mercedes. 2006. 'Architectural Metaphors and Christological Imagery in the Advent Lyrics: Benedictine Propaganda in the Exeter Book?' In *Conversion and Colonization in Anglo-Saxon England*, edited by Catherine E Karkov and Nicholas Howe, 169–211. Tempe, AZ: Arizona Center for Medieval and Renaissance Studies.

Sauer, Hans. 2000. 'The Transmission and Structure of Wulfstan's "Commonplace Book"'. In *Old English Prose: Basic Readings*, edited by Paul Szarmach and Deborah A. Oosterhouse, 339–93. New York: Garland.

Sawyer, P.H. 1957. *Textus Roffensis: Rochester Cathedral Library Manuscript A.3.5, Part I, Early English Manuscripts in Facsimile*, Vol. 7. Copenhagen: Rosenkilde and Bagger.

Sawyer, P.H. 1968. *Anglo-Saxon Charters: An Annotated List and Bibliography*. London: Royal Historical Society.

Scammel, Jean. 1993. 'The Formation of the English Social Structure: Freedom, Knights, and Gentry, 1066–1300'. *Speculum* no. 68 (3): 591–618.

Schulenburg, Jane Tibbets. 1984. 'Strict Active Enclosure and its Effects on Female Monastic Experience'. In *Distant Echoes*, edited by John A. Nichols, 51–86. Kalamazoo, MI: Cistercian Publications.

Schulenburg, Jane Tibbets. 1998. *Forgetful of Their Sex: Female Sanctity and Society, ca. 500–1100*. Chicago, IL: University of Chicago Press.

Schwyter, J.R. 1998. 'Syntax and Style in the Anglo-Saxon Law-Codes'. In *Verschriftung – Verschriftlichung: Aspekte des Medienwechsels in verschiedenen Kulturen und Epochen*, edited by C. Ehler and U. Schaefer, 189–231. Tübingen: Gunter Narr.

Schwyter, J.R. 2010. 'L1 Interference in the Editing Process: Felix Liebermann, the *Gesetze*, and the German Language'. In *English Law Before Magna Carta: Felix Liebermann and Die Gesetze der Angelsachsen*, edited by Stefan Jurasinski, Lisi Oliver and Andrew Rabin, 43–58. Leiden: Brill.

Scragg, Donald. 1977. 'Napier's 'Wulfstan' Homily XXX: Its Sources, Its Relationship to the Vercelli Book and its Style'. *Anglo-Saxon England* no. 6: 197–211.

Scragg, Donald. 1998. *Dating and Style in Old English Composite Homiles, H.M. Chadwick Memorial Lectures*. Cambridge: University of Cambridge, Department of Anglo-Saxon, Norse and Celtic.

Shoemaker, Karl. 2010. *Sanctuary and Crime in the Middle Ages, 400–1500*. New York: Fordham University Press.

Sisam, Kenneth. 1953. 'The Authenticity of Certain Texts in Lambard's *Archaionomia* 1568'. In *Studies in the History of Old English Literature*, 232–59. Oxford: Clarendon Press.

Smith, Mary Frances, Robin Fleming, and Patricia Halpin. 2001. 'Court and Piety in Late Anglo-Saxon England'. *Catholic Historical Review* no. 87 (4): 569–602.

Stafford, Pauline. 1971. 'The Laws of Cnut and the History of Anglo-Saxon Royal Promises'. *Anglo-Saxon England* no. 10: 173–90.

Stafford, Pauline. 1978a. 'Church and Society in the Age of Ælfric'. In *The Old English Homily and Its Backgrounds*, edited by Paul Szarmach and Bernard F. Huppe, 11–42. Albany, NY: State University of New York Press.

Stafford, Pauline. 1978b. 'The Reign of Ethelred II, a Study in the Limitations on Royal Policy and Action'. In *Ethelred the Unready: Papers from the Millenary Conference*, edited by David Hill, 15–46. Oxford: Archaeopress.

Stafford, Pauline. 1989. *Unification and Conquest: A Political and Social History of England in the Tenth and Eleventh Centuries*. London: Edward Arnold.

Stafford, Pauline. 1999. 'Queens, Nunneries, and Reforming Churchmen: Gender, Religious Status and Reform in Tenth- and Eleventh-Century England'. *Past and Present* no. 163: 3–35.

Stanley, E.G. 1985. '*The Judgement of the Damned* (from Cambridge, Corpus Christi College 201 and Other Manuscripts) and the Definition of Old

English Verse'. In *Learning and Literature in Anglo-Saxon England: Studies Presented to Peter Clemoes on the Occasion of His Sixty-Fifth Birthday*, edited by Michael Lapidge and Helmut Gneuss, 363–92. Cambridge: Cambridge University Press.

Stanley, E.G. 2000. 'Anglo-Saxon Trial By Jury'. In *Imagining the Anglo-Saxon Past*, 111–48. Cambridge, England: D.S. Brewer.

Stanley, E.G. 2004. 'Wulfstan and Ælfric: "The true Difference between the Law and the Gospel"'. In *Wulfstan, Archbishop of York: The Proceedings of the Second Alcuin Conference*, edited by Matthew Townend, 429–43. Turnhout: Brepols.

Stenton, F.M. 1970. 'The Thriving of the Anglo-Saxon Ceorl'. In *Preparatory to Anglo-Saxon England*, edited by Doris Stenton, 382–93. Oxford: Oxford University Press. Original edition, 1958.

Stenton, F.M. 1971. *Anglo-Saxon England*. 3d edn. Oxford: Clarendon Press.

Stubbs, William. 1887. *The Constitutional History of England in Its Origin and Development*. 2 vols. Oxford: Clarendon Press.

Thomas, David. 1985. 'Origins of the Common Law, Part II: Anglo-Saxon Antecedents of the Common Law'. *Brigham Young University Law Review* 453–503.

Treharne, Elaine. 2012. *Living Through Conquest: The Politics of Early English, 1020–1220*. Oxford: Oxford University Press.

Trilling, Renée. 2007. 'Sovereignty and Social Order: Archbishop Wulfstan and the *Institutes of Polity*'. In *The Bishop Reformed: Studies of Episcopal Power and Culture in the Central Middle Ages*, edited by John Ott and Anna Trumbore Jones, 58–85. Aldershot: Ashgate.

Whitelock, Dorothy. 1937. 'A Note on the Career of Wulfstan the Homilist'. *English Historical Review* no. 52 (207): 460–5.

Whitelock, Dorothy. 1937–45. 'The Conversion of the Eastern Danelaw'. *Saga Book of the Viking Society* no. 12: 159–76.

Whitelock, Dorothy. 1941. 'Wulfstan and the So-Called Laws of Edward and Guthrum'. *English Historical Review* no. 56 (221): 1–21.

Whitelock, Dorothy. 1942. 'Archbishop Wulfstan, Homilist and Statesman'. In *Transactions of the Royal Historical Society*, 25–46. London: Butler & Tanner.

Whitelock, Dorothy. 1943. 'Two Notes on Ælfric and Wulfstan'. *Modern Language Review* no. 38 (2): 122–6.

Whitelock, Dorothy. 1948. 'Wulfstan and the Laws of Cnut'. *English Historical Review* no. 63 (249): 433–52.

Whitelock, Dorothy. 1955. 'Wulfstan's Authorship of Cnut's Laws'. *The English Historical Review* no. 70 (274): 72–85.

Whitelock, Dorothy. 1959. 'The Dealings of the Kings of England with Northumbria in the Tenth and Eleventh Centuries'. In *The Anglo-Saxons: Studies in Some Aspects of Their History and Culture Presented to Bruce Dickins*, edited by Peter Clemoes, 70–88. London: Bowes & Bowes.

Whitelock, Dorothy. 1961. 'Review of *Die "Institutes of Polity, Civil and Ecclesias-tical": ein Werk Erzbischof Wulfstans von York* by Karl Jost'. *Review of English Studies* no. 12 (45): 61–6.

Whitelock, Dorothy. 1965. 'Wulfstan at York'. In *Franciplegius: Medieval and Linguistic Studies in Honor of Francis Peabody Magoun, Jr*, edited by Jess B. Bessinger, 214–31. New York: New York University Press.

Whitman, James Q. 2008. *The Origins of Reasonable Doubt: Theological Roots of the Criminal Trial*. New Haven, CT: Yale University Press.

Wilcox, Jonathan. 1991. 'Napier's "Wulfstan" Homilies XL and XLII: Two Anonymous Works from Winchester?' *Journal of English and Germanic Philology* no. 90 (1): 1–19.

Wilcox, Jonathan. 1992. 'The Dissemination of Wulfstan's Homilies:The Wulfstan Tradition in Eleventh-Century Vernacular Preaching'. In *England in the Eleventh Century: Proceedings of the 1990 Harlaxton Symposium*, edited by Carola Hicks, 199–217. Stamford: Paul Watkins Publishing.

Wilcox, Jonathan. 2000a. 'The Wolf on Shepherds: Wulfstan, Bishops, and the Context of the *Sermo Lupi ad Anglos*'. In *Old English Prose: Basic Readings*, edited by Paul Szarmach, 395–418. New York: Garland Publishing.

Wilcox, Jonathan. 2000b. 'Wulfstan and the Twelfth Century'. In *Rewriting Old English in the Twelfth Century*, edited by Mary Swan and Elaine Treharne, 83–97. Cambridge: Cambridge University Press.

Wilcox, Jonathan. 2000c. *Wulfstan Texts and Other Homiletic Materials*. Vol. 17, *Anglo-Saxon Manuscripts in Microfiche Facsimile* Tempe, AZ: Arizona Center for Medieval and Renaissance Studies.

Wilcox, Jonathan. 2004. 'Wulfstan's *Sermo Lupi ad Anglos* as Political Perfor-mance: 16 February 1014 and Beyond'. In *Wulfstan, Archbishop of York*, edited by Matthew Townend, 375–96. Turnhout: Brepols.

Williams, Ann. 1996. 'The Spoliation of Worcester'. *Anglo-Norman Studies: Proceedings of the Battle Conference* no. 19: 383–408.

Williams, Ann. 2003a. *Æthelred the Unready: The Ill-Counselled King*. London: Hambledon and London.

Williams, Ann. 2003b. 'A Bell-house and a Burh-geat: Lordly Residences in England before the Norman Conquest'. In *Anglo-Norman Castles*, edited by Robert Liddiard, 23–40. Woodbridge: Boydell.

Wormald, Patrick. 1977. 'The Uses of Literacy in Anglo-Saxon England and Its Neighbors'. *Transactions of the Royal Historical Society* no. 27: 95–114.

Wormald, Patrick. 1978. 'Æthelred the Lawmaker'. In *Ethelred the Unready*, edited by David Hill, 47–80. Oxford, England: B.A.R.

Wormald, Patrick. 1996. 'Maitland and Anglo-Saxon Law: Beyond Domesday Book'. *Proceedings of the British Academy* no. 89: 1–20.

Wormald, Patrick. 1998. 'Frederick William Maitland and the Earliest English Law'. *Law and History Review* no. 16 (1): 1–25.

Wormald, Patrick. 1999a. 'Archbishop Wulfstan and the Holiness of Society'. In *Legal Culture in the Early Medieval West: Law as Text, Image, and Experience*, 225–52. London: Hambledon Press.

Wormald, Patrick. 1999b. '*Laga Eadwardi*: The *Textus Roffensis* and its Context'. In *Legal Culture in the Early Medieval West: Law as Text, Image, and Experience*, 115–39. London: Hambledon Press.

Wormald, Patrick. 1999c. 'The Lambarde Problem: Eighty Years On'. In *Legal Culture in the Early Medieval West*, 139–78. London: Hambledon Press.

Wormald, Patrick. 1999d. *The Making of English Law: King Alfred to the Twelfth Century*. Malden: Blackwell Publishers.

Wormald, Patrick. 1999e. '"*Quadripartitus*"'. In *Legal Culture in the Early Medieval West: Law as Text, Image and Experience*, 81–114. London: Hambledon Press.

Wormald, Patrick. 1999f. 'Wulfstaniana True and False'. In *Legal Culture in the Early Medieval West: Law as Text, Image and Experience*, 247–51. London: Hambledon Press.

Wormald, Patrick. 2004. 'Archbishop Wulfstan: Eleventh Century State-builder'. In *Wulfstan, Archbishop of York: The Proceedings of the Second Alcuin Conference*, edited by Matthew Townend, 9–27. Turnhout: Brepols.

Wormald, Patrick. 2009. 'Anglo-Saxon Law and Scots Law'. *The Scottish Historical Review* no. 88 (2): 192–206.

Digital and internet-based resources

The Anglo-Saxon Penitentials: A Cultural Database, Allen J. Frantzen, www.anglo-saxon.net/penance/

The Dictionary of Old English and Old English Corpus, University of Toronto, www.doe.utoronto.ca

Fontes Anglo-Saxonici, University of Oxford, fontes.english.ox.ac.uk

Parker Library on the Web, Corpus Christi College, Cambridge and Stanford University, parkerweb.stanford.edu

The Production and Use of English Manuscripts, 1060 to 1220, University of Leicester and the University of Leeds, www.le.ac.uk/english/em1060to1220/catalogue/mss.htm

Prosopography of Anglo-Saxon England, King's College, London, and the University of Cambridge, www.pase.ac.uk/index.html

The Sources of Anglo-Saxon Literary Culture, University of Notre Dame, saslc.nd.edu

Wulfstan's Eschatalogical Homilies, Joyce Tally Lionarons, webpages.ursinus.edu/jlionarons/wulfstan/Wulfstan.html

INDEX

Note: legislation is indexed under the king in whose name it was promulgated. Wulfstan's writings are listed under his name, with homilies designated by numbers assigned to them by Napier or Bethurum.